The League of Nations

EDITED BY

RUTH B. HENIG

Lancaster University

BARNES & NOBLE

BOOKS

10 East 53d St., New York 10022
(a division of Harper & Row Publishers, Inc.)

Published in the U.S.A. 1973 by
HARPER & ROW PUBLISHERS, INC.
Barnes & Noble Import Division

Published 1973 by
OLIVER & BOYD
Croythorn House
23 Ravelston Terrace
Edinburgh EH4 3TJ
A Division of Longman Group Ltd

ISBN 0 06 – 492816 – 0 (paperback)
      0 06 – 492815 – 2 (hardback)

Printed in Great Britain by   76 – 353l
Cox & Wyman Ltd, London, Fakenham and Reading

EVIDENCE AND COMMENTARY
Historical Source Books

SERIES EDITORS
C. M. D. Crowder, M.A., D.Phil.
L. Kochan, M.A., Ph.D.

THE LEAGUE OF NATIONS

CONTENTS

GENERAL EDITORS' PREFACE

HISTORICAL WRITING IS based on the control of evidence and commentary. Everything that has happened in the past is potentially historical evidence, and it therefore follows that the historian must apply rigorous selection if his story is to have intelligible form. The inroads of time and common sense greatly reduce the quantity of evidence that is effectively available; but what is left still demands discernment, if its presentation is not to be self-defeating in volume and variety. Even the residue left from this process of irrational and rational refinement does not tell its own story. Documents may speak for themselves, but they say different things to different listeners. The historian's second task is commentary, by means of which he completes the interpretation of the evidence which he has previously selected. Here he makes explicit the insights which have guided his choice of what to include and what to omit. Here he may go beyond what have hitherto been accepted as the common-sense limits of historical territory; the history of public events is extended to the history of private thoughts and beyond this to the historical analysis of instinctive, unreasoned attitudes, and to the gradations of man's experience between these extremes. By this extension of its range, history as a discipline has moved some way to meet sociology, borrowing some of the sociologist's methods to do so.

As a result of the processes by which the historian has become increasingly self-conscious and self-critical, students are introduced nowadays not only to the conclusions drawn from new historical exploration, but to the foundations on which these conclusions rest. This has led in turn to the proliferation of collections of historical evidence for senior students, mainly documentary evidence of a familiar kind rather than the visual and aural records which are made available to younger age-groups.

The question has already been asked whether any further series of this kind is needed. The volumes to be included in this series will effectively prompt an affirmative answer by their choice of significant subjects which, as they accumulate, will provide the basis for comparative study. Each title will authoritatively present sufficient material to excite but not exhaust the curiosity of the serious student. The passages chosen for inclusion must often abbreviate the original documents; but the aim has been to avoid a collection of unconnected snippets. The necessary framework of interpretation is provided, but the student still has the opportunity to form his own judgements, and pursue his own insights. A modest critical apparatus and bibliography and an editorial conclusion will, we hope, direct readers beyond these selections to seek further evidence for use in constructing their own commentary.

CHRISTOPHER CROWDER
LIONEL KOCHAN

ACKNOWLEDGEMENTS

GRATEFUL THANKS ARE due to the following for permission to quote from material in their possession: to the Controller of Her Majesty's Stationery Office for extracts from British government papers and *Hansard*, to Madame Catherine Guillaume and Rosica Colin Limited for a poem by Richard Aldington, to Mr M. Gibson and Macmillan & Company for a poem by Wilfred Gibson, to Macmillan & Company for an extract from Stresemann's *Diaries, Letters and Papers* edited and translated by Eric Sutton, to Mr G. T. Sassoon for a poem by Siegfried Sassoon, to the *Round Table* for an extract from an article in one of their back numbers, to Mr Salvador de Madariaga for an extract from *Disarmament*, to Barrie and Jenkins for extracts from *The Conquest of an Empire* by Emilio de Bono, to the executors of the estate of J. C. Smuts for an extract from his pamphlet, *The League of Nations: a Practical Suggestion*, to the Fabian Society for an extract from a report prepared for its research department in 1916 by Leonard Woolf, and to Oxford University Press for extracts from *Documents on International Affairs* edited by J. W. Wheeler-Bennett.

I am also grateful to the assistants in the Public Record Office and to the librarians in the Royal Institute of International Affairs library and press library for all the help they have given me, to Dr Lionel Kochan for his advice in the preparation of this volume, and to Mrs Christine Ogden for typing out a large part of the manuscript. Most of all I am indebted to my husband who had to bear with me while I was arranging the text and documents, and to my parents without whose sacrifices this book could never have been written.

ABBREVIATIONS

DBFP	*Documents on British Foreign Policy*
DIA	*Documents on International Affairs* edited by J. W. Wheeler-Bennett and published by Oxford University Press under the asupices of the Royal Institute of International Affairs
FO	Foreign Office
L of Ns OJ	*League of Nations Official Journal*
PRO	Public Record Office

INTRODUCTION

VERY LITTLE HAS been written about the League of Nations in the past twenty years. There has been no comprehensive record of its activities since Walters' massive survey,[1] although in the intervening period much new material has become available to historians.[2] Some notable monographs concentrating on particular incidents and activities have appeared,[3] but on the whole, recent analyses of the League of Nations have been the work of political scientists casting around for an introduction to their surveys of the United Nations Organisation or of international organisations in general. This is unfortunate because the image of the League has been distorted by such analyses, and consequently much historical judgement on its record, such as labelling it a failure or an irrelevance to the history of the inter-war period, has been based on a set of false assumptions about the League's powers. In an age when inter-state co-operation is more vital to our survival than ever before, there is much that a study of the League of Nations can tell us about the ways in which states are prepared to co-operate with

[1] F. P. Walters, *A History of the League of Nations*, Oxford University Press, under the auspices of the Royal Institute of International Affairs, 1952. Frank Walters was a member of the League Secretariat at Geneva in the 1920s and 1930s.

[2] Government source material available to researchers now includes the British Cabinet records and Departmental files to within thirty years of the present date, housed at the Public Records Office; photostats of inter-war German archives captured at the end of the second world war, microfilmed and kept at the Foreign Office library in London; French archives up to within thirty years of the present date kept at the Archives Nationales, Paris, and American archives at the United States National Archives, Washington, D.C. Also widely available in bound volumes are *Documents on British Foreign Policy, 1919–39, Documents Diplomatiques Belges, 1919–39, Documents on German Foreign Policy, 1919–45, The Foreign Relations of the United States* from 1919 onwards, *Documents Diplomatiques Français, 1932–9,* and *Documents on International Affairs.*

[3] James Barros, *The Corfu Incident of 1923: Mussolini and the League of Nations*, Princeton University Press, 1965; *The Aland Islands Question: Its Settlement by the League of Nations*, Yale University Press, 1968; *The League of Nations and the Great Powers: The Greek-Bulgarian Incident of 1925*, Oxford University Press, 1970. Antony Alcock, *The History of the International Labour Organisation*, Macmillan, 1971.

1

each other as members of an international body, but such a study must examine the establishment and operation of the League in its historical context to see why it was set up and what it was intended to achieve. Without such a historical approach, it is impossible to come to any meaningful conclusions about the achievements or shortcomings of the League.[4]

The starting-point for any analysis of the League must be an examination of the circumstances in which it was set up and the way in which its constitution was drafted. The fact that it was born out of the waste and futility of the first world war was crucial in shaping its contours. While the opening phrases of its constitution proclaimed a set of universal ideals, the succeeding articles were largely based on the realities of experience gained during the first world war and on assumptions about why the war had broken out and how it could have been prevented. At the same time, the participants in the war had conflicting ideas about the outbreak of the war and the ways in which wars might be prevented or contained in the future. Major differences of opinion were not always satisfactorily resolved in the League Commission which was responsible for drafting the League Covenant at the Paris Peace Conference in 1919, and thus the resulting Covenant contained several provisions for preventing war and promoting international harmony which were not necessarily consistent with each other.

A Commission to draft the League Covenant was set up at Paris in January 1919 on the insistence of Woodrow Wilson, the President of the United States of America, who had advocated the establishment of an international organisation throughout the war years, but who had no very clear-cut ideas about the basis on which it should be organised. The victorious but exhausted principal allies, Britain, France, Italy and Japan, did not share Wilson's enthusiasm for this new venture but were not inclined to oppose him on the issue for a variety of reasons. The project meant so much to Woodrow Wilson that he was prepared to blackmail the allies into participating by threatening to sign a separate peace treaty with the Germans. In turn, however, British, French, Italian and Japanese leaders were able to exploit Wilson's devotion to the League cause by promising their support in return for his approval of their various territorial and political designs. Thus the Italians were able to incorporate large areas of non-Italian speaking territory into their boundaries, and the Japanese were able to secure their hold on

[4] The best analyses of the League in its historical context date from before the second world war: Alfred Zimmern, *The League of Nations and the Rule of Law, 1918–35*, Macmillan, 1936; Charles K. Webster and Sidney Herbert, *The League of Nations in Theory and Practice*, Allen and Unwin, 1933. For a good recent assessment, see Philip Reynolds, 'The League of Nations', in *The New Cambridge Modern History* vol. XII, revised edition, *The Shifting Balance of World Forces, 1898–1945*, Cambridge University Press, 1968.

former German colonies and possessions in the North Pacific and on the Chinese mainland. Less successfully, the French pressed for the Rhine frontier and the British for the cessation of United States naval building. The allies were also committed, to a certain extent, to their publics who had been prevailed upon to make large sacrifices to ensure victory. It was rather unconvincing to assure electorates that their sacrifices had not been in vain because Belgium and Serbia had been liberated, or because the peace-terms were territorially favourable. The existence of the League, however, would be convincing proof that the struggle had been worthwhile, that the first world war had really been a war to end all wars, and that no similar catastrophe would occur again.

So for diverse reasons, the allies agreed to Woodrow Wilson's proposal that a Commission to draft the constitution of the League should be set up as one of the first acts of the Paris Peace Conference and that the resulting constitution would be incorporated into the peace treaties to be concluded with the ex-enemy powers. However, they demonstrated their indifference to the project by refusing to participate at the highest level in the Commission's labours. While Wilson announced his intention of representing the United States personally on the Commission, the British Delegation nominated not Lloyd George, Britain's Prime Minister, or Balfour, the Foreign Secretary, as their representatives, but the former Under-Secretary for Foreign Affairs, Lord Cecil, and the South African Defence Minister, Smuts, who had both shown some enthusiasm for the League project. The French Government were represented not by Clemenceau but by the aged Bourgeois; the Italians followed suit and did not nominate their leading delegates to the Commission. Furthermore, the allies showed a great willingness to allow minor states, like Serbia, Belgium and Portugal, to participate in the drafting of the League constitution, which contrasted markedly with their desire to keep such states out of the discussions on subjects such as reparations and the disarmament of Germany.

Paradoxically, however, the allies had more clear-cut ideas about how the League should be organised than did Wilson. In Britain, statesmen like Cecil, second son of Lord Salisbury, bureaucrats like Hankey, Secretary to the War Cabinet, and writers of the calibre of Leonard Woolf and H. Lowes Dickinson had formulated detailed schemes; Dominion leaders like Smuts had worked out their ideas and published them. The British, French and Italian Governments had set up commissions to look into the schemes already propounded and to recommend viable proposals. On the other hand, in the United States Wilson had not authorised any such official investigations. He had been shown the various plans put forward officially and unofficially in the allied countries and had declared himself unimpressed with all of them. His close adviser and confidant, Colonel House, had worked out some of his own ideas about a viable international organisation, but no official American scheme had resulted. Thus at the start of the Commission's labours, Wilson was not firmly committed to any definite draft constitution, though he had jotted down some of his own ideas on paper, and he was consequently open to persuasion on many points. This gave members of the Commission, such as Cecil and Smuts, the opportunity to press forward their own ideas which were not always endorsed by the Governments they were representing.

The League Commission took as the basis for its discussions a draft constitution formulated by the legal advisers to the British and American delegations, C. J. Hurst and David Hunter Miller respectively, on the basis of informal discussions before the Commission met. The Hurst-Miller draft represented a compromise between the ideas of Wilson and House on the one hand and Cecil and Smuts on the other, and on the insistence of the British delegates it was used in the Commission rather than the draft formulated by Wilson on his arrival at Paris.[5] This procedure immediately put the other delegates on the Commission, particularly the French and Italians, at a disadvantage. In trying to press on the Commission their own proposals they could only proceed by way of amendment to the Hurst-Miller draft in front of them, of which a French translation only became available after the Commission had begun proceedings. This position of weakness was fully exploited by Wilson as chairman of the Commission when he wanted to press forward his own ideas or squash proposals he did not like. Thus the completed Covenant had a distinct Anglo-American flavour, with very few traces of French, Italian or Japanese influence. In order to understand fully the intentions of the framers of the League Covenant, it is necessary to understand what were the main Anglo-American ideas which went into the Covenant and to what extent they were modified by French proposals.

One point on which all delegates agreed was that the League should be an inter-state organisation, with the state constituting the basic unit of League membership. It has often been alleged that the League was not successful because it depended on co-operation between sovereign states for its operation rather than being able to act as a supranational body with the power to compel states to carry out particular actions and policies. It may well be that in the future only such a supranational body with executive powers will be able to save mankind from suicidal destruction, but in 1919 few, if any, statesmen saw the need to constitute this kind of international organisation let alone participate in it. The choice lay between a League based on inter-

[5] A detailed account of the drafting of the Covenant at Paris, together with a large selection of documents, can be found in David Hunter Miller, *The Drafting of the Covenant*, two vols, G. Putnam and Sons, New York, 1928.

state co-operation and no League at all, and in such circumstances it was undoubtedly preferable to have a League, albeit of restricted scope. This was the view of Woodrow Wilson, without whom there would have been no League. He had persistently advocated the establishment of an international organisation, and had used all the economic and political leverage at his disposal, which was considerable as the President of the world's leading economic and political nation, to further the scheme. He advocated it as an alternative to the state of international anarchy which in his view had existed before 1914 and would return again unless the countries of the world organised themselves into a community of states. International anarchy, fed by excessive secrecy, rampant militarism and autocratic government, had caused the outbreak of the first world war and would precipitate another catastrophe unless it was combatted by an international organisation with its emphasis on 'open covenants openly arrived at',[6] justice and morality. Such Wilsonian beliefs coloured the preamble to the Covenant and found expression in Article 18 calling for the registration with the League Secretariat of all treaties or international engagements entered into by members of the League. They reflected his position as the President of a country which was not threatened by any potentially hostile major powers on its frontiers, and which could therefore afford to be idealistic in its hopes for the future conduct of states.

Apart from pious sentiments, however, Wilson had one concrete scheme which he wanted to incorporate into the League Covenant. His idea about it was derived from his experience on the American continent with the Pan-American Union, an organisation set up in the early 1900s to regularise relations between the Latin American states and the United States of America. The basis of this organisation was a mutual guarantee by all members of each others' territorial integrity and political independence; Woodrow Wilson now proposed to make such a guarantee the backbone of the League.

He faced fierce opposition to this intention in the League Commission from the British delegates, particularly from Cecil who repeatedly emphasised the dangers of such a rigid scheme and the necessity for providing some mechanism to allow for peaceful change to take place in the international sphere as conditions changed and treaties became outdated. Wilson remained adamant, insisting that without such a guarantee the League would merely be an ineffective talking shop. He did, however, agree to a small addition to his scheme. If the

[6] The first point in Woodrow Wilson's famous 'fourteen points' speech delivered to Congress on 8 January 1918. The last point called for the formation of 'a general association of nations . . . under specific covenants for the purpose of affording mutual guarantees of political independence and territorial integrity to great and small states alike.' In October 1918, the Germans sued for peace on the basis of this speech and some of Wilson's subsequent addresses.

guarantee was repudiated by a League member, the League Council should advise 'upon the means by which the obligation should be fulfilled.' Wilson's guarantee scheme binding all League members was incorporated in Article 10 of the League Covenant, together with the agreed addition; this concession, however, although not realised at the time, was to render Wilson's whole scheme unworkable in practice. It had already been decided in the League Commission that League Council decisions required the assent of all Council members present at any particular meeting to be binding, and thus the way was open for an aggressor to veto action under Article 10, as Japan did in 1931.

This fatal flaw was not detected in 1919, but Cecil's fears about the severe tensions which a guarantee scheme would generate were widely shared. In the circumstances of 1919, a territorial guarantee endorsed the peace treaties being drawn up at the Paris Peace Conference which were devised to weaken Germany and her late allies. If and when Germany became a member of the League she was unlikely to accept for ever the loss of the Saar, the Polish corridor and Danzig. Furthermore, the situation in Eastern Europe was unresolved. New territorial entities had emerged from the ruins of the Austro-Hungarian and Russian empires, but as yet their frontiers were undefined in several important areas. Both Poland and Lithuania claimed Vilna; Poland and Czechoslovakia were in contention over Teschen. Further east, Bolshevik territorial and political ambitions appeared to menace the new East European entities. Clearly, it would be almost impossible to operate a scheme of territorial guarantee at such a time of flux; opportunities would have to be provided for legitimate adjustment and regulated change.

Cecil was successful in forcing Wilson to accept that treaties might have to be reconsidered by the League, and the League Assembly was charged with the task of reviewing both international treaties and international conditions from time to time to see if they were endangering the peace of the world (Article 19). But once again, as with the guarantee scheme, unanimity amongst the more important members of the League was necessary if changes in the international *status quo* were to be sanctioned, and it was highly unlikely that League powers like France and Poland who had benefited from the 1919 peace treaties would agree to any changes which would result in a weakening of their respective positions.

Thus after 1919 the League was unable to promote a policy of peaceful change, and this was one of the reasons why British statesmen in particular viewed German, Japanese, and to a lesser extent Italian, territorial ambitions sympathetically. It seemed unfair that the *status quo* of 1919 should be enforced for ever. However, the League was provided with another mechanism which could be used to try to alleviate tensions before they reached breaking point, and this also owed its inspiration to the New World, in this case not to Woodrow Wilson but to American senator and lawyer Elihu Root who expounded it to Colonel House.[7] If there was a threat of war, or if any League member felt that some aspect of international relations threatened to disturb international peace or the good understanding between nations on which peace depended, it could notify the League Council or Assembly and urge an investigation to try to resolve the situation. This general and flexible provision which was embodied in article 11 of the Covenant was unlikely to be vetoed by potential aggressors, and in the years after 1919 it proved a most useful means of bringing about League investigation and action.

The British Government's thinking about the role of an international organisation in the post-war world differed strikingly from that of Woodrow Wilson. We have already seen that it was very unhappy about Wilson's guarantee scheme, and Cecil had been successful in pressing forward an article allowing for peaceful change, though not in the form of an amendment to article 10 as he had originally desired. In 1917 Cecil, at the time under-secretary of state for foreign affairs, had also been successful in pressing Lloyd George to set up a Commission headed by an international lawyer, Lord Phillimore, to examine the schemes already propounded for a League of Nations and to formulate, if possible, a practicable outline.[8] The Phillimore Commission's report met with the approval of the British Government, though it was not formally endorsed by the Cabinet at Wilson's request, and its proposals are therefore of great importance in assessing the British Government's contribution towards the drafting of the Covenant.[9]

In the first place, the Phillimore report envisaged the League as an enlarged and institutionalised version of the nineteenth century Concert of Europe, with all the world's leading powers, represented by their ambassadors, concerting together to try to iron out their differences and regulate international affairs as amicably as possible amongst themselves. This concept of the League was heartily endorsed by the British Foreign Office, but came under fire from Wilson and from Smuts in the League Commission. At their insistence, diplomatic representation gave way to representation by leading statesmen from the member states.

More importantly, however, the British Government were overruled

[7] See Zimmern, *The League of Nations and the Rule of Law*, pp 229–32.

[8] Apart from Lord Phillimore, the Commission consisted of three high-ranking Foreign Office officials, Sir Eyre Crowe, Sir William Tyrrell and the Office's legal adviser Cecil J. Hurst, and three historians, A. F. Pollard, Julian Corbett and J. Holland Rose.

[9] See Chapter I, 1, D.

on the question of the composition of the League Council. Since this was to be the League's executive organ, the British Government wanted it to be composed solely of the world's greatest powers who would thus have the opportunity of meeting together frequently to review the international scene and try to resolve its problems. Woodrow Wilson opposed this concept because to him it smacked of pre-war secret diplomacy and dark intriguing among the more powerful nations to dominate their weaker brethren. He found an ally in Smuts who, although he represented the British Government on the League Commission along with Cecil, did not fully share its views. As the representative of a Dominion pressing for greater independence in international affairs, he urged that smaller powers should also be given the opportunity to sit on the League Council with the great world powers, either in rotation or by election from the League Assembly. This view was naturally supported enthusiastically by the representatives on the League Commission of the smaller states, and the British Government's plea for a League Council composed exclusively of great powers was rejected. To the Foreign Office in particular, the presence of four and later six non-permanent members on the executive body of the League lessened its utility as a conference body, especially in the early years of its life when neither Germany nor Russia nor the United States were members. The Foreign Office frequently cited the uneven composition of the League Council as an excellent reason for urging the British Government to by-pass the League altogether and work through some other diplomatic channel such as the Conference of Ambassadors[10] or inter-allied conferences. However, other proposals of the Phillimore Commission concerning the settlement of disputes and the operation of sanctions were received more sympathetically in the League Commission and were incorporated into the League Covenant. According to the Phillimore plan, which was cast in the form of a contract between the participating states, members were not to resort to war without previously submitting their grievance or cause of dispute either to arbitration or to the Conference of the League, depending on its nature, and they were to desist from war while investigations were undertaken. Within a specified period of time, the League would have the responsibility of drafting a report on the merits of the dispute, or of recommending an award, and the parties to the dispute would be asked to abide by the decision reached. If a state resorted to war without submitting its dispute to the arbitration or conciliation processes laid down, or refused to wait while investigations were undertaken, or went to war in

[10] This organisation was set up in 1919 by the allies to deal with any problems arising out of the interpretation or enforcement of the peace treaties which was not dealt with at top-level inter-allied conferences. It was composed of the ambassadors of the war-time allies meeting together periodically at Paris.

defiance of a unanimous League report, or attacked another State who was complying with a League recommendation, sanctions were to be enforced by League members against the offending state. They could be military, naval, financial or economic, but it was generally assumed on the basis of the experience of economic boycotts gained during the first world war that economic and financial measures alone would be sufficient to bring an offending nation to its knees within a reasonably short period.

The Phillimore Commission deliberately left two important loopholes in their scheme. They declined to recommend action in a situation where the League investigators could not agree on the merits of a dispute, and they were reluctant to prescribe sanctions against a state who refused to abide by the award or recommendation of the League, as they doubted whether, in such a situation, member states would fulfil their contract.

These Phillimore proposals were largely incorporated into articles 12–17 of the League Covenant, and represented the British view of how to deal with disputes and in what circumstances to enforce sanctions. This view was strongly coloured by the belief that the sort of mechanisms envisaged by the Phillimore Commission would have averted the outbreak of the first world war. It was generally agreed by British statesmen that if contentious issues such as those which arose in the Balkans and over Alsace-Lorraine could be thoroughly investigated and impartially judged by an international body, nations would be prepared to abide by its recommendations, particularly since the delay in hostilities would allow public opinion in the various countries to bring its influence to bear on securing agreement with the proposed League settlement; it was not anticipated that in fact publics might prove more, not less, belligerent than their Governments. Willingness to comply with the League's recommendations would also be reinforced by the high cost of waging a modern war as evidenced by the experience of the first world war.

This belief in the innate rationality of states and the efficacy of public opinion together with the expectation that states would not be willing to endure again the hardships and expense of the first world war was the product of centuries of relative security reinforced by satisfaction at the terms of the 1919 peace settlement in respect to Great Britain's security.[11] Surely no nation in the future would feel it worth-

[11] The German navy, which had menaced British shores before 1914, was scuttled by its caretaker crew at Scapa Flow in the summer of 1919. Germany's future naval strength was confined by the terms of the Treaty of Versailles to six battleships of the old design, six light cruisers, twelve destroyers and twelve torpedo boats. She was to have no submarines or naval aircraft, and no more than fifteen hundred officers and warrant officers. She was also forbidden to build up an air force, and her overseas colonies were taken away from her.

while to wage war deliberately for territorial gain or to satisfy national prestige. National leaders might want to achieve certain objectives and make belligerent noises in the process, but they would ultimately be content to abide by the League's recommendations. The League's machinery for regulating disputes was based on this optimistic assumption about the limits beyond which nations would not consider it worthwhile to go. There was also an element of fatalism in this belief. The fact that no provision was made in the Covenant to deal with a potential aggressor who waited the requisite number of months, read the League recommendations and then proceeded on his expansionist path reflected the British Government's view that no machinery in the world could stop an aggressor who really meant business. Lord Balfour echoed this sentiment in 1924 when he said, 'the danger that I see in the future is that some powerful nation will pursue a *real politik* in the future as in the past, and the question is whether any machinery that we can create will be sufficient to resist the shock which such unscrupulous efforts will undoubtedly bring on civilisation. ... I do not believe that we have yet found, or can find, a perfect guarantee against this calamity'.[12] Sanctions were only specified for nations who broke the rules formulated by the Phillimore Commission and carefully laid down in the Covenant. Furthermore, they were not automatically to be applied to nations who violated article 10, the article guaranteeing the political and territorial integrity of member states. After the establishment of the League, there was considerable dispute amongst international lawyers as to the exact relationship between article 10 and the sanctions article, article 16, and as to the circumstances in which sanctions should be recommended. To talk about articles 10 and 16 as constituting a 'collective security system', as many political scientists have done, is to ascribe powers to the League which it never possessed. Even if sanctions were agreed upon in a case of flagrant abuse of the provisions of the Covenant, they could only be recommended to the member states by the League Council, and individual countries retained their freedom of decision on whether to follow the Council's advice, and if so, on what sort of sanctions to enforce. Thus the League's sanction provisions were far more limited than is often realised.

Not unnaturally, the French Government was appalled at the laxity of the Phillimore proposals. Their history gave them no reason to believe in the reasonableness of states or to expect that they would comply with internationally-agreed solutions on the grounds of justice

[12] He was chairing a meeting to discuss the Draft Treaty of Mutual Assistance, on 19 February 1924, organised by the British Institute of International Affairs. *Journal of the British Institute of International Affairs*, March 1924, Vol. III pp 80–1.

or morality. They believed that states would be influenced in the formation of their policies principally by their perception of the likely consequences of their actions. If a nation thought it could get away with aggression then it would try to do so. Therefore the only effective preventive action an international organisation could take was concerted military and economic preparation. If the League had fully worked-out military and economic plans and could call on national or League contingents to carry them out at a moment's notice, then potential aggressors might be deterred from action. Thus the scheme outlined by the special committee set up by the French Government to formulate a framework for a viable international organisation put most of its emphasis on sanctions of various kinds and stressed the need for the League to have military forces at its disposal and to operate as an effective executive body.[13] However, both Woodrow Wilson and the British Government delegates demurred at what they considered to be such war-like preparations. They did not believe that to prevent war it was necessary to prepare for war. Indeed they believed the opposite: that to prevent war, it was desirable to promote disarmament.

It was widely thought, especially in Britain and America, that high levels of armaments before 1914 had contributed to the tensions which produced the first world war. It followed logically from this assumption that if states reduced their level of armaments, wars were less likely to occur. Furthermore, nations whose security requirements were well-covered by the 1919 peace settlements, such as Britain, did not want to spend large sums of money on the maintenance of unnecessarily high levels of armaments. The regulation of armaments through the machinery of the League of Nations would keep costs down without endangering security. Thus the British and American delegations agreed on the desirability of using the League of Nations as an agency for the promotion of disarmament 'to the lowest point consistent with national safety and the enforcement by common action of international obligations'. Furthermore, on the insistence of Wilson, backed up by Cecil and Smuts, nations were also to exchange information on the scale of their armaments, their military, naval and aerial programmes, and the condition of such of their industries as were likely to be adaptable to warlike purposes. They were also to try to discourage the manufacture by private enterprise of munitions and implements of war. These latter proposals were not enthusiastically received in the British or French Service Departments, but were embodied in article 8 of the League Covenant.

The French delegates were extremely unhappy about these projected disarmament measures which appeared to them to endanger French security as well as hinder the operation of League sanctions. With the

13 See Chapter I, 1, E.

disarmament of Germany by the Allied and Associated Powers in 1919, France was artificially the stronger country. But any measure of French disarmament, unaccompanied by guarantees of assistance, lessened the disparity in armed force between France and Germany and paved the way to renewed German aggression. Only a strong international body with clearly-defined executive powers could give France the reassurance of instant help against blatant aggression, but the French delegates on the League Commission, despite the support of their Belgian colleagues, were unable to win the majority of the Commission's delegates over to their point of view. Nor were they able to prevent the articles on disarmament from being incorporated into the League Covenant. All they managed to secure was a provision to constitute a permanent Commission to advise the League Council on the execution of disarmament schemes and on military, naval and air questions generally. This was a very faint echo of their original proposals. To the French, therefore, the League as constituted appeared to be far too weak a body to protect France's frontiers in the future. Clemenceau sought more tangible help in the form of a guarantee treaty of assistance from Britain and the United States against unprovoked external aggression, which Wilson and Lloyd George promised in return for the renunciation by the French of their claim to the Rhine frontier.

Thus at the very outset the League was equipped to play many roles. It was cast as a standing international conference, pledged to settle disputes in certain specific ways, a body guaranteeing the existing political and territorial *status quo* and recommending changes where necessary, and an agency for the promotion of disarmament. It was also given specific executive tasks to discharge, arising out of the Paris peace settlements, such as overseeing the Danzig and Saar settlements, protecting the rights of the numerous minority groups scattered throughout the new states of eastern Europe, and administering the mandates system. This latter represented a compromise between Japan and such British Dominions as Australia, New Zealand and South Africa who wanted to annex outright the German possessions they had captured during the war, and Woodrow Wilson who wanted to wipe the colonial slate clean and substitute for annexation the principle of international supervision of backward races. Smuts, who had originally formulated the mandates proposal to apply to the new nations of Central and South-East Europe who would need advice and material assistance from older and more established countries,[14] modified his scheme to break the deadlock which arose particularly between Wilson on the one hand and Hughes, Premier of Australia, on the other. He proposed three classes of mandate, 'A', 'B' and 'C', in which the amount of control exercised

[14] See his pamphlet, *The League of Nations: A Practical Suggestion*, Murray, 1918.

by the mandatory power would differ considerably. In the 'A' class of mandate, the mandatory power was to have only nominal powers of control and supervision, and into this category were placed the ex-Turkish provinces of Mesopotamia, Palestine, Syria and Lebanon. In the 'B' class of mandate, mandatory powers were to have greater powers of supervision and administration, but not as many as in the 'C' category, in which mandatory powers were to rule their charges 'under the laws of the mandatory as integral portions of its territory'. It was no coincidence that in the 'C' category were included all those territories which South Africa, Australia, New Zealand and Japan had wanted to annex, such as German South West Africa, New Guinea, Samoa and the Marianne and Caroline islands. In the 'B' category were placed the ex-German colonies of Tanganyika, the Cameroons and Togoland which neither the British nor the French Governments particularly wished to incorporate into their African empires. However, all mandatory powers were to furnish annual reports on their mandatory activities to a special mandates commission to be set up by the League, so the League was given some degree of supervision even over 'C' category mandates. (Article 22.)

With the active encouragement of the British Government, the League was also cast as a co-ordinating agency for the numerous international scientific and technical bodies which had mushroomed since the beginning of the twentieth century, and was to promote its own humanitarian and economic investigations. It was also to provide the finance for the international labour organisation, an autonomous body set up after the war to try to equalise and improve working conditions throughout the world and promote higher standards of living for working men and women.

From the beginning, therefore, the League wore many different guises and appeared to supporters and sceptics in different lights. To Wilson it was the symbol of a new dawn of just and open international relations based on a firm territorial and political guarantee; to Lloyd George it was a useful mechanism for investigating and settling disputes, and for protecting Britain from a costly arms race especially with the United States; to Clemenceau it was an absurdly idealistic irrelevance. However, domestic opposition in the United States to Wilson's Parisian activities and agreements soon changed these initial attitudes. The refusal of the United States Senate to ratify the Paris Peace Treaties in which the League Covenant constituted the first twenty-six articles, ironically on the insistence of Wilson who feared that otherwise the League would never get off the ground, meant the absence of the world's leading economic and political power from the League of Nations. The guarantee treaty of assistance promised to France also fell to the ground, unratified even by Britain whose participation had been made care-

fully conditional upon American ratification. France was left without
the Rhine frontier and without powerful allies. The League was now
her only hope of security, apart from alliances hastily concluded with
Poland and Czechoslovakia. It must be strengthened and made to
work; article 10 at least provided a foundation on which French delegates could build. The way forward was to tighten the provisions of
articles 12–17 by defining aggression more clearly and spelling out the
circumstances in which sanctions would be enforced and the ways in
which member states would be expected to co-operate. Unless the
League was strengthened along these lines so as to protect France in a
more positive and tangible way against the aggressive action which was
bound to come from the direction of Germany sooner or later, France
could not agree to any measure of disarmament.

The British Government, on the other hand, now viewed the League
with less enthusiasm than before. Without the presence of the American
Government in the League, the British Government considered that
the guarantee of political and territorial integrity contained in article 10
was unworkable and should be tacitly ignored. Indeed the Canadian
Government tried to get the article redefined by assembly resolution in
1923 but was unsuccessful. Far from strengthening the League it was
necessary now to make its procedures more flexible to avoid the possibility of friction with this economic and political giant. There could
be no question of sanctions without United States approval or assistance,
and League activities outside Europe should only proceed slowly and
cautiously, particularly in areas where the United States had great
influence such as South America and the Pacific. Even within Europe,
the main goal should now be peaceful settlement by the League or by
some other agency. The principles of justice and morality were of only
secondary importance.

The League was also less useful to the British Government as a
disarmament agency in the absence of the United States. Naval disarmament, in which the British Government was mainly interested,
would now have to proceed by way of bilateral or multilateral discussions involving principally the United States and Japan. Though the
regulation of armies and air forces through international agreement was
of some importance to Britain, it was not considered by most statesmen
to be worth the French price of making peace enforcement by the
League a more automatic process. Cecil, with his Draft Treaty of
Mutual Assistance in 1922, and the Labour Government delegates to
the League Assembly in 1924 with their contribution to the Geneva
Protocol, were prepared to contribute to the strengthening of the League
against potential aggression in return for the implementation of disarmament schemes, but their example was not followed by any other
British delegates. Indeed, there were British political leaders and

advisers who considered that membership of the League without the presence of the United States was useless, and Lloyd George tried to organise a rival organisation which would include the United States, but his efforts failed. Britain stayed in the League not out of conviction but rather out of cowardice. The public believed in it, and to disavow it might be to court electoral disaster. Baldwin admitted as much in 1923 and 1924 when he included in his Cabinets as Lord Privy Seal Lord Cecil to be in charge of League affairs 'as a kind of guarantee to supporters of the League in this country that the policy they so much desire is safe.'[15]

Unfortunately the British Government, along with other members of the League, took no steps to educate their public about the potentialities and limitations of the League or about its different roles. They glossed over the fact that the Covenant was a complex document which contained several provisions for preserving peace, some of which they endorsed and some of which they wanted to ignore. There were, indeed, some articles of the Covenant whose interpretation caused disagreement amongst the world's leading international lawyers; there were some League resolutions which were ambiguous or unclear. But Governments did not reveal their uncertainties or doubts openly to their publics, and their reluctance to spell out the implications of League membership as they interpreted them was bound to weaken the effective functioning of the League by raising exalted expectations which could not be fulfilled, or feeding fears about the League's powers which were not justified.

At times of crisis, such as during the Manchurian incident of 1931, the public feared or expected powerful reprisals by the League against Japan, and were disappointed. They did not realise that the effective functioning of the League in the Pacific area was dependent on the economic and naval co-operation of the United States, or that the British Government placed the maintenance of good relations with the United States above its responsibilities as a member of the League. They watched Japan overrun Manchuria, and concluded gladly or sadly that the League had been unable to prevent aggression and was thus a failure.[16] Had the British Government been more explicit about the way it interpreted its responsibilities under the Covenant, the public's expectations would have been more realistic and its attitudes more helpful to the Government and to the working of the League. There might have been a clearer assessment of the League's role in that particular crisis, and in the many others which succeeded it.

. . . . .

[15] See Keith Middlemas and John Barnes, *Baldwin: A Biography*, Weidenfeld and Nicolson, 1969.
[16] See R. Bassett, *Democracy and Foreign Policy*, Cass, 1968.

However much excuse there might have been in the past for an inadequate assessment of the League in its many roles there is none today. Indeed the problem facing the League analyst is the enormous volume of documents at his disposal since the introduction in Britain and in many other countries of the thirty-year rule. It has been extremely difficult, in editing this volume, to decide which documents to include and which to omit from the voluminous mass now available. There is, of course, a lot of duplication and overlapping of material, and for this reason it is advisable for the League historian to tackle the collections of documents in a certain order.

The richest vein of League material is undoubtedly to be found in the Public Record Office in London, in the Foreign Office files on the League of Nations, and I have included some extracts from these files. After 1922, the Western Department of the Foreign Office was responsible for receiving and analysing reports of League activities, and its files contain not only the vast bulk of League material issued from Geneva but also the suggestions and comments of Foreign Office officials and Government ministers in charge of foreign affairs.[17] Apart from the League of Nations files, interesting material can also be found in the personal Foreign Office files of successive inter-war foreign secretaries, in the files of the Committee of Imperial Defence, in the Disarmament and Colonial Office files, and in files dealing with specific countries and problems such as health. Combing through all the files likely to yield interesting information is an extremely arduous and time-consuming task but it does bring to light the many functions of the League and the ways in which British government officials and statesmen regarded each one.

Extracts from the enormous mass of Foreign Office files are contained in the relatively compact volumes of the British foreign policy documents, arranged in four series and covering at present the years 1919–22 (Series I), 1926–7 (Series Ia), 1929–33 (Series II), and 1938–9 (Series III). The most interesting volumes for the League historian are those covering the Manchurian dispute, and I have included some extracts from these volumes. Unfortunately, the gaps between the series cover both the Corfu crisis of 1923 and the Abyssinian affair of 1935–6. The latter omission is the more serious since, at the time of writing, the Foreign Office files on the Abyssinian affair were not available at the Public Record Office but were in the possession of the Foreign Office itself.

Apart from departmental files, the Public Record Office also houses

---

[17] Before 1922, the Cabinet Office handled all League correspondence and channelled it to and from the various interested Government departments. Thus the Foreign Office was not always in touch with League activities before 1922.

the Cabinet records, a collection of minutes of Cabinet meetings and papers prepared in various Government departments for the consideration of the Cabinet. These records, while less detailed than those of the Foreign Office, reveal the attitudes to the League not only of different foreign and colonial secretaries but also of the Prime Ministers and other Cabinet ministers of the inter-war period, and show in many crucial instances why certain policies were pursued to the exclusion of others. Scattered around the country are also some private collections of source material amassed by statesmen in office. Of particular interest to League historians are the Cecil and Balfour papers at the British Museum, the Fisher papers at the Bodleian Library in Oxford, the Lloyd George and Bonar Law papers at the Beaverbrook Library in London, and the Baldwin papers at New College, Cambridge.

Other countries are also slowly making available their state papers and collecting together important documents. Unfortunately the most complete collection, outside Britain, is in the United States and can therefore shed only marginal light on League proceedings. However, British foreign office files do help the student who is shaky in foreign languages or unable to travel abroad. They contain many précis of conversations between British statesmen and officials and their foreign counterparts, and despatches from British ambassadors and chargés d'affaires abroad, which illuminate very clearly in some instances the attitudes and policies of other nations towards the League.[18]

There is, of course, a complete set of League records covering every meeting of the League Council, Assembly and Assembly Committees, and every activity and investigation undertaken by League officials. This exhaustive documentation, published throughout the League's existence in Geneva and distributed throughout the world, was until recently the most useful available source of information about the League, and still remains an invaluable source of reference on which I have drawn heavily. Another collection of documents which was of great value to contemporary historians before the opening of the inter-war Foreign Office files is the series of *Documents on International Affairs* published annually under the auspices of the Royal Institute of International Affairs and covering League of Nations affairs in some detail. There are also some interesting British Government white papers on relatively obscure areas of League activity such as mandates and international labour activity. Records of House of Commons and House of Lords debates, while somewhat tedious and predictable, do mirror accurately if guardedly the attitudes and policies towards the League of the Government and Opposition, and of the different political parties and factions, especially at times of crisis such as during the Abyssinian affair.

[18] See Chapter II. 2. D and Chapter II. 3. A.

Though such collections of documents obviously provide the League historian with his staple diet, there are other appetising tit-bits for him to sample. Newspapers of the day, especially the more racy ones, put an interesting gloss on current affairs, and can be tracked down at the National Newspaper Library at Colindale, London, or in the newspaper library at the Royal Institute of International Affairs. Autobiographies and biographies of statesmen, diplomats and writers are fascinating for what they say and for what they leave unsaid. Analyses of contemporary events written as they occurred and published soon afterwards are helpful, though unfortunately they rapidly become unobtainable as they go out of print. Annual reference works, party manuals and manifestoes, novels and poems all contribute to an understanding of the inter-war period and its prevailing atmosphere and attitudes which help the League historian to put his subject into perspective.

With all this abundance of material now available it surely cannot be long before the League of Nations becomes a focus of interest to contemporary historians and an object of study in its own right. When official files have been combed through and digested, it should be possible to produce an authoritative account of its many activities and an accurate assessment of its achievements and shortcomings, as well as numerous monographs and detailed studies of particular crises and incidents of great value to historians, political scientists and students of current affairs.

I

A LIVING THING IS BORN

ALTHOUGH MEN HAD long dreamed of constructing some sort of international framework which would attempt to preserve peace among potentially antagonistic states, it took the appalling waste and futility of the first world war to translate this dream into reality. Sickened by the senseless slaughter of long years of trench warfare, statesmen and writers in Europe and America came together to draw up schemes for an international organisation which would prevent such a catastrophe from occurring again. The crippling economic and material cost of waging the war forced Britain and her Allies to contract large loans in the United States of America, and by the end of the war the Old World found itself heavily in debt to the New. This relationship was reflected in the fact that the Germans sued for peace in 1918 on the basis of the American President's peace programme, contained largely in his famous fourteen points; point fourteen called for the establishment of a post-war international organisation. Woodrow Wilson utilised his position of superiority at the Paris Peace Conference to push the establishment of the League of Nations to the forefront of the conference programme, and by his insistence secured the incorporation of the twenty-six articles of the League Covenant into each of the peace treaties concluded in 1919. Ironically, domestic opposition to Wilson and to the prominent role he was marking out for the United States of America in the post-war world resulted in the refusal of the American Senate to ratify the Treaty of Versailles. Thus, from the outset, the League of Nations was deprived of the support of the world's most powerful nation.

I.1 IDEAS ON AN ORGANISATION TO PREVENT FUTURE WARS

The phrase 'League of Nations' was reputedly first coined in August, 1914, by the writer and lecturer H. Lowes Dickinson, and during the ensuing four terrible years many politicians, writers and academics formulated schemes embodying their own personal ideas on post-war international organisation. Notable amongst advocates of a League of Nations was Sir Robert Cecil, younger son of Lord Salisbury, and Under-Secretary of State for Foreign Affairs under both the Asquith

19

and Lloyd George wartime administrations. In 1916 he urged the Cabinet to consider his 'Proposals for the Maintenance of Future Peace', and he then persuaded his cousin Lord Balfour, the Foreign Secretary, to appoint a committee under the international lawyer Lord Phillimore, to examine proposals for a League of Nations and to formulate a practicable scheme. Amongst the schemes considered by this committee was one on 'International Government' drawn up by Leonard Woolf in conjunction with the Fabian Society. The conclusions of the Phillimore Committee on the constitution and functions of a feasible League of Nations were endorsed by the Lloyd George coalition Government in 1918 as a suitable basis for a post-war international organisation. Meanwhile the French Government also set up a Commission to work out a framework for an international organisation, and its conclusions were markedly different from those of the Phillimore Committee. Both schemes were submitted to President Wilson for his observations, and he confessed himself unimpressed by their contents. The outline which fired his imagination, and furnished him with new ideas to incorporate into his own hitherto woolly thoughts on a League was Smuts' 'The League of Nations: A Practical Suggestion', which was specifically designed by the South African Defence Minister to lift the whole discussion about post-war international organisation from a theoretical plane into the realm of practical politics.[1]

I.1.A   Three War Poems.
        (i)   *Bombardment* : RICHARD ALDINGTON

            Four days the earth was rent and torn
            By bursting steel,
            The houses fell about us;
            Three nights we dared not sleep,
            Sweating, and listening for the imminent crash
            Which meant our death.

            The fourth night every man,
            Nerve-tortured, racked to exhaustion,
            Slept, muttering and twitching,
            While the shells crashed overhead.

            The fifth day there came a hush;
            We left our holes

---

[1] Lord Riddell, in his *Intimate Diary of the Peace Conference and after* (Gollancz, London, 1933) on p. 279 quotes Lloyd George as saying in 1921, 'I gave him (Wilson) Smuts' plan and begged him to consider it. He intimated that he did not want any assistance but, after reading Smuts' memorandum, swallowed it whole. . . .' In *The Truth About the Peace Treaties*, vol I (Gollancz, 1938) on p. 620, Lloyd George refers to the Smuts paper as 'the model upon which the Covenant of the League was built'.

And looked above the wreckage of the earth
To where the white clouds moved in silent lines
Across the untroubled blue.

(ii)   *Attack*: SIEGFRIED SASSOON

At dawn the ridge emerges massed and dun
In the wild purple of the glow'ring sun,
Smouldering through spouts of drifting smoke that shroud
The menacing scarred slope; and, one by one,
Tanks creep and topple forward to the wire.
The barrage roars and lifts. Then, clumsily bowed
With bombs and guns and shovels and battle-gear,
Men jostle and climb to meet the bristling fire.
Lines of grey, muttering faces, masked with fear,
They leave their trenches, going over the top,
While time ticks blank and busy on their wrists,
And hope, with furtive eyes and grappling fists,
Flounders in mud. O Jesus, make it stop!

(iii)   *A Lament*: WILFRED WILSON GIBSON

We who are left, how shall we look again
Happily on the sun, or feel the rain,
Without remembering how they who went
Ungrudgingly, and spent
Their all for us, loved, too, the sun and rain?

A bird among the rain-wet lilac sings—
But we, how shall we turn to little things
And listen to the birds and winds and streams
Made holy by their dreams,
Nor feel the heart-break in the heart of things?

I.1.B   *Memorandum on Proposals for Diminishing the Occasion of Future
Wars*, (Autumn 1916) written by Lord Cecil and presented to
the Cabinet. (PRO reference number: FO371/3082).

It is estimated that the total number of killed and wounded in this war
approaches 50,000,000—more than the population of the British
islands—and that of these 7,000,000 have been killed. . . . We have so
far spent between 2,000 and 3,000 millions of pounds. Assuming our
Allies have spent as much and our enemies half as much again the
total expenditure has been not less than some 8,000 or 9,000 millions,
and may well have been much more. . . . Taken altogether, the impoverishment of the world by waste of life, waste of labour, and destruction of material has been appalling. Human suffering has resulted on a

scale unprecedented in the history of the world. . . . A small battle recorded as the capture of a few yards of trench involves the death by torture of hundreds, perhaps thousands of young men, the maiming or blinding of as many more, and for the lucky ones horrible wounds inflicted by jagged fragments of high-explosive shells. Perhaps even harder to bear are the anxiety, the grief and the bereavement which fall on the women at home.

. . . It is not too much to say that it has endangered the fabric of our civilisation, and if it is to be repeated the whole European system may probably disappear in anarchy. It is surely, therefore, most urgent that we should try to think out some plan to lessen the possibility of future war. . . .

What . . . can be done? The only possible way out appears to be to try to substitute for war some other way of settling international disputes. Two expedients suggest themselves: arbitration and conference of the Powers—European Concert. The difficulty of arbitration is to discover the arbitrators to whom sovereign powers will be content to submit questions of vital importance. The same objection does not apply to conferences. But, as was found in the present war, no machinery exists to force unwilling powers to agree to a conference and await its decision. It would be simple to include in the Treaty of Peace a general agreement to that effect. But what if a group of Powers were determined on war, how are they to be compelled to enter a conference? In other words, what is to be the sanction? A provision that all the Powers shall combine to punish by force of arms a breach of the treaty will probably by itself be ineffective. As far as Europe is concerned, there will always be a tendency for the Powers to form themselves into two groups more or less equal in strength, and if one of these becomes aggressive it may and probably will ignore all treaties. Under these circumstances the risks of war are so great that few countries would enter it merely in support of treaties and international right, and the settlement of the dispute will be left to war between the Powers immediately concerned. If, however, an instrument could be found which would exert considerable pressure on a recalcitrant Power without causing excessive risk to the Powers using it, a solution of the difficulty might perhaps be found. I believe that in blockade as developed in this war such an instrument exists. No doubt for its full effect an overwhelming naval power is requisite. But much could be done even by overwhelming financial power, and with the two combined no modern State could ultimately resist its pressure. Suppose in July 1914 it had been possible for the Entente Powers to say to Germany and Austria, 'unless the ultimatum to Serbia is modified or a conference is called, we will cut off all commercial and financial intercourse from you', it is very doubtful whether the Central Powers would have proceeded. If the United States could have been induced to join in such a declaration, the effect would have been enormously increased. And though it is certainly hopeless to expect America to fight in a European quarrel unless her interests are directly affected, it does not seem so certain that she would refuse to join in organised economic action to preserve peace. It is assumed as a necessary condition of this proposal that a territorial settlement of a reasonable sort is arrived at in the treaty, and its maintenance is guaranteed by the signatory Powers. . . .

I append a rough draft to explain the working of the scheme.

Proposals for Maintenance of Future Peace

The High Contracting Powers further agree that the territorial arrangements hereinbefore set forth shall remain unaltered for the next five years. At, or if any of the High Contracting Powers so demands then before, the end of that period a conference of the High Contracting Powers shall be summoned, and any rearrangements of territory which have become necessary or desirable shall be then considered and, if agreed upon, shall be forthwith carried out.

If any difference or controversy shall arise between any of the High Contracting Powers with respect to the meaning of any of the articles of this treaty, or with respect to the rights of any of the parties thereto, or with respect to any other matter, a conference of the Powers shall forthwith be summoned, and the controversy shall be submitted to it, and no action shall be taken by any of the parties to the controversy until the conference has met and considered the matter, and has either come to a decision thereon or has failed for a period of three months after its meeting to come to such a decision. Any decision agreed upon at such conference shall be maintained and enforced by all the High Contracting Powers as if it were one of the articles of this treaty.

Each of the High Contracting Powers guarantees and agrees to maintain the provisions of this treaty if necessary by force of arms, and in particular undertakes that if any Power shall refuse or fail to submit any controversy to a conference as provided in the last preceding article of this treaty, or shall otherwise infringe any of the provisions of this treaty, each of the High Contracting Powers shall thereupon cut off all commercial and financial intercourse with the wrongdoing Power, and as far as possible shall prevent such Power from having any commercial or financial intercourse with any other Power, whether a party to this treaty or not; and it is hereby further agreed that for the purpose of enforcing this provision, any of the High Contracting Powers may detain any ship or goods belonging to any of the subjects of the wrongdoing Powers or coming from or destined for any person residing in the territory of such Power, and with the same object may take any other similar step which may seem desirable or necessary.

I.1.c   Leonard Woolf prepared two reports for the Fabian Research Department, which were published in 1916 under the title *International Government*. The following extract is taken from the first report, entitled *An International Authority and the Prevention of War*.

A deliberate co-ordination of the machinery of international relationship is . . . absolutely essential as a first step towards preventing war. . . .

The existing international system of the world is founded upon the theoretical sacredness of the independence and the sovereignty of independent sovereign States. That is why, in my search for an International Authority, I have assumed that the constituents of that authority will be independent sovereign States. It is certain that today, in this demi-civilised world, no State will agree to come into an international system unless its independence and sovereignty are safeguarded. . . .

It is possible to see how the Conference can develop logically . . . into a real organ of an International Authority. These occasional and tentative assemblies of national representatives must become regular and permanent. They will have the right and the power to make general rules of international conduct, and to consider and pronounce decisions upon all differences and disputes which are not referred to a judicial tribunal. The rule that every dispute in which negotiation has failed must come before either a tribunal or a Conference will be the pivot of the international system, and this co-ordination of machinery will be the foundation of international organisation. But, since the units of the International Authority are independent sovereign States, they alone are masters, and must retain that mastership of their own independence and sovereignty. They can therefore, without fear of endangering their 'vital interests' or 'national honour', agree to be bound by the decisions of such conferences, and to maintain the right of the majority to bind the minority only where the decision would not affect the independence, or territorial integrity, or would not require an alteration in the internal laws of the State.

. . . It is hardly practical, in the present condition of the world, to discuss the possibility of anything like a permanent international police force. . . . We are only just feeling about for an International Authority, and all that we can hope for at this stage is that the nations will agree upon and declare what methods the Authority has the right to use in order to enforce those fundamental obligations upon which this system of international society rests.

I.1.D   The Interim Report of the Phillimore Committee was completed
by early 1918, and printed for the Cabinet. (It can be found in
the PRO, reference number G.T. 4454, Cab 24/50.)

1. We had the honour to be appointed by you as a Committee to
enquire particularly from a judicial and historical point of view into
the various schemes for establishing by means of a League of Nations,
or other device, some alternative to war as a means of settling international disputes, to report on their practicability, to suggest amendments, or to elaborate a further scheme if on consideration it should be
deemed possible and expedient, and to report to you the result of our
deliberations.

2. We have held nine meetings in which our attention has been
directed mainly to the various proposals for a League of Nations which
were formulated in the sixteenth and seventeenth centuries and to
those which have been put forward since the recent revival of the movement. . . .

4. The earlier projects which aimed at setting up a kind of European
Confederation with a supernational authority we have after consideration rejected, feeling that international opinion is not ripe for so drastic
a pooling of sovereignty, and that the only feasible method of securing
the object is by way of co-operation or possibly a treaty of alliance on
the lines of the more recent schemes.

5. We have accordingly carefully considered those schemes, all of
which substitute, in place of the earlier idea of confederation, a system
working by means of a permanent conference and an arbitral tribunal.
None of them, however, in their entirety appear to your Committee
to be practicable or likely to meet with acceptance. We have therefore, drafted a Convention in which, while embodying their leading
ideas, we have endeavoured to avoid their more obvious stumbling
blocks.

6. On the assumption that a League of Nations may be regarded as a
possible solution of the problem, we now submit this draft as the best
we have been able to devise, to serve as a basis for an interchange o
views. . . .

7. The primary object of the proposed alliance will be that whatever
happens peace shall be preserved between members of the alliance. The
secondary object will be the provision of means for disposing of disputes which may arise between the members of the alliance. Our draft
treaty, therefore, divides itself into four parts; Articles 1 and 2, which
stand very much by themselves, are to provide for the avoidance of war;
Articles 3 to 12, for the pacific settlement of international disputes;
Articles 13 to 17, for the relations between the allied States and States
not party to the Convention; while Article 18 provides that this treaty
shall override all others.

8. The mutual covenant not to go to war is contained in Article 1. We have not covered all cases. We have provided that no State shall go to war without previously submitting the matter to arbitration or to the Conference of the League, nor while the discussion is pending in debate, nor shall seek any further satisfaction than that which the award or the recommendation of the Conference requires. This leaves untouched the case in which the Conference can make no recommendation, but we are in great hope that this event will be rare. There will be every inducement to the Conference to find a mode of escaping from war, and, at any rate, the time will be so long drawn out that passions will have cooled. The other case omitted is when a State that has given cause of offence refuses to abide by the award or the recommendation of the Conference. It might be suggested that in this case the whole power of the League should be used to enforce submission, but we have felt a doubt whether States would contract to do this, and still greater doubt whether, when the time came, they would fulfil their contract. . . .

9. It will be noted that the proposed moratorium only extends to actual warfare. Some writers have suggested that there should be no warlike preparations during the period. We have rejected this

(a) because it would be difficult to ascertain what were warlike preparations;

(b) because we would designedly give an opportunity to the most peaceful State which had not kept its armaments up to a high pitch to improve them during the period of the moratorium, in this way discounting to some extent the advantages which a State which kept up excessive armaments would otherwise have had.

10. Article 2 contains the sanction proposed. We have desired to make it as weighty as possible. We have, therefore, made it unanimous and automatic, and one to which each State must contribute its force without waiting for the others, but we have recognised that some States may not be able to make, at any rate in certain cases, an effective contribution of military or naval force. We have accordingly provided that such States shall at the least take the financial, economic, and other measures indicated in the Article. . . .

14. The next questions which enter into consideration in Articles 7, 9, 11, and 12 are whether the decisions of the Conference must be unanimous, and whether, if any resolutions may be passed by a majority, the voting strengths of the States should differ. We have concluded to eliminate the States parties to the dispute, but the precedents in favour of unanimity are so invariable that we have not seen our way to give power to a majority, or even a preponderant majority, to issue a definite recommendation. . . . We have been rather loath to frame a scheme

under which our own country should be rendered liable to have a recommendation passed against it by a majority vote in a matter vitally affecting the national interests, and ... we have also felt that if some of the enemy Powers are ever to come into this League they would equally be unwilling to submit themselves to such a liability. ...

DRAFT CONVENTION

(There will be a Preamble reciting that the object of this Convention is to create a League of Nations which will, if possible, prevent all wars in the future.)

Avoidance of War

Article 1. Each of the Allied States (being the parties to this Convention) agrees with the other Allied States collectively and separately that it will not go to war with another of the Allied States
  (a) without previously submitting the matter in dispute to arbitration or to a Conference of the Allied States; and
  (b) until there has been an award or a report by the Conference ... and also that it will not go to war
  (c) with another of the Allied States which complies with the award or with the recommendation (if any) made by the Conference in its report.

Article 2. If, which may God avert, one of the Allied States should break the Covenant contained in the preceding Article, this State will become *ipso facto* at war with all the other Allied States, and the latter agree to take and to support each other in taking jointly and severally all such measures—military, naval, financial, and economic— as will best avail for restraining the breach of covenant. Such financial and economic measures shall include severance of all relations of trade and finance with the subjects of the covenant-breaking State, prohibition against the subjects of the Allied States entering into any relations with the subjects of the covenant-breaking State, and the prevention, so far as possible, of the subjects of the covenant-breaking State from having any commercial or financial intercourse with the subjects or any other State, whether party to this Convention or not.

For the purpose of this Article, the Allied States shall detain any ship or goods belonging to any of the subjects of the covenant-breaking State or coming from or destined for any person residing in the territory of such state and shall take any other similar steps which shall be necessary for the same purpose.

Such of the Allied States (if any) as cannot make an effective contribution of military or naval force shall at the least take the other measures indicated in this Article.

Pacific Settlement of International Disputes

Article 3. If a dispute should hereafter arise between any of the Allied States as to the interpretation of a treaty, as to any question of international law, as to the existence of any fact which if established would constitute a breach of any international obligation, or as to the nature and extent of the reparation to be made for any such breach, if such dispute cannot be settled by negotiation, arbitration is recognised by the Applied States as the most effective and at the same time the most equitable means of settling the dispute.

Article 4. But if the Allied States concerned do not agree that the dispute is suitable for reference to arbitration or do not agree as to the question to be referred or as to the composition of the tribunal of arbitration, or if for any other reason a reference to arbitration should prove impracticable, any one of the Allied States concerned may make application to the Conference of the Allied States to take the matter of the dispute into consideration. . . .

Article 8. The function of the Conference shall be to ascertain the facts with regard to the dispute, and to make a recommendation based on the merits of the case, and calculated to ensure a just and lasting settlement. The recommendation shall not have the force of a decision. . . .

I.1.E   The Report of the Committee appointed by the French Government to examine the basis on which a League of Nations might be constituted, was completed in June 1918. (This can be found in the PRO reference number: FO 371/3439.)

I.   STATEMENT OF THE PRINCIPLES TO BE TAKEN AS BASIS OF THE LEAGUE OF NATIONS.

. . .

2. The object of the League of Nations shall not be to establish an international political State. It shall merely aim at the maintenance of peace by substituting Right for Might as the arbiter of disputes. It will thus guarantee to all States alike, whether small or great, the exercise of their sovereignty.

3. The scope of the League of Nations is universal, but, by its very nature, it can only extend to those nations which will give each other all necessary guarantees of a practical and legal nature, and which, in loyal fulfilment of their given word, solemnly undertake to be bound by certain rules in order to maintain peace by respecting Right, and to guarantee the free development of their national life.

Consequently, no nations can be admitted to the League other than those which are constituted as States and provided with representative institutions such as will permit their being themselves considered responsible for the acts of their own Governments.

4. The League of Nations shall be represented by an international body, composed of the responsible heads of Governments or of their delegates.

This international body shall have the following powers:

(1) It shall organise an international tribunal.

(2) It shall effect the amicable settlement of disputes between the States members of the League by means of mediation. . . .

(3) In the event of an amicable settlement proving impossible, it will refer the matter to the International Tribunal, if the question at issue is open to a legal decision; otherwise it shall itself decide the matter.

(4) It shall enforce the execution of its decisions and those of the International Tribunal; at its demand every nation shall be bound, in agreement with the other nations, to exert its economic, naval, and military power against any recalcitrant nation.

(5) Every nation shall likewise be bound, at the demand of the International Body, to exert, in common accord with the other nations, its economic, naval and military power against any nation which, not having become a member of the League of Nations, shall attempt, by any means whatsoever, to impose its will on another nation.

5. The International Tribunal shall pronounce on all questions submitted to it, either by the International Body or by a State having any dispute with another.

It shall decide and pronounce upon questions of law at issue between States, on the basis of custom or of international conventions, as well as of theory and jurisprudence.

In cases of violation of such law, it shall order the necessary reparation and sanctions.

II. DIPLOMATIC, LEGAL AND ECONOMIC SANCTIONS

1. *Diplomatic Sanctions*

These sanctions . . . fall under three headings:—

(a) The suspension or breaking off of the diplomatic relations existing up to that period between such State and other member States of the League of Nations;

(b) The withdrawal of the *exequatur* granted to the consuls of such State:

(c) The exclusion of the State in question from the benefit of any international conventions to which it may be a party.

2. *Legal Sanctions*

On the other hand, certain sanctions of a legal nature will enable the League of Nations ... to enforce respect of the principles which it is called upon to protect....

3. *Economic Sanctions*

Other sanctions of an economic nature can be employed by the League of Nations, by which it will be enabled to excerise an efficient control over the recalcitrant State, by various measures which may extend to placing it under an absolute commercial, industrial, or financial ban.

The principle measures in question are:—

(a) *Blockade*, consisting in the prevention by force of any commercial intercourse with the territory of the State in question.

(b) *Embargo*, i.e., the seizure and temporary sequestration, in the ports and territorial waters of the member States, of ships and cargoes belonging to the delinquent State and its nationals, as also the seizure of all goods destined for such State.

(c) Prohibition of the supply of raw materials and foodstuffs indispensable to its economic existence.

(d) Prohibition of the issue by such State of public loans in the territories of the member States; refusal to allow stock issued elsewhere to be quoted on the official Exchange, and even withdrawal of any previous permission for the quotation of the stock of such State.

The sanctions thus provided will be all the more efficacious and their application will be all the more prompt, in that the member States will have previously arranged to protect themselves against any reprisals to their prejudice, by means of an economic organisation adapted to facilitate their co-operation and mutual assistance....

III. MILITARY SANCTIONS

(i) *International Forces*

The execution of the military sanctions on land or at sea shall be entrusted either to an international force, or to one or more Powers, members of the League of Nations, to whom a mandate in that behalf shall have been given.

The International Body shall have at its disposal a military force supplied by the various member States of sufficient strength:—

(1) to secure the execution of its decisions and those of the International Tribunal;

(2) to overcome, in case of need, any forces which may be opposed to the League of Nations in the event of armed conflict.

(ii) *Strength of International Contingents*

The International Body shall determine the strength of the international force and fix the contingents which must be held at its disposal.

Each of the member States shall be free to settle as it deems best the conditions under which its contingent shall be recruited. . . .

(iii) *Permanent Staff*

A permanent international Staff shall investigate all military questions affecting the League of Nations. Each State shall appoint the officer or officers who shall represent it in a proportion to be determined later. . . .

(iv) *Functions of the Permanent Staff*

It shall be the duty of the permanent international Staff to deal, under the supervision of the International Body, with everything relating to the organisation of the joint forces and the eventual conduct of military operations. It will in particular be charged with the task of inspecting international forces and armaments in agreement with the military authorities of each State, and of proposing any improvements it may deem necessary, either in the international military organisation or in the constitution, composition, and methods of recruiting of the forces of each State. . . .

IV. Scope and Functions of the International Body

(i) *Maintenance of Peace between the Member Nations*

The Council shall devise and apply all means for the prevention of international disputes. . . .

2. The International Council shall, either at the demand of the parties or at the instance of a third State, effect an amicable settlement of differences, menacing peace between the member States; in default of any such demand, it shall be bound to take the initiative as regards such settlement.

3. It shall, in the first place, proceed either by means of good offices and of mediation . . . or by reminding the disputant States that the permanent Court is open to them.

4. Should no amicable settlement be thus obtained, the International Council shall consider whether the question is of a legal nature, in

which case it shall order the disputant States to submit their differences to the Court of International Jurisdiction, which is competent to deal with the matter in the terms of Section iv of the First Hague Convention. . . .

5. The International Council shall ensure the execution of the decisions of the International Court, if necessary, by resorting to the application of diplomatic, legal, economic, and military sanctions.

6. Should the International Council consider that the matter is not of a nature to be finally settled by a legal decision, it shall deal with the question direct.

It shall in the first instance attempt to promote an amicable settlement, and, should it not itself be successful in so doing, it shall define the terms according to which the dispute shall be settled in a manner which shall respect the rights of each State and the maintenance of Peace.

This decision shall be notified to the States concerned, it being intimated to them that as from such date no dispute exists between the contestant States, but between the entirety of the member States and the State, which, by refusing to accept such decision, violates the very principles of the League. Should the State concerned refuse to accept the decision after having been summoned to do so, the International Council shall notify to it the coercive measures of a diplomatic, legal, economic, or military nature to be taken against it within a specified time. . . .

I.1.F   *The League of Nations: A Practical Suggestion* was a pamphlet written by J. C. Smuts in late 1918 to popularise the concept of a League of Nations, and to widen its rather restricted scope as envisaged in previous schemes.

. . . If the League is ever to be a success it will have to occupy a much greater position and perform many other functions besides those ordinarily assigned to it. Peace and war are resultants of many complex forces, and those forces will have to be gripped at an earlier stage of their growth if peace is to be effectively maintained. To enable it to do so, the League will have to occupy the great position which has been rendered vacant by the destruction of so many of the old European empires and the passing away of the old European order. And the League should be put into the very forefront of the programme of the peace conference, and be made the point of departure for the solution of many of the grave problems with which it will be confronted.

To my mind the world is ripe for the greatest step forward ever made in the government of man. And I hope this brief account of the League will assist the public to realise how great an advance is possible today as a direct result of the immeasurable sacrifices of this war.

If that advance is not made, this war will, from the most essential point of view, have been fought in vain. And greater calamities will follow. . . .

During this war a great deal of attention has been given to the idea of a League of Nations as a means of preventing future wars. The discussion of the subject has proceeded almost entirely from that one point of view, and as most people are rather sceptical of the possibility of preventing wars altogether, the League has only too often been looked upon as Utopian, as an impractical ideal not likely to be realised while human nature remains what it is. . . .

An attempt will be made in this sketch to give an essential extension to the functions of the League; . . . to view it not only as a possible means for preventing future wars, but much more as a great organ of the ordinary peaceful life of civilisation, as the foundation of the new international system which will be erected on the ruins of this war, and as the starting point from which the peace arrangements of the forthcoming conference should be made. Such an orientation of the idea seems to me necessary if the League is to become a permanent part of our international machinery. It is not sufficient for the League merely to be a sort of *deus ex machina*, called in in very grave emergencies when the spectre of war appears; if it is to last, it must be much more. It must become part and parcel of the common international life of states; it must be an ever visible, living working organ of the polity of civilisation. It must function so strongly in the ordinary peaceful intercourse of states that it becomes irresistible in their disputes; its peace activity must be the foundation and guarantee of its war power. . . .

The real work of the League will . . . be done by its council, whose constitution and powers ought therefore to be very carefully considered. This council would have to be a comparatively small body, as it is not possible to have executive action taken and most difficult contentious administrative work done through a large body. . . . The Great Powers will have to be permanent members of it. Thus the British Empire, France, Italy, the United States of America, and Japan will be permanent members, to whom Germany will be added as soon as she has a stable democratic Government. To these permanent members I would suggest that four additional members be added in rotation from two panels, one panel comprising the important intermediate Powers below the rank of Great Powers, . . . and the other panel comprising all the minor states who are members of the League. . . .

The Powers represented on the council should send to it representatives of the highest standing and authority. These representatives should be the Prime Ministers or Foreign Secretaries. . . . On really important occasions either the Prime Ministers or Foreign Secretaries should ... attend personally. And, in any case, they should attend one annual meeting at which there should be a free and frank interchange of views and a review of the general policies of the council. It should also be the invariable practice to call into consultation any state not represented on the council whose interests are directly affected by any decision proposed to be taken by the council. If the most important leaders in the Governments of the Powers attend the sittings of the council as often as possible, and proper consultation of others interested takes place, the council cannot fail to command the highest prestige and authority, and to become the executive committee of the whole body of sovereign states in their international relations and activities. The more confidence it commands, the less will be the inclination among the Powers to enter into private intrigues or understandings apart from the regular machinery of the council, and the smoother will become the working of the new system of world government.

... as long as members of the League submit their disputes for inquiry and report or recommendation or decision by some outside authority, their obligations to the League will be satisfied, and thereafter they will be free to take any action they like, and even to go to war.

This may appear a weak position to take up; and yet it is not deemed expedient to go any further. The utmost that it seems possible to achieve in the present conditions of international opinion and practice is to provide for a breathing space before the disputants are free to go to war; to create a binding moratorium or period of delay, during which the parties to the dispute agree not to proceed to extremes but to await the results of the inquiry or hearing to which their case has been referred. The general opinion is that states will not be prepared to bind themselves further; and even if they do, the risk of their breaking their engagements is so great as to make the engagement not worth while and indeed positively dangerous. The common view is that, if such a period of deliberation and delay is established, there will be time for extreme war passions to cool down, and for public opinion to be aroused and organised on the side of peace. And in view of the enormous force which public opinion would exert in such a case, the general expectation is that it will prove effective, and that the delay, and the opportunity thus given for further reflection and the expression of public opinion, will in most cases prevent the parties from going to war. . . .

The moratorium must extend not only for the period of the inquiry and until a decision or report has been rendered, but for a reasonable time after such rendering. . . . The breaker of the moratorium ... should ... become *ipso facto* at war with all the other members of the League ... which will sever all relations of trade and finance with the law-breaker, and prohibit all intercourse with its subjects, and also prevent as far as possible all commercial and financial intercourse between the subjects of the law-breaker and those of any other state, whether a member of the League or not. . . . The effect of such a complete automatic trade and financial boycott will necessarily be enormous . . . I do not think the League is likely to prove a success unless in the last resort the maintenance of the moratorium is guaranteed by force. The obligation on the members of the League to use force for this purpose should . . . be absolute, but the amount of the force and the contribution from the members should be left to the recommendation of the council to the respective Governments in each case. . . .

If the future peace of the world is to be maintained, it will not be sufficient merely to erect an institution for the purpose of settling international disputes after they have arisen, it will be necessary to devise an instrument of government which will deal with the causes and sources of disputes. The need is there, and the end of the great war has brought an unequalled opportunity for dealing with it . . . mankind is once more on the move. The very foundations have been shaken and loosened, and things are again fluid. The tents have been struck, and the great caravan of humanity is once more on the march. Vast social and industrial changes are coming—perhaps upheavals which may, in their magnitude and effects, be comparable to war itself. A steadying, controlling, regulating influence will be required to give stability to progress and to remove that wasteful friction which has dissipated so much social force in the past, and in this war more than ever before. These great functions could only be adequately fulfilled by the League of Nations. Responding to such vital needs and coming at such a unique opportunity in history, it may well be destined to mark a new era in the government of man, and become to the peoples the guarantee of peace, to the workers of all races the great international, and to all the embodiment and living expression of the moral and spiritual unity of the human race.

I.2 THE DRAFTING OF THE COVENANT

The drafting of a constitution for the new international organisation was, at Woodrow Wilson's insistence, tackled during the early weeks of the Paris Peace Conference, by a special League of Nations Commission chaired by Woodrow Wilson himself, and numbering amongst its members Cecil and Smuts, representing the British Empire, and Bourgeois representing France. The Commission took as the basis for its deliberations a draft constitution prepared by the legal advisers of the United States and British Empire delegations, David Hunter Miller and Cecil J. Hurst respectively, and embodying the ideas of Wilson, his close advisor House, Cecil and Smuts. Other delegations not unnaturally felt that their views were being ignored and the French representatives in particular pressed vigorously for substantial modifications which would incorporate their own ideas. However, their efforts were to a great extent resisted, and the resulting League Covenant was largely the product of Anglo-American thinking on the subject of international organisation.

I.2.A An extract from the English minutes of the proceedings of the Commission on the League of Nations, concerning the 10th meeting, 13 February 1919 (PRO. cf. also the reproduction of these minutes in vol. II of *The Drafting of the Covenant*, by D. H. Miller).

Mr Bourgeois said that the only way in which the French Delegation could state its point of view was through the medium of amendment, inasmuch as the text of the French proposals for a League of Nations had not been used as the basis of discussion. . . .

Article 9 was presented by Lord Robert Cecil as a separate article in the wording set out above: 'A permanent commission shall be constituted to advise the League of the execution of the provisions of Article 8 [dealing with reduction of armaments] and on military and naval questions generally.'

Mr Bourgeois recalled the fact that the French Delegation had proposed an amendment to article 9 on the following lines: 'A permanent body shall be created in order to plan and prepare the military and naval programme, by which obligations imposed upon the High Contracting Parties by the present Covenant shall be enforced, and in order to give immediate effect to it in any urgent situation that may arise.'

Lord Robert Cecil observed that the French proposal aimed at the creation of an international General Staff, which should study military and naval questions, as well as the means by which effective action might be secured. The League of Nations, however, could not be considered as an alliance against Germany. Nothing would more quickly imperil peace. Furthermore, no country would agree to the establishment of an international General Staff, empowered to interfere with its own military and naval programme.

Mr Bourgeois explained the purposes of this amendment. It was in no way intended to create an international army stationed at, or operating from, a given point. It was simply the question of creating an understanding between the military authorities of the different nations associated in the League, so that they might be ready to furnish part of their national forces quickly in case of sudden attack from a nation either within or without the League.

If such an understanding were not provided, there would be the danger of finding one's self in a state of disorganisation, like that in which the free nations found themselves when Germany invaded Belgium. It was therefore necessary, above all, to provide an organisation, no matter what name were given to it, whose chief object would be to ensure prompt and effective military action on the part of the League of Nations. Such a provision, he thought, was absolutely necessary, not only for the safety of nations exposed to 'geographic risks', but also for the defence of the League itself.

Mr Larnaude [the second French representative], in support of these remarks, said that if the League of Nations was going to impose a regime of peace upon all people, it was necessary that it be known that the League possessed the means of bringing this about. Such a result, however, would be impossible to attain unless a central organisation should be built up during times of peace, which should be ready to act at once against an obstinate or bellicose Power.

Mr Vesnitch [Serbia] . . . as far as the French amendment was concerned it introduced the idea of distrust among the members of the League by assuming that one of them might violate the Covenant, and that a strict control was necessary.

Mr Bourgeois answered that . . . the essential thing was the idea of a military and naval organisation built up during times of peace by the League of Nations. If this was not done, the League would be caught off its guard.

Mr Hymans [Belgium] was not very much impressed by the apprehensions voiced by Mr Vesnitch concerning evidences of mistrust within the League of Nations. It would be right and proper at least to demand adequate guarantees, and especially for the countries, which, like Belgium, were most exposed because of their geographical position. That could hardly offend the susceptibilities of anyone. . . .

The amendment was defeated by vote. Article 9 was adopted.

I.3   THE WITHDRAWAL OF THE UNITED STATES OF AMERICA

The reception of the draft League covenant in the United States of America was mixed. Personal hostility to President Wilson, resentment at the growing power of the Presidential office as against other constitutional bodies, and widespread reluctance to assume onerous worldwide obligations after the end of the war were exploited by certain of Wilson's political opponents who drew up a formidable list of reservations to the Treaty of Versailles. The British Government, alarmed at the possibility that the United States might not ratify the Treaty of Versailles, sent Lord Grey to Washington to try to avert this potential catastrophe. His mission, however, was a failure. An ailing Woodrow Wilson would not accept any of the reservations proposed by the Senate, and a two-thirds majority was not obtained for the Treaty of Versailles as it stood. Instead, separate peace treaties were concluded between the United States and the ex-enemy countries, and one of the world's leading powers thus dissociated itself, from the outset, from the new international organisation.

I.3.A   A list of reservations drawn up by the United States Senate to the Treaty of Peace with Germany, as at the end of 1919.

1. The United States so understands and construes Article 1 that in case of notice of withdrawal from the League of Nations, as provided in said Article, the United States shall be the sole judge as to whether all its international obligations and all its obligations under the said Covenant have been fulfilled, and notice of withdrawal by the United States may be given by a concurrent resolution of the Congress of the United States.

2. The United States assumes no obligation to preserve the territorial integrity or political independence of any other country or to interfere in controversies between nations—whether members of the League or not—under the provisions of Article 10, or to employ the military or naval forces of the United States under any article of the Treaty for any purpose, unless in any particular case the Congress, which, under the Constitution, has the sole power to declare war or authorise the employment of the military or naval forces of the United States, shall by act or joint resolution so provide.

3. No mandate shall be accepted by the United States under Article 22 Part 1, or any other provision of the Treaty of Peace with Germany, except by action of the Congress of the United States.

4. The United States reserves to itself exclusively the right to decide what questions are within its domestic jurisdiction, and declares that all domestic and political questions relating wholly or in part to its internal affairs, including immigration, labour, coast-wise traffic, the tariff, commerce, the suppression of traffic of women and children and in opium and other dangerous drugs, and all other domestic questions are solely within the jursidiction of the United States and are not under this Treaty to be submitted in any way either to arbitration or to the consideration of the Council or of the Assembly of the League of Nations or any agency thereof, or to the decision or recommendation of any other Power.

5. The United States will not submit to arbitration or to inquiry by the Assembly or by the Council of the League of Nations provided for in said Treaty of Peace any questions which in the judgement of the United States depend upon or relate to its long established policy commonly known as the Monroe doctrine; said doctrine to be interpreted by the United States alone, and is hereby declared to be wholly

outside the jurisdiction of said League of Nations and entirely un-
affected by any provision contained in the said Treaty of Peace with
Germany. . . .

7. The Congress of the United States will provide by law for the
appointment of the representatives of the United States in the Assembly
and the Council of the League of Nations. . . . and until such participation and appointment have been so provided for and the powers and
duties of such representatives so defined, no person shall represent the
United States under either said League of Nations or the Treaty of
Peace with Germany or be authorised to perform any act for or on
behalf of the United States thereunder. . . .

9. The United States shall not be obligated to contribute to any
expenses of the League of Nations, or of the secretariat or of any commission, or committee, or conference, or other agency, organised under
the League of Nations or under the Treaty, or for the purpose of carrying out the Treaty provisions, unless and until an appropriation of
funds available for such expenses shall have been made by the Congress
of the United States.

10. If the United States shall at any time adopt any plan for the limitation of armaments proposed by the Council of the League of Nations
under the provisions of Article 8, it reserves the right to increase such
armaments without the consent of the Council whenever the United
States is threatened with invasion or engaged in war.

11. The United States reserves the right to permit, in its discretion,
the nationals of a Covenant-breaking State, as defined in Article 16 of
the Covenant of the League of Nations, residing within the United
States or in countries other than that violating said Article 16, to continue their commercial, financial, and personal relations with the
nationals of the United States. . . .

13. The United States withholds its assent to Part XIII (Articles
387–427 inclusive) [ILO provisions] unless Congress by act or joint
resolution shall hereafter make provision for representation in the
organisation established by said Part XIII, and in such event participation of the United States will be governed by and conditional on the
provisions of such act or joint resolution.

14. The United States assumes no obligation to be bound by any
election, decision, report, or finding of the Council or Assembly in
which any member of the League and its self-governing dominions,
colonies, or parts of the Empire in the aggregate have cast more than
one vote, and assumes no obligation to be bound by any decision, report
or finding of the Council or Assembly arising out of any dispute
between the United States and any member of the League if such
member or any self-governing dominion, colony, empire, or part of
empire united with it politically has voted.

I.3.B   Memordandum by Cecil Hurst, Legal Adviser to the British
         Foreign Office, on the American Reservations to the Peace
         Treaty, dated 18 November 1919. (DBFP Series I, vol V, no.
         399.)

Collectively the effect of the reservations to the Treaty of Peace now
adopted by the Senate of the United States would be to create the
situation that the United States should be allowed to come into the
peace settlement upon a footing different to that upon which the other
Powers come in. . . . To accept now the reservations desired by the
United States Senate would inevitably give rise to the impression
among the other signatories of the Treaty of Peace, and more especially
among the smaller Powers, that there is to be one rule for the United
States and one rule for the rest of the world. . . .

The principle for which the Allied Powers at Paris purported to be
struggling, and the basis upon which they posed as contracting, was
that of substituting the principle of sharing in common the obligations
of the civilised States for the condition of affairs which had prevailed
up to the time of the war of mere individual regulation of international
relations. Once the principle is admitted that one or more of the great
Powers is to stand outside the settlement, the inevitable result must be
to reintroduce the old state of affairs with all the uneasy conditions
which have prevailed in Europe for the last two decades.

On the other hand, the failure of the attempt to effect the peace
settlement in common deprives the work that was done of a great part
of its value, and means that much of it must be done again. Questions
like disarmament can only be dealt with by all the civilised States
acting together. If the attempt made in the Covenant of the League of
Nations to settle this problem has no success, the world must return
to the condition of competition in armaments limited only by financial
considerations. The United States is now so rich that no other Power
could keep pace with her in a competitive struggle for armaments. For
the British Empire, depending on its fleet for security, the outlook
would be particularly disquieting; consequently any chance there may
be of ultimately bringing in the United States ought not to be lost, but
it should be the whole Treaty or nothing, for any reservations imply
the admission of a principle which is fatal to the whole basis upon
which the Treaty was prepared.

Dealing with the reservations individually, the first is to Article X.
Under this article, as drafted, the members of the League undertake to
preserve against external aggression the territorial integrity of other
members of the League. Under the reservation no obligation is to be
imposed upon the United States under this article without the consent
of Congress on each occasion. In consequence, therefore, if Congress
refused its assent to action being taken the United States would take

no part in the protection of the other members of the League. The President is probably right in saying that the effect of this reservation is to cut the heart out of the Covenant. It may well be that in practice the United States would move in flagrant cases, being forced thereto by public opinion at the moment, but the importance of the reservation is that it would destroy the feeling of confidence which the existence of the obligation would afford to the smaller States more liable to external aggression than an island empire like Japan or a vast continental republic like the United States. The doctrine preached at Paris was that the small States must trust to the League to protect them, but the small States cannot trust to the League unless they know that the members of the League are pledged definitely to support them. If the United States are entitled to stand out, other countries may claim the same liberty, and so long as that is possible, the small States may feel that they can trust to nothing but to their own right hand, and that they must arm and train in self-defence.

To the British Empire the exclusion of the United States from the obligation under Article X means that burdens might have to be supported single-handed which no Government would lightly undertake without an assurance that the other great States would do their part, more particularly its great commercial rival across the Atlantic. Great Britain cannot take part in a war without diverting its shipping and its commerce from their normal channel, and if the United States are to be free to stand out, the Americans would use the opportunity to seize trade opportunities which Great Britain was forced to forego.

There is the further danger that a country with world-wide trade like the United States might find the interests of her citizens adversely affected by the operations which were undertaken in support of one party under Article X and be driven into an attitude of opposition and to taking the other side in the struggle. . . .

The importance of the reservation with regard to the Monroe Doctrine depends to a great extent upon the question whether the South and Central American Republics come into the League of Nations or not. If they came in and the United States stayed outside, the provision already appearing in the Covenant (Article XXI) that the Covenant is not to be deemed to affect the Monroe Doctrine, would operate only in cases where all parties concerned admitted that the Monroe Doctrine applied. The Monroe Doctrine is merely a policy which varies from time to time, and if the South American Republics threw in their lot with the League it is not probable that they would admit a very extended operation to it. For them to accept the reservation in its present form would mean the acceptance by them of the principle that the Monroe Doctrine is to be interpreted by the United States alone. It is inconceivable that States like the A.B.C. Powers (i.e.

Argentina, Brazil and Chile) should agree to this. To my mind, unless the United States come in without reservations to the League of Nations the Monroe Doctrine is certain to give rise to so much friction as to render the Covenant unworkable, and I should be afraid that this fact will become so apparent to the other American Republics that they will hesitate to come into the League at all unless the United States do the same. . . .

The next reservation deals with the American representatives in all commissions, &c., under the Treaty of Peace. From the point of view of other Powers this reservation is of less importance. It is merely an attempt on the part of Congress to tie the hands of the Executive Government. . . .

The next reservation, dealing with the expenses of the League, is also a domestic matter of small importance to other Powers. The objection to it is that which appertains to all reservations, that it purports to enable the United States to fail to carry out the obligations of the Treaty without violating it.

The [next] reservation deals with the limitation of armaments, and provides that even if the United States adopts any plan for the limitation of armaments as proposed by the Council of the League, she shall be free whenever she is threatened with invasion, or whenever she is engaged in war, to increase such armaments. To my mind, this reservation destroys the chief merit of the League of Nations. The state of Europe before the war was one in which the perpetual increase in armaments and the continual state of tension that was arising between the European Powers were interacting upon each other in a way that rendered it impossible to say which was the cause and which was the effect; in practice armaments had grown to an extent which ensured tension, and periods of tension were becoming so frequent that the increase of armaments was inevitable. . . . Nothing was likely to stop it except the introduction of a state of affairs which would create sufficient confidence in the minds of the Powers to render arming in self-defence unnecessary . . . if every nation is to be entitled to increase the armaments beyond the agreed limitation whenever it considers itself threatened with invasion it is obvious that on the Continent of Europe the scheme outlined in Article VIII of the Covenant is not worth the paper on which it is written. It may well be that the scheme in Article VIII is itself incapable of realisation, but in any event it cannot work unless all accept it literally.

The [next] reservation deals with the economic boycott. The economic boycott was the weapon wherewith the League intended to coerce an aggressive or recalcitrant member. The complexities of modern commerce have rendered no nation self-supporting. On the other hand, there is no nation whose individual contribution to the commerce of the world is vital to all the rest; consequently an economic boycott, if it could be worked, was certain to be effective. An economic boycott with the Americans standing outside it is certain to mean that the Americans will endeavour to trade with the boycotted country. The drafting of Article XVI of the Covenant is very unsatisfactory because it is not made sufficiently clear that the prohibition of intercourse between nationals of the one party and nationals of the other is merely complementary to the prohibition of trade between the two countries; but whatever the precise effect of the article, it is essential that the United States and American citizens should not be allowed to trade in any way in which other members of the League and the nationals of those members are prohibited from doing. Any claim for special treatment for the citizens of an active commercial Power like the United States is bound to bring the whole machine of the economic boycott to grief. . . .

The papers this morning state that President Wilson has announced his intention to refuse to accept the reservations passed by the Senate. In that case the United States Government will not ask the other Powers whether or not they are prepared to accept these reservations. It is to be hoped that President Wilson will stand by the statements he has made. If he does not, His Majesty's Government will then be face to face with the question whether they are prepared to undertake the responsibilities which the Covenant of the League of Nations entails upon them if the United States decline to participate.

The Covenant cannot be separated from the rest of the Treaty, and, great as the responsibilities and obligations which the Covenant entails may be, it seems that the loss of the Treaty would be a great disaster. In these circumstances the suggestion which was recently made that His Majesty's Government should couple their ratification of the Treaty with a declaration that they will withdraw from the League at the end of the period of two years provided for in Article I ought to be seriously considered. To me it seems the only way out of the difficulty. It could be made subject to an intimation that if all the other civilised Powers joined the League it would be withdrawn, and also with a suggestion that unless they had done so a conference of all the Powers who signed the Treaty of Peace with Germany and all those who were invited to become original members of the League should take place to arrive at an agreed substitute for the existing Covenant.

The existing Covenant of the League is not by any means an ideal instrument, and if, within two years it were possible to substitute an improved and simplified draft for the existing one, it would be a great advantage.

II

CONCILIATION OR COERCION?

THE WITHDRAWAL OF the United States from the League of Nations left as its leading members Britain, France, Italy, Japan, and from 1926, Germany, all of whom had different views about its potential role in international affairs. There was general agreement, however, that the attitudes of such powerful non-League states as the United States and Russia must be carefully considered before any major activities could be undertaken by the League.

II.1 ANGLO-FRENCH FRICTION

The failure of the United States to ratify the Treaty of Versailles also meant the withdrawal, by Britain as well as the United States, of the offer of assistance against unprovoked aggression made to Clemenceau at the Paris Peace Conference by Wilson and Lloyd George as a substitute for the Rhine frontier for which the French were pressing. French feelings of insecurity about the potential menace of a resurgent Germany were therefore intensified, and successive French Governments turned to the League as a source of extra security, pressing for the conclusion of economic and military agreements amongst members in readiness for any attack on an individual League member. British Governments, however, unhappy about the territorial arrangements laid down by the Treaty of Versailles, seemingly perpetuated by Article X of the League of Nations, and concerned that the League should not constitute a source of friction between Britain and the United States, resisted French attempts to tighten the machinery of the League, and tried to limit its principal activities to the prevention or regulation of international crises by the enforcement of the statutory period of delay, to allow for impartial investigations and the cooling of tempers.

II.1.A France's desire for additional security through the machinery of the League of Nations was stressed in this speech by a French delegate to the 1921 League Assembly, M. Noblemaire. (*L of Ns O J.*)

... we need to provide for, and to study, the common action which will have to be exercised by the Council in virtue of Article 16, since

I need hardly point out we lack the means of control or police that would render the decisions of the League effective. We all want our action to be effective; we do not want anybody to be able to ridicule us.

... we desire security ... the security which is due under the Covenant if it is loyally observed. ... I am bound to say, quite frankly, that at the present moment we do not feel that the securities are adequate.

... The German disarmament is nearly completed, but the impossibility of re-armament is no less an essential condition of security. What is the use of destroying obsolete weapons if people may, in the meanwhile, manufacture improved weapons of greater destructive power? ... we require more than a material disarmament; what we want is a moral disarmament.

... we are spectators of a strange duel, a duel between the spirit of war and revenge on the one hand, and the spirit of work and peace on the other—a struggle between the Junkers and the democrats. We can only feel secure ... when the German Republic is established on a stable foundation, and when it is filled with the idea of justice, dignity and liberty, which are the ideals of the League of Nations. But, unfortunately, this duel is not yet concluded, and meanwhile we must keep our weapons in readiness. ... France is obliged to be military for the present, and to continue to be so in order to avoid the resumption of war. She does not want to have lost a million and a half of lives for nothing.

II.1.B   The British conception of the principle role of the League is well summed up in this extract from a *Round Table* article, 'Europe, the Covenant and the Protocol' 1924 (see J. R. M. Butler: *Lord Lothian, 1882–1940*, p. 324 for a suggestion about possible authorship).

The one serious defect in the Covenant ... is the element of compulsory obligation, the attempt to promote peace by binding members to take economic or other sanctions, under an automatic legal process, and irrespective of the merits of the dispute in question. The British Commonwealth is concerned, and deeply concerned, in disputes over the Danzig corridor, the Russo-Polish frontier, the Hungarian or Bulgarian boundaries, Bessarabia, and the Tyrol, the position in China or Persia or Central America. All these questions affect it either directly or because any outbreak of war over them affects international trade and might expand into a world war. But its attitude towards them must depend upon its view of the merits of each case when it arises and of its effect on its own vital interests. If it thinks that Poland has no right to vast areas inhabited by Russians, it is useless to try to bind it automatically to take sanctions against Russia in order to preserve the territorial integrity of existing Poland intact. If it thinks that Hungary has been deprived of its legitimate rights under the treaties, it will never go to war to maintain an injustice. And similarly with every dispute in every part of the world. The vital matter in every case is the merits, and it is their own view of the merits, and not any legal obligation, that will and ought to decide the action which members of the League will take to enforce compliance with the terms of the Covenant on their neighbours.

This criticism of the Covenant in no way implies any lack of support of the League of Nations. The League of Nations is by far the most effective and hopeful instrument for the prevention of war and the promotion of international understanding that the world has yet seen. Its main features, the Council, the Assembly, the Secretariat, the World Court, the mechanism for arbitration and inquiry, the International Labour Office, are steadily increasing in utility and effect, and ought to be increasingly employed as the channels for international intercourse. Without the League there would be no hope of averting another world war. But, in our judgement, the compulsory sanctions are a hindrance and not a help to the League. They are certainly the principal reason why certain great nations stay out of the League.

The essential thing is not to try to tie the hands of members beforehand, in accordance with some automatic formula or obligation, but to provide machinery which, with the greatest possible speed, will give publicity to all the facts, will educate and mobilise public opinion about them and will provide as long as possible a delay before hostilities can break out. That is the only way in which democratic peoples will ever take effective action in international affairs. Autocracies can declare war and make peace, and the people will follow. But self-governing peoples will only assume the terrible responsibility of doing things which may lead to war when the rights and wrongs are understood, and a moral and not a mere legal obligation to act appears.

The main problem of the League procedure centres about the problem of securing delay. . . . If adequate delay can really be secured after notification of a dispute likely to lead to war, the greatest menace to the general peace of the world will have been removed. If the League can secure such delay and the reference of the matter in dispute to a commission of inquiry, or arbitration, for full public investigation and report, even though the conclusions of that commission are not binding, it will succeed in its main purpose. For nine months' delay and public inquiry into the merits will in nine cases out of ten lead to one of three results. Either the dispute will be amicably settled, or the rest of the nations will combine to insist, with overwhelming force, on acceptance by one of the parties of a just solution, or if they are divided in opinion about the merits, they will agree on measures which will isolate a local appeal to arms, and so prevent it spreading into a world war.

. . . we are driven to the conclusion that it is essential to disembarrass the League system of automatic sanctions in every shape and form. The League is fundamentally a conference system between independent sovereign States. Its effectiveness depends partly on the facilities it affords for consultation between the principal Ministers of nations and the mechanism it has created for inquiry, arbitration and judicial inquiry, and partly on the willingness of its members to take action which will deter nations from trying to solve their problems by force, and encourage them to adopt pacific means. The worst way of attaining this end is to try to tie the hands of members to specific obligations irrespective of the rights and wrongs of the case or of the actual circumstances at the time. The best way is to leave the full responsibility for decision about their action on the individual members, while affording to them the fullest possible opportunity of understanding the issues at stake, and the reasons why they should act.

We therefore urge that the nations of the Commonwealth should make a declaration at the earliest possible time under Article 1 of the Covenant that they do not intend to be bound by any obligations to use sanctions, or to defend frontiers, of an automatic or legal kind, and that any sanctions which they do take in conjunction with the League and under the Covenant will be based upon their own free judgement of the merits of the dispute and in the light of the circumstances of the time. . . .

II.2 ATTEMPTS TO STRENGTHEN THE COVENANT

The wording of the League Covenant gave nations the legal right to go to war if, after a League inquiry by an *ad hoc* Commission into the circumstances of the dispute, the League Council could come to no unanimous decision on the rights and wrongs of the case. Even in cases of flagrant abuse of the provisions of the Covenant, the League Council could only 'advise' League members on what military measures to undertake. Not unnaturally, French governments wanted to tighten up what they regarded as glaring loopholes in the League Covenant, and took up an intransigent attitude towards any measure of disarmament until League security provisions were more precisely delineated. To achieve progress in the sphere of disarmament, successive British statesmen were forced to grapple with the problem of French insecurity, and first Lord Cecil, in his Draft Treaty of Mutual Assistance, and then Ramsay Macdonald and the Labour Delegates to the 1924 League Assembly through the Geneva Protocol, attempted to soothe French nerves by reinforcing the machinery of the League. However, vociferous opposition to these attempts from the British Service Departments, the Committee of Imperial Defence, and the Dominions, and only luke-warm responses from other important League members such as Holland and Italy, rendered both schemes abortive. Instead, the sensitive Franco-Belgian-German frontiers were dealt with through the Treaty of Locarno, as a result of which Germany became a League Member in 1926.

II.2.A Cecil's proposals for a Draft Treaty of Mutual Guarantee, dated 1 July 1922, (PRO reference number FO371/11070) with comments by Hurst and Villiers of the Foreign Office.

1. The High Contracting Powers hereby agree that if any one of them is attacked, all the others will forthwith take such action as may have been agreed upon under Article 4 of this Treaty, or if there is no agreement, as may be most effective for the defence of the Party attacked, provided that this obligation shall not come into force unless the naval, military and air forces of the party attacked shall have been reduced in accordance with the terms of the Treaty.

2. In consideration of the undertaking contained in the immediately preceding Article, each of the High Contracting Powers shall forthwith reduce its naval, military and air forces in the manner and to the extent set out for each High Contracting Power in the annex.

3. It shall be the duty of the Permanent Armaments Commission to take into consideration any circumstances in the International situation, which may seem to it likely to disturb the peace of the world, and to advise the council of the League as to what steps, if any, should be taken to deal with such circumstances in accordance with the general purpose and objects of this Treaty.

4. In the event of any of the High Contracting Powers regarding themselves as menaced by the preparations or action of any other state whether party to this Treaty or not, it may so inform the Secretary General of the League of Nations who shall forthwith summon a meeting of the Council of the League, and if the Council by not less than a three-quarters majority shall be of opinion that there is reasonable ground for thinking that the said preparations or action do constitute a menace as alleged they shall make such representations to the Governments creating the menace, in respect of such preparations or action as they may think right, and shall direct the Permanent Military Commission of the League or a Committee thereof to submit plans for assistance to be given by the High Contracting Powers to the party menaced. Such plans if approved by a three-quarters majority of the Council shall forthwith become binding on the High Contracting Parties. Providing that neither under this nor any other article of this Treaty shall any of the High Contracting Parties not being a European

state be bound to furnish any naval, military or air force in Europe, or not being an American state in America, or not being an Asiatic state in Asia, or not being an African state in Africa.

5. Each of the High Contracting Parties agrees to receive such naval, military and air representatives of the League of Nations as the Council may desire to appoint and undertakes to give to these representatives such facilities and information regarding armaments as the Council may from time to time require. If it shall at any time appear to a majority of the Council that the naval, military or air forces or preparations of any of the High Contracting Parties are in excess of those agreed to under the annex of this Treaty, the Council shall so inform the party in question and if a majority of the Council is not satisfied within six months that the naval, military and air forces of the said party have been brought into accordance with this Treaty, they shall suspend the said party from all its rights under this Treaty under such conditions as the Council shall think right and may take any other measures including, if thought right, a recommendation to the High Contracting Powers that penalties similar to those provided in Article 16 of the Covenant shall be put in force against the said party. . . .

Hurst [Legal Advisor to the Foreign Office minuted on 31 July 1922]. The main difficulty about any scheme for disarmament or . . . intended to facilitate disarmament, is political.

France at present obstructs the cause of disarmament. . . . If France is regarded as refusing to disarm because no other course is consistent with her safety, because at any moment she may be left single handed to face a resurrected Germany, and single handed because the failure of America to ratify the Help-to-France Treaty of 1919 has lost her the aid she was promised by Great Britain and the United States of America and because Article 10 of the Covenant of the League has turned out to be a broken reed, it is obvious that any scheme which helps the cause of disarmament by helping France to disarm deserves benevolent consideration at the hands of His Majesty's Government.

If on the other hand France is regarded as profiting by the disappearance of the German menace to aid her in securing the hegemony of Europe in the manner that Louis Quatorze and Napoleon strove for it, it is obvious that any scheme which may lull other Powers into a sense of false security by weakening their own forces and trusting to the protection of an ill formed confederacy is very dangerous. History shows that self-seeking among confederates is too rife for confederacies to provide any protection against determined aggressors.

If the latter of these views prevails—viz, that there is no genuine desire in France for peace and disarmament—an attractive disarmament scheme is particularly dangerous in gatherings like the Assembly of the League at Geneva which are the happy hunting ground of the crank and the enthusiast. The scheme now put forward by Lord Robert Cecil should be obstructed and opposed unless it is considered that France will honestly accept and loyally abide by and fulfil any scheme of this sort to which she puts her name.

Cecil's scheme is dependent for its successful working on a feeling of confidence among all the States who join that every other State will play the game.

Do the circumstances of Europe today justify any such feeling? Could Poland for instance, feel confident that if she reduced her forces as desired and were attacked by Russia, France would send her battalions across Europe to help her?

A treaty of this sort can have no sanctions; if the obligations entered into were not carried out the state attacked would be left in the lurch. It is noteworthy that though this scheme provides that a state arming in excess of the amount allowed may be subjected to an economic blockade, no attempt is made to provide a similar penalty in the event of a State which fails to move to support another who is attacked. . . .

There must be effective machinery to ensure that states will move in each other's support when a 'casus foederis' arises and when one of their number is attacked. Without it that sense of security is not going to be engendered which alone can render disarmament genuine and safe.

At the same time the scheme is not one lightly to be set aside; if the rest of the League is content to accept it, it would ill-become an island power which is least exposed to the risks which beset the powers on the continent of Europe and least dependent on external assistance to frustrate its adoption. If France is regarded as genuinely anxious for peace in Europe the scheme merits at the least sympathetic consideration at Geneva. If it is thought to merit more there are some details in the scheme which require further consideration.

[Villiers minuted, on 3 August 1922] . . . I do not believe that at the present moment of chaos and unrest in Europe, public opinion here will agree to any far-reaching measure of disarmament, still less to binding ourselves to come to the rescue with such armed forces as we have of, say, Hungary threatened by Czechoslovakia. That some scheme such as that adumbrated by Lord Robert Cecil will eventually be adopted can hardly be doubted by anyone who believes in human progress. But the time has not come yet—it may come in our grandchildren's days, but not in ours.

At Geneva our attitude should be one of mild approval and benevolence, coupled with a determination to shelve any such proposals *sine die*.

II.2.B   A Naval Staff Memorandum, July 1923, on the Treaty of Mutual
Guarantee (PRO reference number FO371/9420).

. . . .

2. . . . The Treaty of Mutual Guarantee if ratified would throw large
and unknown commitments upon the British Navy. The British Navy
would certainly always be the first Force to be called upon. . . .

3. It is the considered opinion of the Naval Staff that to carry out
the provisions of such a Treaty would, in fact, necessitate an increase
in our Naval Forces. Provision would have to be made for meeting the
commitments under the Treaty as these commitments might arise
when the services of the Fleet were required elsewhere, and, without
an increase, our Forces would be insufficient to cope with a war between
this Country and an adversary in a distant part of the world.

4. The Naval Staff are opposed to portions of the Navy being practically at the disposal of the League for a series of campaigns of indefinite
duration and magnitude. In the twenty years prior to 1914 there were
many important wars into which this Country was not drawn, and if
we attempted to avert and suppress a similar series of wars in the
future the Navy would be continuously employed on war service,
which might well cause losses in ships thus reducing us below the
One Power Standard at possibly a critical time.

5. The obligations under the Treaty to render assistance to a Country
attacked may in the Treaty be limited in principle to those Countries
situated in the same part of the globe, but the regional aspect of the
Guarantee is unlimited in the case of a world-wide Empire, and the
Royal or Dominion Navies would be liable to be called upon to enforce
the Treaty and to furnish a quota of ships in any sea in the event of a
menace of war. One of the gravest consequences of the Treaty might
be that the British Navy might be called upon to exercise pressure on
the United States, which is outside the League, should that Country
menace a small American Power which is in the League. . . .

II.2.C   Memorandum on Treaties of Mutual Guarantee and the Reduction of Armaments by Leopold Amery, 1st Lord of the Admiralty, July 1923 (PRO reference number FO371/9420).

. . . such a Treaty, whatever its shape, can only add unnecessarily to
our military commitments and increase the danger of dragging us into
wars in which we have no real interest, without in the slightest degree
promoting either our own peace and security or those of other Nations
or leading to any reduction of armaments. . . .

Any treaty of mutual guarantee must, in fact, be a guarantee of the
status quo established by the recent Peace Treaties. No other guarantee
would be acceptable to any of our late Allies; and, for the same reason,

no such guarantee could really be acceptable to any of our late enemies. We should be committed by it to intervening by force in order to maintain, in every detail, a settlement which, by the very nature of the circumstances under which it was concluded, could not be wholly equitable or deserve permanence in respect to many of its features. We should be stereotyping the rigid division of Europe into two camps, instead of giving reasonable free play to the forces which will gradually, by a series of minor upheavals, bring about the necessary readjustment.

... The dangers which confront us are in the Pacific, on the Afghan Frontier, in the Middle East, in Africa. In none of these are we likely to receive any assistance from the European Powers, whose peace we guarantee, that would justify the reduction of our exiguous forces by one ship or one battalion. In Europe, on the other hand, except for the possible menace of air invasion from France, we are in no danger whatever. Why on earth should we get committed to intervening in conflicts which we should otherwise keep clear of, as we kept clear of every European war between 1815 and 1914, with the one exception of the Crimean War which concerned us not as a European but as an Eastern Power?

Lord Robert Cecil, indeed, frankly contemplates a treaty under which the guarantee is confined to separate continents. That is a point of view which, carried to its logical conclusion, would mean the dissolution of the British Empire, and its replacement by a political organisation of the world in continents. Against such an artificial and unnatural conception I would set the conception of strengthening that world-wide pact of mutual guarantee, based on a policy of peace and purely defensive armaments, and on an enduring community of ideals and methods, which is known as the British Commonwealth, and of associating it as closely as possible with that other great Commonwealth of kindred outlook, the United States.

It may be said that some such treaty as is advocated is a necessary corollary of the Covenant of the League of Nations and that our acceptance of the one compels us to endeavour to carry out the other. That argument raises a fundamental issue with regard to the existence of the League of Nations itself. The people of the United States rejected the League of Nations because, reading the clauses of the Covenant literally, as they are accustomed to read the articles of their own constitution, they feared that they would be involved by it in commitments and responsibilities which they were not prepared to face. We, here and elsewhere in the Empire, accepted the League because we believed, and believed rightly, that the method of conference and discussion among nations would tend to promote peace by better mutual understanding. We ignored the fears which influenced Americans, because we attached no real importance to the form of the clauses which they regarded as so pregnant with concealed menace. But if we are told that our acceptance of the League compels us to draw from those very clauses the conclusions which America rejected, and that the general obligation to work for peace and disarmament is to issue in a rigid compact for the maintenance of the present territorial settlement, and for intervention in every case of 'aggression', then I am certain that the people of this country and of the Dominions will decide that the United States were right in their misgivings, and will come to regard the League of Nations ... as a League for repression and interference of which we should do well to wash our hands as speedily and as completely as possible.

II.2.D   Summary by the British Ambassador in Holland, Sir Charles Marling, of the attitude of the Netherlands Minister for Foreign Affairs towards the Treaty of Mutual Guarantee (PRO FO371/ 10568).

... the question which had to be answered was, briefly, whether an unconditional obligation to afford military assistance should be established and undertaken. The Covenant of the League of Nations left the application of military sanctions to the sovereign decision of each individual member. According to the guarantee treaties there would be an absolute obligation to afford military assistance, and the decision would be vested in the council. If the treaty were concluded, it would probably amount to the States being bound to afford military aid to a country at war, without any corresponding gain in the direction of a restriction of armaments. Apart from this consideration, the report of the Permament Consultative Commission showed that the general obligation to afford such aid would only be of real value if it had been elaborated beforehand by means of special arrangements. It was clear that this general obligation, implying the loss of individuality and a risk of the Netherlands being dragged into the wars of third parties, was not compatible with the policy which Holland should pursue if her existence was not to be endangered. Furthermore, if the general obligation were undertaken, the position of the Netherlands would not become easier, if, as was done in the case of the negotiations about the revision of the treaties of 1839, efforts were made once more, but this time with reference to the general obligation, to concern the country in a regional military arrangement. These objections were the graver if it were considered that the general obligation to afford military assistance would operate not only in the case of actual aggression, but also whenever, in the opinion of the council, any State anticipated a commencement of hostilities owing to the aggressive policy of another State. This stipulation was obviously liable to abuse for political and military objects, and also dangerous, as possibly involving the Netherlands in disputes between other countries without war having broken out.

On these grounds, the Minister for Foreign Affairs was of opinion that there was every reason for very serious consideration before the Netherlands participated in the proposed arrangement. Moreover, there was reason to fear that the conclusion of the Guarantee Treaty would not only be in conflict with the Covenant of the League of Nations, but in the long run might even force that covenant into the background and render it ineffective.

II.2.E   The British Government sought the views of its Dominions on the merits of the Geneva Protocol, before making a final decision as to their action. The replies from South Africa and Canada express the hostility to the Protocol shared by all the Dominions (PRO reference number FO371/11066).

[Governor-General of Canada to British Secretary of State for Colonies, 4 March, 1925].

After careful examination of the Geneva Protocol by members of the Cabinet and by Inter-departmental Committee our Government has come to conclusions which may be summarised as follows:

First, that we should continue to give whole-hearted support to the League of Nations and particularly to its work of conciliation, co-operation and publicity. Second, that we do not consider it in the interests of Canada, of the British Empire, or of the League itself to recommend to Parliament adherence to the Protocol and particularly to its rigid provisions for application of Economic and Military sanctions in every future war. Among the grounds for this conclusion is the consideration of the effect of non-participation of the United States upon attempts to enforce sanctions and particularly so in the case of contiguous countries like Canada. . . .

[Governor-General of South Africa to British Secretary of State for Colonies, 26 January, 1925].

Ministers after careful consideration of the proposed Protocol regret to have to inform British Government that they feel themselves unable to accept the same or to recommend its acceptance by Parliament. The reasons which have led Ministers to arrive at this conclusion may without going into details be stated as follows:—

1. It seems generally admitted, and Ministers share that feeling, that the League of Nations as at present existing with America, Germany and Russia standing aloof cannot over any length of time achieve its great and primary object of ensuring peaceable world, and must, unless these great nations become members, necessarily as time goes on

assume more and more the character of political alliance. To accept Protocol ... would be only to make it more difficult for countries at present outside the League, notably America, to become members, and would consequently contribute very materially to making it impossible for League to attain its real object(s) and so give an additional impulse to the diversion of its activity(ies) in the direction of an alliance, having as its object the maintenance of a balance of power.

2. It is quite impossible even approximately to calculate or tell in advance what are going to be the obligations and consequences direct and indirect which may accrue from an acceptance of the Protocol or what may be the many and various international complications to which it may give rise.

3. By accepting the Protocol the character of the League will be so modified that no nation being a member of it, subject to the provisions of the Protocol, can rightly be said any longer to retain its full measure of sovereign rights. This, Ministers deem a matter of very grave concern, in view more particularly of [the] indefinite character of the obligations which are sought to be imposed and of the practical consequences it may have for the weaker nations not possessing influence derived from power to add prestige and weight to their interpretation of the obligations thus assumed.

4. Ministers feel convinced that while public feeling in the Union may be taken as sincerely in favour of a real and genuine League of Nations, it is generally felt that the League, as it is at present, has not yet arrived at that stage, and that to have obligations of the Union under Covenant extended any further is not in the interests of this country.

5. In matters of such a grave nature as the relationship and obligation(s) of nation(s) League professedly instituted with a view to the guardianship of the peace of the world, but under present conditions more especially the protector of the circumstances and requirements of particular nations and countries. Ministers feel that they are called upon to exercise particular vigilance and to bestow particular attention upon the peculiar position and interests of South Africa, and are of the opinion that these interests demand that no international obligations should be entered into which may entail a participation and interference by the Union in matters which do not, or only remotely, concern her and whereby her real and proper interests may eventually be jeopardised. . . .

II.2.F   Sir Austen Chamberlain's speech to the League Council at Geneva, 12 March 1925, in which he outlined British Government objections to the Geneva Protocol (PRO reference number FO371/11070).

His Majesty's Government have given the most anxious consideration
to the protocol which was provisionally accepted last October by the
Assembly of the League of Nations and submitted by the Council to
the various States members of the League. . . .

The declared object of the protocol is to facilitate disarmament, and
it proposes to attain this most desirable end:

(1) by closing certain gaps in the scheme originally laid down in
the covenant for peaceably settling international disputes, and

(2) by sharpening the 'sanctions', especially the economic sanctions,
by which, under the existing system, aggression is to be discouraged and aggressors coerced. . . .

His Majesty's Government are . . . immediately concerned to enquire
how far the change in the covenant affected by the protocol is likely
to increase the responsibilities already undertaken by the States members of the League. . . . Fresh classes of dispute are to be decided by
the League; fresh possibilities of defying its decisions are thereby
created; fresh occasions for the application of coercive measures follow
as a matter of course, and it is, therefore, not surprising that, quite
apart from the problem of disarmament, the question of 'sanctions'
should be treated at length in the clauses of the protocol.

. . . surely it is most unwise to add to the liabilities already incurred
without taking stock of the degree to which the machinery of the
covenant has been already weakened by the non-membership of
certain great States. For in truth the change, especially as regards the
'economic sanctions', amounts to a transformation. The 'economic
sanction', if simultaneously directed by all the world against a State
which is not itself economically self-sufficing, would be a weapon of
incalculable power. This . . . was the weapon originally devised by the
authors of the covenant. To them it appeared to be not only bloodless,
but cheap, effective and easy to use, in the most improbable event of
its use being necessary. But all this is changed by the mere existence of
powerful economic communities outside the limits of the League. It
might force trade into unaccustomed channels, but it could hardly
stop it, and, though the offending State would no doubt suffer, there is
no presumption that it would be crushed, or even that it would suffer
most.

. . . The protocol purports to be little more than a completion of the
work begun, but not perfected, by the authors of the covenant. But
surely this is a very inadequate description of its effects. The additions
which it makes to the original document do something quite different
from merely clarifying obscurities and filling in omissions. They destroy
its balance and alter its spirit. The fresh emphasis laid upon sanctions,
the new occasions discovered for their employment, the elaboration of
military procedure, insensibly suggest the idea that the vital business of

the League is not so much to promote friendly co-operation and reasoned harmony in the management of international affairs as to preserve peace by organising war, and (it may be) war on the largest scale. Now, it is unhappily true that circumstances may be easily imagined in which war, conducted by members of the League, and with its collective assistance and approval, will become a tragic necessity. But such catastrophes belong to the pathology of international life, not to its normal conditions. It is not wholesome for the ordinary man to be always brooding over the possibility of some severe surgical operation, nor is it wise for societies to pursue a similar course ... it certainly seems to His Majesty's Government that anything which fosters the idea that the main business of the League is with war rather than with peace is likely to weaken it in its fundamental task of diminishing the causes of war without making it in every respect a satisfactory instrument for organising great military operations should the necessity for them be forced upon the world.

... It may perhaps be replied that ... some scheme of sanctions is certainly necessary. Without it a League of Nations would be as insecure as a civilised society without magistrates and police. International engagements which cannot be internationally enforced are little better than a sham. Those, therefore who object to the plan proposed in the protocol are bound to suggest a better.

... How is security and, above all, the feeling of security to be attained? ... The brooding fears that keep huge armaments in being have little relation to the ordinary misunderstandings with which the League is so admirably fitted to deal. They spring from deep-lying causes of hostility, which for historic or other reasons divide great and powerful States. These fears may be groundless; but if they exist they cannot be effectually laid, even by the most perfect method of dealing with particular disputes—the machinery of inquiry and arbitration. For what is feared in such cases is not injustice but war—war deliberately undertaken for purposes of conquest and revenge. And, if so, can there be a better way of allaying fears like these than by adopting some scheme which should prove to all the world that such a war would fail?

Since the general provisions of the covenant cannot be stiffened with advantage, and since the 'extreme cases' with which the League may have to deal will probably affect certain nations or groups of nations more nearly than others. His Majesty's Government conclude that the best way of dealing with the situation is, with the co-operation of the League, to supplement the covenant by making special arrangements in order to meet special needs. That these arrangements should be purely defensive in character, that they should be framed in the spirit of the covenant, working in close harmony with the League and under its guidance, is manifest. And, in the opinion of

His Majesty's Government, these objects can best be attained by knitting together the nations most immediately concerned, and whose differences might lead to a renewal of strife, by means of treaties framed with the sole object of maintaining, as between themselves, an unbroken peace. Within its limits no quicker remedy for our present ills can easily be found nor any surer safeguard against future calamities. . . .

II.3 ATTITUDES TO THE LEAGUE OF POWERS WITH EXPANSIONIST DESIGNS

While France sought to strengthen the provisions of the Covenant, other powers, notably Italy, Japan and Germany, desired to minimise its coercive powers and prevent its interference with their expansionist aims. In Japan, until the late 1920s, successive civilian Governments were able to check the aggressive designs of the military forces and enforce at least nominal adherence to the clauses of the Covenant, but in Italy after Mussolini's accession to power in 1922, his Government adopted an attitude of outright hostility to the restrictions on national ambitions imposed by the League. Mussolini tried to undermine the authority of the League by his seizure of Corfu and his denial of the competence of the League to deal with the crisis. Thereafter, his attitude remained one of contempt, and of determination to proceed with his plans for empire-building when the time was ripe.

Germany, admitted to the League in 1926, was wholly preoccupied with the task of lifting the restrictions imposed by the Treaty of Versailles, and modifying the east European territorial settlement laid down in 1919. Membership of the League was valued only in so far as it could further these primary national objectives.

II.3.A   Italy's attitude to the League after 1922 is well summed up in this despatch from the British Ambassador at Rome, to the Foreign Office, 19 October 1923 (PRO reference number FO371/8900).

Signor Francesco Coppola, a prominent nationalist writer and one of the Italian supplementary delegates at the recent Assembly of the League of Nations, has contributed two articles to the *Idea Nazionale* (16 and 19 Oct) on the subject of Italy's relation to the League.

. . . he lays stress (1) on Italy's inadequate representation on the Secretariat of the League which leaves this machinery entirely at the service of British and French policy; (2) on the fact that Italy has no 'clients' among the smaller powers. 'Small nations are not wanting whose interests would attract them into Italy's orbit, but no systematic scheme of attraction has been pursued by the Italian Government either at Geneva or Rome'.

But beyond these considerations Italy 'cannot but see in the League a force antithetical to the vital necessities of her own future expansion'. The League is an organism for the maintenance of peace: i.e. of the territorial integrity of all states, in their present limits, 'while Italy is suffocated in its narrow and poor country, and (since the Fascist Revolution) an object of diffidence and hostility to states who wish to impede her expansion. It is only natural that England and France should seek to defend the League, standing as they do at the climax of their fortunes. It is equally natural that Italy, deprived as she is of the fruits of her great victory, should regard the League as an international instrument for her own repression.'

Under these circumstances, what policy should Italy pursue? . . . It would be well to leave the League if she has an opportunity of doing so in such a way as would effectively destroy it; but not otherwise. Again, she might identify herself within the League with the other Powers who are its 'victims'—but this would diminish her force and her prestige, and cannot seriously be considered. Rather, her best course is to remain within the League as one of the great conquering powers and to take every opportunity of hastening on the destruction of its present pretensions and reducing it to a merely technical body. Italy must place herself at the head of the reaction against the pseudo-pacifist pseudo-democratic spirit which inspires the League. She must make a compromise with the League as it exists in order to destroy the idea which it represents.

II.3.B This letter from Stresemann to the former German Crown Prince, dated 7 September 1925, is to be found in his collected papers (*Diaries, Papers and Letters*, edited by Eric Sutton, Vol. II, pp. 503–5).

On the question of Germany's entry into the League I would make the following observations:

In my opinion there are three great tasks that confront German foreign policy in the more immediate future—

In the first place the solution of the Reparations question in a sense tolerable for Germany, and the assurance of peace, which is an essential promise for the recovery of our strength.

Secondly, the protection of Germans abroad, those ten to twelve millions of our kindred who now live under a foreign yoke in foreign lands.

The third great task is the readjustment of our Eastern frontiers; the recovery of Danzig, the Polish corridor, and a correction of the frontier in Upper Silesia.

In the background stands the union with German Austria, although I am quite clear that this not merely brings no advantages to Germany, but seriously complicates the problem of the German Reich.

... Our anxiety on behalf of Germans abroad is an argument in favour of our joining the League. . . . In Geneva we shall speak on behalf of German civilisation as a whole, because the whole of the Germanic world sees in us its refuge and protector. The objection that we shall be outvoted on the League proceeds from the false assumption that, on the Council of the League, . . . any outvoting is possible. The decisions of the League Council must be taken unanimously. Germany is assured of a permanent seat on the Council. . . . Poland, Czecho-Slovakia, Jugo-Slavia, and Rumania, who are all bound by international treaties to take care of their minority population, *i.e.* more especially the German minorities, would not so disgracefully ignore their obligations if they knew that Germany could bring all these derelictions before the League. Moreover all the questions that lie so close to German hearts, as for instance, War Guilt, General Disarmament, Danzig, the Saar, etc., are matters for the League of Nations, and a skilful speaker at a plenary session of the League may make them very disagreeable for the Entente. France, indeed, is not very enthusiastic at the idea of Germany's entering the League, while England is anxious for it, in order to counteract France's hitherto predominant influence on that body.

The question of a choice between East and West does not arise as the result of our joining the League. Such a choice can only be made when backed by military force. That, alas, we do not possess. We can neither become a Continental spear-head for England, as some believe, nor can we involve ourselves in an alliance with Russia. . . . The most important thing for the first task of German policy mentioned above is the liberation of German soil from any occupying force. We must get the stranglehold off our neck. On that account, German policy, as Metternich said of Austria, no doubt after 1809, will be one of finesse and the avoidance of great decisions.

II.4 ATTITUDES TO THE LEAGUE OF NON-MEMBERS

The fact that the Soviet Union and the United States of America stayed aloof from the League throughout the 1920s increased the difficulties facing the League and further limited its potential scope for action. The bellicose noises made by leading Bolsheviks in the early 1920s were gradually toned down as the Soviet Union was drawn increasingly into the orbit of League activities, especially disarmament. The Government of the United States, however, refused to be drawn into close contact with the League and emphasised its independent position by pursuing a parallel course to that of the League, directed towards the maintenance of peace but secured through other mechanisms such as the 1928 Kellogg-Briand Pact which bound its signatories to renounce war as an instrument of national policy.

II.4.A Speech by Chicherin at the Third Soviet Congress, 14, May, 1925 (*Stenograficheskii Ofchet*, p. 83).

... A little episode has just occurred which has given rise to a still stronger campaign against us, to the accusation that we want to break the peace and stir up trouble everywhere. A conference was called at Geneva by the League of Nations to regulate the international trade in arms. We declined to take part in this conference, for reasons which anyone can understand. The League of Nations, which is in fact a coalition of the victor Powers who wish to impose their will on other States, convened this conference. We do not categorically boycott the League always. There have been cases when we have agreed to enter into negotiations with the League for technical or for humanitarian purposes, such as the reduction of the burden of armaments. But in this case the draft convention on the international trade in arms which the League sent us showed clearly that what they had in mind was to strengthen the dominion of the imperialist States over the weaker States and the oppressed peoples. What the draft amounted to was that the trade in arms should be strictly regulated between the designated Governments, and all licenses for the export of arms should be sent to a central office set up by the League of Nations. This meant control by a group of imperialist Powers dominating the League of Nations over the entire international arms trade. ... We refused to take part in this conference which, while appearing to regulate the trade in arms, really strengthened to the utmost the rule of the imperialist Powers over the weaker peoples. This served as an excuse for a new and extremely furious campaign against us. You have probably read in the newspapers that the Geneva Press, connected with the permanent home of the League, is beginning to clamour for the transformation of the League of Nations into some kind of universal alliance against the USSR, justifying this by the fact that our absence from this conference prevented the dominant States from putting through this plan. If the USSR does not take part in the conference, then there is practically no hope for it. Using this as its basis, the press connected with the League is beginning to call for a kind of crusade, led by the League of Nations, against the USSR.

II.4.B Extract from President Hoover's Armistice Day Address at Washington, 11 November 1929 (DIA 1929, p. 244–5).

... Recently we have covenanted with other civilised nations, not only to renounce war as an instrument of national policy, but also we have agreed that we shall settle all controversies by pacific means. But the machinery for the pacific settlement of disputes among nations is as yet inadequate. We need to strengthen our own provisions for it. Our State Department ... must be strengthened and supported as the great arm of our Government dedicated to the organisation of peace. We need further to extend our treaties with other countries, providing methods for reference of controversies to conference, to inquiry as to fact, or to arbitration, or to judicial determination.

We have need to define the rules of conduct of nations, and to formulate an authoritative system of International Law. We have need, under proper reservations, to support the World Court in order that we may secure judicial determination of certain types of controversies and build up precedents which add to the body of International Law. By these agencies we relegate a thousand frictions to orderly processes of settlement, and by deliberation in action we prevent their development into national inflammation.

We are also interested that other nations shall settle by pacific means the controversies arising between them. From every selfish point of view the preservation of peace among other nations is of interest to the United States. In such wars we are in constant danger of entanglement because of interference with the widespread activities of our citizens. But, of far more importance than this, our ideals and our hopes are for the progress of justice through the entire world. We desire to see all humanity relieved of the hideous blight of war and of the cruelties and injustices that lead to war. We are interested in all methods that can be devised to assure the settlement of all controversies between nations.

There are today two roads to that end. The European nations have, by the Covenant of the League of Nations, agreed that if nations fail to settle their differences peaceably, then force should be applied by other nations to compel them to be reasonable. We have refused to travel this road. We are confident that, at least in the Western Hemisphere, public opinion will suffice to check violence. This is the road we propose to travel. What we urgently need in this direction is a further development of methods for the reference of unsettled controversies to joint inquiry by the parties, assisted by friendly nations, in order that action may be stayed, and that the aggressor may be subjected to the searchlight of public opinion.

III

DISARMAMENT

ONE OF THE major roles of the League of Nations was expected to be the promotion of disarmament by providing a framework within which member nations could conclude agreements about armament limitation which could be progressively extended. It was widely felt in 1919 that high levels of armaments, apart from being economically wasteful, bore much of the responsibility for the outbreak of war in 1914 and that substantial reductions in the level of armaments would reduce the likelihood of a major war in the future.

III.1 THE CASE FOR DISARMAMENT

In 1919, wide sections of informed opinion throughout the world paid lip service to the ideal of disarmament, as a shocked reaction to the waste of the first world war, and a determination not to waste depleted economic resources in the future, or because of sincerely-held moral convictions. Furthermore, the clauses in the Treaty of Versailles which laid down stringent conditions about the future level of German armaments were prefaced by the observation that these measures were to prepare the way for a general limitation of armaments. While this was not interpreted by internationl lawyers as a legally-binding obligation, it was felt by many statesmen, particularly in Britain, to constitute a morally-binding obligation to pursue vigorous disarmament policies.

III.1.A In his book *Disarmament* (OUP, London, 1929) the Director of the League of Nations Disarmament Section during the first years of the League's existence, Salvador de Madariaga, stressed the wasteful, immoral aspects of armaments.

... the world ... is nowadays spending in preparing for war 600 times the sum which it devotes to preparing for peace.

What becomes of these sums? They are spent in men and in material. Now this material is the most expensive in the world. While we grudge the quality of the material we grant our schools, hospitals, astronomical observatories, we lavish our best steel, our choicest woods, our finest optical appliances, our purest chemicals, on the soldier, the sailor, and the airman who ask for them. And these costly guns, these expensive aeroplanes, these extravagant battleships, how long do they last? The life of an aeroplane engine is measured in hours; the number of shots a gun can shoot is smaller than the number of dollars it costs. The life of a battleship may be represented by a number of years smaller than the number of millions of dollars which went for its making. All the skill, patience, attention, devotion, all the precious human life which goes to the making of these destructive machines, is not only directed to wrong uses, but to fleeting uses. ... Save vice, nothing is so wasteful in the world as war and the preparation for it. ...

As for the men, ... the armament system implies of course huge sums spent in food, clothes, and salaries for soldiers, sailors, and airmen, that is to say, for unproductive services. Yet the material loss is even greater. For these men are all diverted from productive occupations, so that to the yearly sum represented by their salaries must be added the value which their labour would have reached in the market, indeed the whole value of the goods and services which, left to live a productive life, they might have created.

Nor is that all. These men, thus diverted from creative occupations, are made to learn a trade which ... it is impossible to describe otherwise than as organised and disciplined, systematic and wholesale murder.

III.1.B In this extract from his *Fontainebleau Memorandum*, written in March 1919 and published as a Government White Paper (Cmd 1614) in 1922, Lloyd George emphasised the role which the League should play in the field of disarmament. The alternative was a renewed, costly arms race which Britain could ill-afford in the circumstances of 1919.

An essential element ... in the peace settlement is the constitution of the League of Nations as the effective guardian of international right and international liberty throughout the world. If this is to happen, the first thing to do is that the leading members of the League of Nations should arrive at an understanding between themselves in regard to armaments. To my mind it is idle to endeavour to impose a permanent limitation of armaments upon Germany unless we are prepared similarly to impose a limitation upon ourselves. I recognise that until Germany has settled down and given practical proof that she has abandoned her imperialist ambitions, and until Russia has also given proof that she does not intend to embark upon a military crusade against her neighbours, it is essential that the leading members of the League of Nations should maintain considerable forces both by land and sea in order to preserve liberty in the world. But if they are to present a united front to the forces both of reaction and revolution, they must arrive at such an agreement in regard to armaments among themselves as would make it impossible for suspicion to arise between the members of the League of Nations in regard to their intentions towards one another. If the League is to do its work for the world it will only be because the members of the League trust it themselves and because there are no rivalries and jealousies in the matter of armaments between them. The first condition of success for the League of Nations is, therefore, a firm understanding between the British Empire and the United States of America and France and Italy that there will be no competitive building up of fleets or armies between them. Unless this is arrived at before the Covenant is signed the League of Nations will be a sham and a mockery. . . . It will be regarded, and rightly regarded, as a proof that its principal promoters and patrons repose no confidence in its efficacy. But once the leading members of the League have made it clear that they have reached an understanding which will both secure to the League of Nations the strength which is necessary to enable it to protect its members and which at the same time will make misunderstanding and suspicion with regard to competitive armaments impossible between them its future and its authority will be ensured. It will then be able to ensure as an essential condition of peace that not only Germany, but all the smaller States of Europe undertake to limit their armaments and abolish conscription. If the small nations are permitted to organise and maintain conscript armies running each to hundreds of thousands, boundary wars will be inevitable and all Europe will be drawn in. Unless we secure this universal limitation we shall achieve neither lasting peace, nor the permanent observance of the limitation of German armaments which we now seek to impose.

III.1.c In a Foreign Office Memorandum of 1926 (PRO reference number FO371/11878) Lord Cecil stressed the morally binding nature of German disarmament on the other signatories of the Treaty of Versailles.

1. By the Treaty of Versailles the Germans are bound to carry out a drastic scheme of disarmament. That they have substantially done, according to the view of the British experts. They were also bound by the Treaty to maintain their condition of disarmament. Is that second obligation perpetual and unconditional, or does it depend upon the fulfilment of the promises made by the Allies before the signing of the Treaty, and in its clauses, that they, too, would carry out a scheme of disarmament?

2. By the Preamble to the disarmament clauses of the Treaty they are described as the first step towards world disarmament. The actual words are as follows—

> In order to render possible the initiation of a general limitation of the armaments of all nations, Germany undertakes strictly to observe the military, naval and air clauses which follow.

It is contended that all the succeeding clauses must be read subject
to this initial declaration and that in consequence although the Germans were bound to carry out the measures of disarmament indicated,
the Allies were also bound to carry out a measure of disarmament
after the German disarmament had been effected or otherwise the
Treaty would have provided that the Germans should be for ever
kept in a condition of inferiority to the other nations of Europe.

3. Before accepting these obligations Germany wrote the letter of
29 May 1919, in which she offered to accept her own disarmament and
even to carry it rather further than was asked provided she were
immediately admitted to the League of Nations and further that
within two years 'the other States also, in accordance with Article 8 of
the enemy Covenant of the League of Nations, undertake to reduce
their armaments and to abolish universal military service'. It was in
reply to that suggestion that the Allies wrote:—

> The Allied and Associated Powers wish to make it clear that
> their requirements in regard to German armaments were not
> made solely with the object of rendering it impossible for Ger-
> many to resume her policy of military aggression. They are also
> the first step towards that general reduction and limitation of
> armaments which they seek to bring about as one of the most
> fruitful preventives of war, and which it will be one of the first
> duties of the League of Nations to promote.
>
> They must point out, however, that the colossal growth in
> armaments of the last few decades was forced upon the nations
> of Europe by Germany. As Germany increased her power, her
> neighbours had to follow suit unless they were to become im-
> potent to resist German dictation or the German sword. It is
> therefore right, as it is necessary, that the process of limitation
> of armaments should begin with the nation which has been
> responsible for their expansion. It is not until the aggressor has
> led the way that the attacked can safely afford to follow suit. . . .
> Germany must consent unconditionally to disarm in advance of
> the Allied and Associated Powers; she must agree to immediate
> abolition of universal military service, a definite organisation and
> scale of armaments must be enforced. It is essential that she
> should be subjected to special controls as regards the reduction
> of her armies and armaments, the dismantling of her fortifica-
> tions, and the reduction, conversion or destruction of her mili-
> tary establishments.

It will be noticed that in this reply the Germans are required to 'consent
unconditionally to disarm in advance of the Allies'. The German
contention will be that they have disarmed, and that they have done it

in advance of the Allies, that that is all they were required to do unconditionally. The remainder of their obligation, the obligation to remain disarmed was undertaken in consideration of the express assurances that their disarmament was the 'first step towards that general reduction and limitation of armaments which the Allies seek to bring about as one of the most fruitful preventives of war'. There is always a difficulty where the two parties to a negotiation have each given undertakings with respect to a particular matter to say whether those undertakings are dependent on one another or not. It seems to me fairly clear that morally they are: legally the point may be more doubtful. . . .

III.2 THE CASE AGAINST DISARMAMENT

Even in the immediate aftermath of the first world war there were some people who felt that the ideal of disarmament was unrealisable, even if desirable, and that prevailing human attitudes and technical difficulties were bound to prevent any scheme for disarmament from being successfully implemented.

III.2.A Memorandum written in 1916 by Sir Eyre Crowe, subsequently to become Permanent Under Secretary of the Foreign Office (PRO reference number FO371/3082).

. . . It is an attractive proposition that at any given moment the world would be as well off, and each nation as strong relatively to the rest, if all their existing armaments were, and remained, proportionately reduced, so that the balance of force, whatever it might be at the time, would be maintained. But so soon as any attempt is made to put this theory into practice, insuperable difficulties appear.

A limitation of armaments is possible in three ways: (a) a numerical limitation of the units of force, that is, soldiers, guns, ships, aeroplanes, etc.; (b) a limitation of the kind of force to be employed, such as prohibition of explosive bullets, of armed submarines or airships, of poisonous gases, of particular types of guns or torpedoes or explosives, etc.; (c) a limitation of the amount of money to be spent annually on armaments.

It can be shown that at any rate so long as these several kinds of limitation are not combined and employed together, even the primary object of maintaining the balance of force would not be attained. A limitation of numbers and units presents, to start with, an extraordinarily complicated problem. All modern States, except the United States, have adopted the principle of general and compulsory service. How, under that system, can the number of soldiers be limited otherwise than by the size of the population? It may be said that only so-and-so many, or such-and-such a proportion, shall be called to the colours. But what does serving with the colours mean? What about passing successive batches of men into the reserves of various classes? What about swelling the numbers of trained men by shortening the term of service with the colours whilst intensifying the training; by extending the age limits for liability to serve; and by other devices of a similar kind? It is really impossible to conceive how the actual fighting strength represented by the number of trained and partially trained men could be regulated except by minutely laying down the exact conditions on which every national army is to be organised and trained. This is hardly a feasible proposition. But even supposing it was possible to give practical effect to it, the purpose would not be achieved. For a limitation of numbers can always be counteracted by qualitative increases in the fighting values of particular engines or methods of warfare. As these relative fighting values vary with the progress of science and invention, an equilibrium could only be preserved by standardising each kind of weapon and instrument, which would be quite impracticable. Similarly, the prohibition or restricted scope of particular vehicles of force, implements, or contrivances could be set off by the multiplication of others. Again, the limitation of expenditure on armaments may become ineffective or immaterial as a result of the discovery or invention of simpler and less expensive methods of destruction. One maxim gun served by three men is in certain circumstances more formidable than 100 men carrying rifles and certainly cheaper, and it is conceivable that a few big guns firing shells of special power may be a good substitute for parks of less effective artillery.

To some extent these objections could be met by insisting on the simultaneous application of all the three methods of limitation. But more serious difficulties remain to be overcome. They are twofold.

There is, firstly, the question of general confidence in the good faith of all the parties. This confidence does not exist. There is good reason why it should not exist. History and the nature of things and men afford the explanation. Nor is there any prospect that it will exist in the future. That being so, who is to see and guarantee that the limitations are really applied with scrupulous honesty? What is to prevent their being evaded or countered by the ingenuity of practical men, whose ideas about the sanctity of words written on scraps of paper may or may not be strictly puritanical? It has been suggested that there might be an international body exercising control in each country. But this only removes the difficulty one step further back. Who is to guarantee the honesty and efficiency of the international body; and how can individual governments or statesmen be prevented from hoodwinking the international body? To these questions there is no satisfactory answer.

The second objection is more fundamental. Any general limitation of armaments implies that every State accepts for itself a definite standard of force, not to be exceeded. This standard cannot be equal for all. The armaments of Montenegro cannot be the same as those of Russia. What should be the proportion of armed strength to be allotted to the several countries? By what test should the different standards be measured and fixed: population, area, shipping, wealth, climate, geographical factors, or what? It will be recognised, on reflection, that there is no abstract rule or system on which a proportionate standard could be based. There remains only the empirical method of accepting the existing distribution of force as indicating the normal, to be varied, if necessary, in such a manner as to preserve the same proportion between the different States.

The existing proportionate distribution of force is the outcome of history, of past wars and territorial arrangements. It is the result of victories and defeats, of national achievements and of national disasters. At every given moment there are States who hope to retrieve past errors and misfortunes, and who strive to build upon stronger foundations the power of their nation. Such ambitions are natural and just. The nation that has them not is despised. To perpetuate indefinitely the conditions prevailing at a given time would mean not only that no States whose power has hitherto been weak relatively to others may hope to get stronger, but that a definite order or hierarchy must be recognised, in which each State is fated to occupy a fixed place. Is this a condition which can be expected to meet with general acceptance? And is the termination of a life-and-death struggle like the present war, which will presumably end in establishing a decided superiority of one side or the other, the appropriate moment for fixing the hierarchy of States according to the condition of their respective armaments? Supposing the Central Powers to be absolutely defeated, are we to fix their proportion of permitted armaments at the figures resulting from such defeat? It would be only fair to ask the question, What would be the attitude of our own country supposing for a moment that we were the defeated party? No one can doubt that in such a calamitous contingency our enemies would insist on the practical disappearance of our fleet. What then should we think of a proposal to limit armaments on the basis of no fleet, or only a weak fleet, for England? If forced to subscribe to such conditions, should we expect that future generations of Englishmen would feel themselves bound in honour to respect the sanctity of such an arrangement?

Are we then, if victorious, to re-establish the proportions generally prevailing before the war, and so prolong or renew the conditions which made German aggression possible? This alternative need only be stated in order to be rejected. But would the other alternative of a standard based on the result of the present war be accepted by our enemies if they are utterly defeated? And if forced to accept it, will they do so honestly, whole-heartedly, without any mental reservation?

At the same time, who will undertake to fix the standard of armed strength for China, for Holland, for Mexico, for the United States? Can it be seriously believed that standards so fixed now could survive a general revolution in China, a quarrel over the Dutch Indies between Holland and Japan, or an American invasion of Mexico? Such events—none of them improbable—would scatter to the winds the papers on which the agreements for fixing the proportionate amounts of armaments had been written. . . .

There are strong and obvious reasons against inviting the Powers to enter into an agreement for any purpose, however humane and ideal, unless and until the way is seen clear to the achievement of that purpose by the adoption of some definite and thought-out plan. It is the conviction that no such plan can at present be suggested which impels me to urge most strongly that we should refrain from bringing forward again the question of a limitation of armaments, which has landed us in such embarassing difficulties before.

III.3 PRACTICAL DIFFICULTIES: SECURITY FIRST

The question of disarmament was inextricably bound up with that of security; no country was willing to disarm unless and until it felt secure. For a British Government this meant no naval disarmament below a certain level; for a Polish Government no arms limitation until fear of Russian expansionist ambitions was allayed; for a Belgian or French Government no substantial measure of disarmament until reassurance about speedy assistance against renewed German aggression was forthcoming. Uncertainty about the extent of German disarmament exacerbated suspicions and prolonged tension; successive French and Belgian Governments, and many well-informed sources in other countries including Britain, cited authoritative evidence of widespread German evasion of the Versailles restrictions, most alarmingly through military and industrial collaboration with the Russian Government. Not surprisingly, it was not until 1926, in the rosy aftermath of the Locarno agreements, that the Preparatory Commission for Disarmamant set to work, with the help of American and Russian delegates, to draw up a programme for a League disarmament conference, an arduous process which took five years of long and tedious negotiations.

III.3.A Draft Instructions to Viscount Cecil for his guidance in attending a meeting of the Preparatory Commission for the Disarmament Conference, Geneva, May 1926, issued by the British Government (PRO reference number FO371/11883).

The Preparatory Commission which you are to attend on behalf of His Majesty's Government meets on 18 May. Its business is to explore the principles on which a scheme for the general reduction and limitation of armaments might be formulated in accordance with article 8 of the Covenant for the consideration in an International Conference of the Governments concerned. . . .

. . . there is one . . . point to which it is advisable to draw attention, namely, the present situation of the armaments maintained by this country in relation to any future schemes of reduction or limitation of armaments.

(a) Our Imperial naval forces were considerably reduced after the war—indeed, millions of tons of warships were scrapped—and then a further considerable reduction was brought about by the Washington Agreement. By this agreement a definite limit was imposed on the defensive power of the larger surface vessels, i.e., battleships, battle cruisers, cruisers and aircraft carriers, but similar restrictions were not applied either to submarines or to aircraft. You should endeavour to correct this omission. Up to date nothing has been done to limit the power of attacking the trade routes, either from the air or under the water, and so long as that is the case it becomes more and more incumbent that our naval forces shall be numerous enough to defend the Mercantile Marine, on whose maintenance the Empire so largely depends. Before any further limitation of our naval forces could be considered, international agreement should be obtained as to the number, size and gun armament of submarines. Even if this could be effected, it must be remembered that our trade routes are very long and vulnerable. To protect them a certain number of cruisers are essential, whatever naval forces other Powers may have. The Admiralty are therefore of the opinion that, even if a general agreement for the reduction of naval forces were secured, the British Empire must have very special treatment in regard to its number of cruisers. It would, however, in any case, be feasible for us to agree with other nations upon a lower limit to the size of cruisers and to the calibre of guns which they were permitted to carry. It would also be feasible to limit the size of torpedoes to be carried in all ships.

Very considerable economies might follow such an agreement, which would presumably also affect the gun armaments of aircraft carriers and submarines.

(b) Our Army is notoriously small, having regard to our world-wide commitments and the length of our land frontiers throughout the Empire; and from the standpoint of disarmament its strength compares favourably with the forces maintained by many other States. The size of our land forces is not regulated by the size of those of any other

Power, and it does not therefore seem capable of reduction in consequence of an agreement with other military Powers.

(c) Even to a greater extent than the Royal Navy our Air Forces were reduced—almost to the vanishing point—immediately after the war. Since then a progressive programme of development has been adopted which aims at providing us with an air force comparable to that of our nearest neighbour by 1930. Recently this date of completion has been postponed till 1935. His Majesty's Government would welcome any scheme of reduction and limitation which would result in a measure of equality being established between the air forces maintained by ourselves and the other countries of Europe. It is for consideration, pending the adoption of a universal scheme for limitation and reduction of Air Armaments, whether resort could not be made to a specific agreement between Great Britain and one or more of the other European Powers....

... The real menace to security in many areas is the competition which exists between neighbouring Powers in the maintenance of excessive armaments, and measures such as are contemplated by Article 16 for dealing with acts of aggression after they have taken place do little towards the removal of this menace, which can only be brought about by an effective agreement for a Reduction of Armaments and their subsequent Limitation. His Majesty's Government, therefore, could only contemplate contributing to additional or more precise guarantees of security in exchange for definite and substantial guarantees that a genuine scheme of Disarmament will be enforced, and that the degree to which this country would assist an attacked State should be made dependent on the extent of the policy of Disarmament agreed upon by the Conference and on the measure in which that policy is put into effect.

III.3.B Speech of the Polish delegate, M. Sokal, in the Preparatory Commission for Disarmament, Geneva, 1926. (*L of Ns O J*, 1926).

... the technical and political aspects of the problem of disarmament are closely allied. The reason for this is that it is not the armaments themselves which are the real cause of danger, but ... the causes are of a political and psychological nature. If all States were willing to bind themselves not to resort to war and to settle all questions between them by peaceful means, then effective disarmament might become a reality much sooner than at present seems possible. We must not forget the three principles which are bound up together—arbitration, security and disarmament. Certain countries have done a great deal towards arbitration, my own among them. With regard to guarantees of security we are only at the beginning of our journey, and of course every progress we make towards security will necessarily result in a diminution of armaments. Unfortunately, however, Poland is not in as good a position so far as security is concerned as, for instance, Switzerland, which has almost complete security through her system of international guarantees laid down in Treaties.

Poland would be the first to reduce her armaments could she obtain such effective international guarantees for her security. My country, however, like many others, is only at the beginning of its security and can therefore be only at the beginning of its disarmament. We hope one day we shall arrive at a degree of security which will enable us to reduce our armaments and reach the position referred to by the hon. delegate of the United States, of having only one soldier per thousand inhabitants.

I should like to say that the desire to provide for our security by treaties of guarantee and other effective means is the fundamental basis of the foreign policy of every Polish Government. I do not think I need lay stress on the particular difficulties which beset us, more especially in view of the fact that not all our neighbours are Members of the League of Nations, and are not taking part in the work for peace of the League.

We must also remember that States which do not possess natural frontiers are sometimes compelled to provide for their security by fortifications, to replace the natural frontiers which they unfortunately lack.

We should now consider, I think, what we can do in practice. We cannot limit the resources of a country so far as its population, its natural riches, its industrial equipment or means of transport are concerned. We realise it is not possible in practice to limit those, but we can and should consider what we can in fact do. One thing we can certainly do is to facilitate the working of the procedure of the Council in case of aggression. The Council should be enabled to take a decision with regard to the aggressor as speedily as possible, and be able to make the Covenant of the League effectively respected. At the present moment, however, I fear that the regulations of the Council do not provide for a procedure which would be sufficiently speedy. . . .

. . . We must first take account of security, and then proceed towards disarmament by stages. There are so many questions bound up with national disarmament that we cannot merely take the course which seems mathematically and logically correct. We must consider existing practical conditions. I think one of the chief services which our Commission could render to the League of Nations would be to suggest some procedure for making the action of the Council in case of aggression more speedy and more effective.

III.3.c Speech by M. de Brouckère, the Belgian delegate to the Preparatory Commission for Disarmament, 1926 (*L of Ns OJ*).

> The Members of the League recognise that the maintenance of peace requires the reduction of national armaments to the lowest point consistent with national safety and the enforcement by common action of international obligations.

What inference are we to draw from that? Supposing that a country has a very large population and is very wealthy and has a very large area. If you consider its armaments are excessive it simply means it has not been observing that undertaking which it accepted in the Covenant. It has got an armament which is larger than the lowest point consistent with national safety. Similarly, if a smaller State claims that it is insufficiently armed the inference is that you ought not to reduce it below what is the lowest point consistent with its national security. I have lately read a very important book which deals with this question, and the author has examined all the various methods of disarmament and all the possible bases for disarmament, and he concludes that when you have done all within your power, you have to establish some plan, and when that plan is submitted to different countries, you will have to adjust the different claims by means of negotiations; therefore it appears to me that all mathematical calculations are really of no effect. ... We want to get on to the more realistic stage when you come to discuss with the individual countries the question of reduction, and when you ask them specifically what reduction they are prepared to make, when you ask them ... what they are prepared to put on the table. That must be the real basis of the reduction of armaments, and that is the only method which really offers any effective hope for disarmament.

Now what arguments are you going to use towards a State in such a situation? Take my own country, for example. Suppose the League of Nations says: 'We consider that you are entitled to have an army of such-and-such a number; you shall have so many guns, so many rifles, so many regiments of infantry and so on.' Well, probably, as is the way in diplomatic negotiations, the first reply of the Government concerned would be that we do not think that is sufficient; and what arguments are you going to use to convince them in that situation? Will you say, 'Oh, but the armament we have laid down represents a certain percentage of your population, or a certain percentage of your expenditure?' Obviously not. The only argument which you could effectively use would be with reference to their security. The Government will reply: 'We do not feel ourselves sufficiently secure,' and you will have to convince them that the forces which you are prepared to allow them to maintain are sufficient for their defence against a possible aggressor in the existing situation of the world and taking count of the potential strength of the aggressor from whom they desire to be protected. The

League of Nations will say to them, 'You have got certain Treaties: you have got the Covenant of the League of Nations; you have got the agreements of Locarno . . . and if you take account of that you will see that your security is adequately provided for.' It is at that stage that I think you will need a certain amount of calculations, because you will have to make some calculations to show them that the assistance which they are going to get under these agreements is sufficient to compensate them for the reduction of armaments. So after this, what may be called the rather academic phase of the discussion, the chief consideration must be the provisions of Article VIII; that is to say the chief consideration must be to leave every country the national armaments which are consistent with national safety, and in doing so you must take count of the possibility of attack from certain directions, and the possibility of assistance from certain directions.

III.3.D   Letter from General J. H. Morgan, British Military Representative on the Inter-Allied Council and GOC British 'effectives' sub-committee of the Control Commission for the Disarmament of Germany, 1919–23, to the editor of the weekly German journal, *Die Menschheit*, published in its issue of 20 February 1925, at Wiesbaden.

. . . why does the Reichswehrministerium persistently refuse to disclose its recruiting returns? . . . These alone can establish how many men are being called up for training by the Reichsheer [Regular Army], and for five years they have been constantly refused. Why? The reason given is that they are a matter of 'inner service' which does not concern us. But is it no concern of ours to know how many men are being trained in the use of arms? And if there is nothing to conceal, why conceal it?

In the second place, why do the Reichswehrministerium refuse to show us those registers of armament production which were snatched from under our very noses at Spandau? They alone can serve to establish what your gun establishment was in 1919 and what it is now.

Thirdly, why does the Reichswehrministerium insist on retaining control of the vast network of military establishments, artillery depots, munition depots, supply depots, remount depots, which supplied the needs of the old army and are altogether superfluous for the needs, the legitimate needs, of the new? Your Government does not expropriate these, it does not alienate them, it does not sell them, it does not convert them—it either leaves them idle or lets them to a tenant at will. They are available for the mobilization of a vast army at almost any moment. A trifling sum of 200,000 gold marks is all that appears in the *Reischshaushaltsplan* [Budget] for 1924 as the proceeds of a sale of some two or three of them. What is being done with all the rest?

Fourthly, why is the Reichswehrministerium paying no less than twenty-two officers in the Ministry alone, without taking account of the generals in the Wehrkreis commands, as lieutenant-generals and major-generals? Why are all the captains in the Reichsheer with over two years' service drawing the pay of majors, and the oberleutnants drawing the pay of captains? Why is your Government maintaining an establishment of *Feldwebels* and *Unteroffiziers* [Sergeant majors and sergeants or corporals] sufficient for an army thrice, and more than thrice, the Treaty strength? To a soldier there is only one explanation of these things and that is that this army is, and is destined to be, a cadre for expansion.

What of your 'Security Police'? . . . they are, by one statute after another, made interchangeable with the Reichsheer in pay, promotion, pensions, grades, and a dozen other things, so that the two forces match one another even as the wards of a lock match the key which fits it. Behind every Reichsheer soldier there stands, like a silhouette, a 'police official'.

As to your army expenditure—and I have studied your Budget—I will only say this: if your army is really as small as your Government say it is, then your Government is the most extravagant Government in the world; and if your Government is not extravagant, then your army is far larger than it ought to be. Your Reichsheer, in theory small in stature, projects in reality a gigantic shadow across the map of Germany, and the shadow is the greater reality of the two. That shadow is the old army. Everything that an ingenious brain could devise and a subtle intellect invent, down even to giving the companies of infantry of the new army the numbers and badges of the regiments of the old, has been done to ensure that, at a touch of a button, the new army shall expand to the full stature of its predecessor. The proofs in my possession are overwhelming.

Your Government tells us repeatedly that our work is done and that there is nothing left to find out. They tell us that the Treaty of Versailles has been loyally executed. How then do they explain the astounding paradox that every time a store of hidden arms in a factory is revealed to the Commission by a pacifist workman, the workman, if discovered, is immediately arrested and sentenced to a long term of penal servitude? . . . If . . . the military clauses of the Treaty 'are part of the law of Germany', these unfortunate workmen were merely assisting in the execution of the law. If these concealments of arms are not approved by the German Government, why are the workmen who disclose them ruthlessly punished and the factory owners who conceal them allowed to go free?

III.3.E Memorandum prepared for Vansittart, Permanent Under Secretary at the Foreign Office, 1931, about German–Russian co-operation (PRO reference number FO371/15224, C3786).

On 24 April 1926, i.e. soon after her entry into the League, Germany signed a treaty with the Soviet Union at Berlin, whereby each side pledged itself to (a) remain neutral in the event of the other being attacked; and (b) remain outside any coalition with third parties formed for the purpose of imposing an economic or financial boycott on the other. In an exchange of notes attached to this treaty Germany undertook to oppose any efforts within the League directed against the Soviet Union. This treaty caused a violent flutter in the European dove-cote until, upon calmer reflection, it was found that its obligations were of a negative character and did not necessarily conflict with those assumed by Germany under the Covenant. It appears that, as at Rapallo, Germany had become alarmed by the conclusion of certain agreements between the members of the Little Entente, and that fortified by the Locarno Treaties she felt able to consolidate her relations with the Soviet Union on her own terms and without the dangerous intimacy that would have resulted from a treaty of alliance such as the Russians ardently desired. . . .

Military

There is close collaboration between the German and Soviet military authorities. . . . At the end of [1929], . . . it looked as though the 'Easterners' in the German military party had got the upper hand. Russian officers were invited to German manoeuvres (which were not attended by Allied officers), and German officers regularly attended the Soviet manoeuvres.

Under the Wirth Government there had been efforts at co-operating with the Soviet Union in the manufacture of war material. German technicians assisted in the making of poison gases in the Soviet Union and in return Soviet war material was supplied to Germany. The socialists in the Reichstag insisted on an inquiry. The facts were admitted and the whole scheme abandoned.

During 1930 evidence was forthcoming that Reichswehr officers were being illegally seconded for flying service in Russia with the knowledge of the German authorities. . . .

III.4 THE DISARMAMENT CONFERENCE OF 1932

At the end of 1930, the Preparatory Disarmament Commission adopted a draft Disarmament Convention to serve as a basis for discussion at the forthcoming General Disarmament Conference. Both Russia and

Germany voted against the adoption of the Convention, to express their disapproval of the very limited progress achieved by the agreed proposals. However, the same difficulties, fears and tensions which had hampered the work of the Preparatory Commission, served to obstruct the labours of the Conference, and were reinforced by the gloom and despondency caused by the Great Slump. Countries bordering on Germany demanded more effective security before adopting serious measures of arms reduction; Germany demanded equality of treatment on armaments, since her neighbours were not displaying any serious intention of disarming. In this kind of atmosphere, proposals such as that put forward by President Hoover to the Conference were bound to prove abortive, and not surprisingly, many observers became increasingly cynical about the willingness of major nations to agree to any serious measures of arms limitation.

III.4.A A French Memorandum of July 1931, setting forth the French
       view of the course which the Disarmament Conference should
       take (L of Ns OJ, 1931).

The Governments that are due to take part in the General Conference for the Limitation and Reduction of Armaments have been requested by the Council of the League of Nations to forward to the Secretariat before 15 September certain particulars concerning the state of their armaments and any information of a nature to enlighten the Conference of 1932 concerning them.

... The Government of the Republic consider it advisable to set forth the principles and methods of French policy as regards the limitation of armaments, the extent to which they have already applied them since signing the League Covenant, and, finally, those conditions the fulfillment of which they deem necessary if the Conference of 1932 is not to disappoint the hopes it has awakened.

I

... Article 8 of the Covenant is ... based upon two fundamental conceptions which it is important to emphasise.

The first is the idea of 'common action'.

In a system of international solidarity like that of the League of Nations each State must have sufficient armaments to protect itself against aggression until this 'common action' can begin to function: if left to its own unaided resources, a State, unlawfully attacked, must be sufficiently armed not to be overwhelmed before having had time to mobilise the whole of its national forces. It will therefore be possible for the reduction of armaments to be the more substantial in proportion as the setting in motion of the contemplated 'common action' is less uncertain and likely to be more prompt. ...

Viewed from this angle, the limitation of armaments, in conjunction with the development of the systems for the peaceful settlement of disputes and with mutual assistance, is a means of organising peace. But, in order that it may be carried into effect, the principle of common action must supersede in the minds of the nations that of individual defence. It implies that the League is considered by them as a living reality, invested with positive responsibilities and possessed of effective power.

Concurrently—and this is the second essential idea upon which it is based—Article 8 of the Covenant clearly states that the point below which national armaments cannot be reduced depends upon the degree of security enjoyed by the nation concerned.

A proper estimate of this safety must take into account not only the manner in which the 'common action' of the League will operate, but also the geographical situation and circumstances of each nation.

Article 8 of the Covenant therefore clearly lays down the principle that, as regards the reduction and limitation of armaments, there can be no hard and fast rules; the armaments of each State constitute an aggregate which must necessarily be adapted to its own particular case; the notion of diversity governs the work to be undertaken. Any levelling or automatic equalisation of forces is, for this very reason, excluded *a priori*, for equality of armaments as between two States would only be justifiable in the unlikely event of their geographical situation and circumstances being identical. . . .

II

Since the coming into force of the Covenant, France has of her own accord proceeded to reduce her armaments, taking into account, on the one hand, her geographical situation and the circumstances for which her armaments are intended to provide and, on the other, of the progress achieved in the organisation of security.

The particular circumstances of French national defence are well known.

Having thrice suffered invasion in the course of a hundred years, and with extensive frontiers lying open to attack, more particularly those frontiers in close proximity to which are concentrated the resources most essential to her economic life and national defence, France must have at her disposal land forces sufficient to protect her as surely and as promptly as their sea forces protect Naval Powers.

In addition, France is called upon to maintain order in an overseas Empire peopled by 60,000,000 inhabitants, covering an area equal to twenty-three times that of the home country, some parts of which are not yet entirely pacified. She is therefore obliged to maintain two specially trained forces, one in her dependencies, of the smallest size compatible with assuring their security in normal times, and a similar force in the home country, which would be available in case of emergency.

In close conjunction with national defence on land, the protection of the sea frontiers, both at home and overseas, and of the essential communications between these various territories requires the co-operation of a navy sufficiently powerful to dispense the Government of the Republic from the necessity of maintaining in every part of their Empire forces sufficient to cope alone with domestic disturbances which might conceivably coincide with a foreign aggression. The level, therefore, of the naval forces of France directly affects that of her land as well as that of her air forces.

Called upon to ensure the air defence of the home country, and to co-operate with the land and naval forces, the air service contributes in addition to the policing and protection of the overseas territories, which otherwise would require still larger land forces.

This interdependence of the three great categories of armaments is therefore extremely important for France; she must constantly consider them in combination with each other if she is properly to estimate the consequences which a measure adopted for one might have on the others.

As for security—an essential factor dominating the entire problem of the limitation and reduction of armaments and acting . . . as a mainspring for the functioning of Article 8 of the Covenant—the French Government have, in the last ten years, unceasingly striven to make clearer, stronger, and more tangible the conception of how this primary requisite is to be assured. They had all the more reason to devote their energies to this purpose that one of the foremost guarantees of French security, provided for and relied upon by the framers of the Peace Treaty, was from the very first inexistent. In consequence they have unreservedly associated themselves with every effort undertaken at Geneva for the purpose of defining more clearly and developing on a general plane the principles of arbitration and mutual help laid down in the Covenant.

The value of those efforts it is by no means their intention to belittle today.

It must, however, be noted that the slow rate of progress hitherto achieved has not tended to speed up the task of reducing armaments. . . .

III.4.B Speech by General Groener in the Reichstag, 9 March 1931. (*Frankfurter Zeitung*, 10 March 1931, translated in *DIA*, 1931, pp. 53–4.)

... The reason given for Germany's disarmament in the Treaty of Versailles was that it would render possible the initiation of a general limitation of the armaments of all countries. Germany has done her part. We have disarmed to a degree unexampled in history. But the other Powers undertook to follow us along the way of disarmament. Authoritative statesmen in those countries have admitted that this was a legally binding obligation. We have the right to demand that the inequality of armament caused by the disarmament already effected by Germany should be rectified by corresponding action on the part of the other Powers in accordance with their obligations under the Treaty. We have the right to demand the same degree of security as other countries. We put forward our demand for general disarmament ... in the interests of peace and the reconstruction of Europe, the most urgent task of our time. Germany is ready, and has always been ready, to co-operate actively in any form of disarmament which is acceptable on the basis of equality.

M. Maginot has claimed that France has already done something in the way of disarmament. He compares the number of French divisions with the number in 1913, and points to the reduction in men serving with the Colours, owing to the substitution of one year's military service for three. We cannot recognise these alterations in the organisation of the French Army as disarmament. They represent, rather, a carefully worked out change of system embodying the lessons of the War and technical developments and increasing, not diminishing, the actual striking power of the French Army. The value of an army is determined not by the length of service but by the intensity of training, the strength of trained reserves, and the amount and quality of material. In 1912, with two years' service, the French Army was 640,000 strong. Today there is only one year's service with the Colours but the strength of the Army is almost the same. Nearly half the Army, at least 230,000 men, serve more than the legal period and prove a highly qualified training staff. Newly created civilian bodies have taken all mobilisation, stores, and other clerical work off the soldiers' hands, and 30,000 civilian employees relieve the soldiers of fatigue duties. Boys are prepared for military service to a degree hitherto unknown. Consequently, France is in a position to give her soldiers a complete military training, even with one year's military service. Do the thousands of tanks, aeroplanes, and guns, the tens of thousands of machine-guns, suggest disarmament? France also has masses of other material in store. How many units she can form from her trained reserve and arm with that material is indicated by the fact that the number of generals and senior staff officers is one and a half times as large as before the War, in spite of the reduction in the number of divisions. French military expenditure has risen unceasingly since the War. All these undeniable facts show that France has not begun to disarm, for by means of her new army organisation she has, perhaps, created the strongest and most effective instrument of war in the world.

III.4.c Message of President Hoover to the Disarmament Conference, June 1932, containing proposals for disarmament. (Minutes of the General Commission, *League Document*, 1932.)

The time has come when we should cut through the brush and adopt some broad and definite method of reducing the overwhelming burden of armament which now lies upon the toilers of the world. This would be the most important world step that could be taken to expedite economic recovery. We must make headway against the mutual fear and friction arising out of war armaments which kill human confidence throughout the world. We can still remain practical in maintaining an adequate self-defence among all nations. We can add to the assurances of peace and yet save the people of the world from ten to fifteen billions of wasted dollars during the next ten years.

I propose that the following principles should be our guide.

First: The Briand-Kellogg Pact to which we are all signatories can only mean that the nations of the world have agreed that they will use their arms solely for defence.

Second: This reduction should be carried out, not only by broad general cuts in armaments, but by increasing the comparative power of defence through decreases in the power of the attack.

Third: The armaments of the world have grown up in mutual relation to each other; and, speaking generally, such relativity should be preserved in making reductions.

Fourth: The reductions must be real and positive. They must effect economic relief.

Fifth: There are three problems to deal with—land forces, air forces, and naval forces. They are all inter-connected. No part of the proposals which I make can be dissociated one from the other.

Based on these principles, I propose that the arms of the world should be reduced by nearly one-third.

Questions of status, as distinguished from quantitative questions, involve considerations of national pride and dignity, which deeply touch the heart of a people and keep alive resentment which would otherwise die down and give place to more kindly feeling. In the interests of general appeasement, therefore, it is much to be desired that any such questions should be disposed of by friendly negotiation and agreed adjustment, not involving either disregard of treaty obligations or the increase in the sum total of armed force. But this desirable consummation cannot be attained by peremptory challenge or by withdrawal from deliberations which are about to be resumed. It can only be reached by patient discussion through the medium of conference between the States concerned.

Land Forces. In order to reduce the offensive character of all land forces as distinguished from their defensive character, I propose the adoption of the presentation already made at the Geneva Conference for the abolition of all tanks, all chemical warfare, and all large mobile guns. This would not prevent the establishment or increase of fixed fortifications of any character for the defence of frontiers and sea coasts. It would give an increased relative strength to such defence as compared with attack.

I propose, furthermore, that there should be a reduction of one third in the strength of all land armies over and above the so-called police component.

The land armaments of many nations are considered to have two functions. One is the maintenance of internal order in connection with the regular police forces of the country. The strength required for this purpose has been called the 'police component'. The other function is defence against foreign attack. The additional strength required for this purpose has been called the 'defence component'. Under the Treaty of Versailles and the other peace treaties the armies of Germany, Austria, Hungary and Bulgaria were reduced to a size deemed appropriate for the maintenance of internal order, Germany being assigned 100,000 troops for a population of approximately 65 million people. I propose that we should accept for all nations a basic police component of soldiers proportionate to the average which was thus allowed Germany and these other States. This formula, with necessary corrections for Powers having colonial possessions, should be sufficient to provide for the maintenance of internal order by the nations of the world. . . .

Air Forces. All bombing planes to be abolished. This will do away with the military possession of types of planes capable of attacks upon civil populations and should be coupled with the total prohibition of all bombardment from the air.

Naval Forces. I propose that the treaty number and tonnage of battleships shall be reduced by one third; that the treaty tonnage of aircraft-carriers, cruisers, and destroyers shall be reduced by one quarter; that the treaty tonnage of submarines shall be reduced by one third; and that no nation shall retain a submarine tonnage greater than 35,000 tons. . . .

These proposals are simple and direct. They call upon all nations to contribute something. The contribution here proposed will be relative and mutual. . . . It is folly for the world to go on breaking its back under military expenditure, and the United States is willing to take its share of the responsibility, by making definite proposals that will relieve the world.

III.4.D *Izvestia* on the results of the Disarmament Conference (No. 205, 26 July 1932, p. 1).

After five years of preparation and six months of work, the labours of the Disarmament Conference have come to an end, having accomplished nothing. ... What then did the Geneva conference do in the course of six months? All the capitalist countries presented declarations camouflaged in pacifist phrases which defended their own specific programmes of armament. The most characteristic was the programme of French imperialism. French imperialism refused to agree to any limitation on armaments and proposed instead to place the most powerful instruments of warfare in the hands of a special army controlled by the League of Nations. The French proposal did not aim at the limitation of armaments, but rather at the legalisation by the League of Nations of all instruments of warfare that had been invented by postwar militarists.

In view of the fact that as a result of the Versailles Treaty Germany is the least armed of all the imperialist states, it insisted on parity in case no agreement was reached on the limitation of armament.

Italy, taking into account its difficult financial situation, was prepared to give up a number of costly modern instruments of warfare. The United States and England did not advance any special programme for the limitation of armaments but simply paraded a series of humanitarian proposals for easing the burdens of war on the civilian population.

Only the Soviet Union presented a clear and exact programme of disarmament, pointing out that disarmament alone will safeguard the people of the world from the unheard of calamities of modern warfare. But in view of the fact that this proposal of the Soviet Union was rejected by all the capitalist countries, the Soviet Union advanced a plan whereby armed forces were to be cut down to half their present size, and some preferential conditions granted only to small countries which fear attack by large powers. This proposal also was rejected.

After several oratorical battles at the plenum of the conference and at the sessions of the General Commission, the conference went to sleep for several months. The Technical Commissions alone held sessions. These Technical Commissions, naturally, could not make any headway because the question of disarmament is not a technical but a political one. Therefore the Technical Commissions were simply marking time, trying to find the proper definition for a dreadnought or a tank. ...

III. 5 THE NAZI CHALLENGE

The unhappy labours of the disarmament conference were finally doomed to failure by political changes in Germany. The assumption of power by the Nazis was marked by an immediate stiffening of German intransigence and belligerent demands, especially at the Geneva disarmament conference. Close observers of the German scene were quick to point to the change in attitude and atmosphere in Germany, and it came as no surprise when the German Government announced its intention of withdrawing from both the disarmament conference and the League of Nations. The first Government to appreciate fully the serious implications of the Nazi challenge was that of the Bolsheviks, and it lost no time in realigning its foreign policy, and joining the League to try to strengthen potential resistence to what it foresaw would be German expansionist designs.

III.5.A Sir Horace Rumbold, retiring British Ambassador in Berlin, to Sir John Simon, British Foreign Secretary, 30 June 1933 *DBFP* Series II, Vol. V, No. 229).

... This despatch is an attempt at a general appreciation of the situation here on the eve of my departure from this post.

... Hitlerism ... is a reaction from what are alleged to be the criminal shortcomings and international outlook of all German Governments since 1919. It has, therefore, gone to the other extreme and produced an aggressive nationalism which is accompanied by a seemingly profound contempt for and disregard of foreign opinion. ...

Hitler has now been in power for five months and appears to have firmly riveted his hold on the country. The first phase of the revolution witnessed the destruction of the Communist party and organisation, the partial hamstringing of the Social Democratic party, the attack on the Jews and the establishment of concentration camps to contain opponents of the present regime. The second phase of the revolution, which began a few days ago, has been marked by an accelerated *tempo*. ...

Visitors from abroad usually ask where this policy is leading and who is the driving force in the Nazi party. Some competent observers doubt whether the Nazi party itself knows what its goal is. The leaders, when pressed, almost invariably take refuge in verbiage and generalities. The outside world is best acquainted with the three chiefs, Hitler, Goering and Goebbels. All three are notoriously pathological cases, Hitler and Goering as a result of wounds and hardships in the war, Goebbels as a result of a physical defect and neglect in childhood. ...

One looks in vain for any men of real worth amongst the other leaders, who are seemingly recruited from a bad class. Dr. Ley, the leader of the labour front ... recently gave the Labour Conference at

Geneva a taste of his quality. He is a man with all the aggressive and brutal characteristics of a low-class Prussian. He is a drunkard. Herr Rust, the Minister of Education, is of the same kidney, and amongst others, the names of Herr Frick in Prussia, Herr Klagges [Prime Minister of Brunswick] in Brunswick and of Herren Wagner [Bavarian Minister of Interior] and Frank in Bavaria occur to the mind as examples of Nazis who will not hesitate to adopt the most ruthless methods and outlandish ideas ... these men have succeeded in creating an atmosphere of terror which is increased by the difficulty, for Germans, of obtaining authentic information about what is going on. Nobody can foresee the actions of leaders who ... seem to possess authority to incarcerate anyone at a moment's notice ... the prevalent feeling is one of great insecurity. ...

During the last few days I have seen practically all my principal colleagues and have been struck by the unanimity of their views on the present situation. They are bewildered by the whirlwind development of Hitler's internal policy, and view the future with great uneasiness and apprehension. ...

Unpleasant incidents and excesses are bound to occur during a revolution, but the deliberate ruthlessness and brutality which have been practised during the last five months seem both excessive and unnecessary. I have the impression that the persons directing the policy of the Hitler Government are not normal. Many of us, indeed, have a feeling that we are living in a country where fanatics, hooligans and eccentrics have got the upper hand, and there is certainly an element of hysteria in the policy and actions of the Hitler regime.

III.5.B   Memorandum on Germany and Disarmament written by Brigadier Temperley, 1933, and circulated to the Cabinet (*DBFP* Series II, Vol. V, No. 127).

The time has come when Germany's attitude to disarmament and the attitude of the United Kingdom towards Germany ought to be reviewed. In the past there has been much sympathy with Germany and public opinion was in favour of granting her equality of status by degrees and in proportion to evidence of good behaviour; even France had realised that the end of the disarmament clauses of the Peace Treaty was in sight. ... While no one believed that they had been kept with complete fidelity, the breaches which could be proved in open court were individually not great, though their cumulative effect was not inconsiderable. Germany had not been idle during these years and with great ingenuity had carried out a steady erosion of the disarmament clauses, in some cases with permission but more frequently without. ...

Public opinion has been well aware of the continuous breaches of the treaty but was disposed to regard them as the not unexpected reaction by a high spirited people against their penal character. It was ready to go forward, in spite of these evasions, with a first step towards equality of status, though France was naturally more hesitant. So long as Bruening could retain his precarious hold upon the Chancellorship and continue with some form of parliamentary government, there remained a certain amount of faith in Germany's pacific intentions. . . .

Within a few weeks of his arrival, Hitler has carried out a revolution and made himself complete master of Germany. The country has given itself up to a delirium of reawakened nationalism and of the most blatant and dangerous militarism. Fuel has been added to the flames by an orgy of military parades and torch-light processions and by a constant stream of patriotic wireless addresses delivered by masters of the art of propaganda, including Hitler himself. Behind all this surge and fury, Hitler has been swiftly consolidating his position. . . . The whole country has been Hitlerised and the swastika flag flies side by side with the old banner of the Reich on all public buildings and Embassies.

On the military side, Storm detachments of the Nazis and Stahlhelm have been converted into auxiliary police. As the Nazi detachments were recruited from the most desperate and violent elements of the unemployed, they do not seem particularly suitable for police work, the more so since arms have been placed in their hands. Their numbers are probably in the vicinity of 75,000. They are to undergo military training similar to that given to the militarised police. The incorporation of these troops in the police is, of course, a flagrant violation of the Peace Treaty. It is believed that the total strength of the Nazi Storm detachment is 300,000 men. . . . It has just been announced that the Chancellor has issued a decree calling up all youths of 20 years of age annually for national labour service for twelve months beginning on 1 January 1934. This will produce an annual contingent of 350,000. The Secretary of State for Labour Service announces that every youth must do his year in the Labour Service before passing on to military service, *when conscription has been reintroduced.* . . . The alleged objects of inculcating discipline and patriotism and providing physical training and productive work, as well as such training described as 'Defence Sport', are the merest camouflage for intensive military training. It cannot be doubted that arms will be in their hands before long and instruction will be given in their use. All this is an equally flagrant violation of the Peace Treaty. The Stahlhelm has been forcibly absorbed into the Nazi Army and the military activities of these bodies will certainly be intensified. Goering has put a number of air personnel into uniform, and the formation of an Air Force seems to be actively proceeding.

D

On the material side it is understood that the Air Ministry have identified at least 125 fighting machines in existence or being made, exclusive of some 60 believed to be at Lipetsk in Russia. Information has been received from secret sources that an order has been given by the Reichswehr Ministerium to the Dornier works for 36 twin-engined night bombers. The cost of these orders is to be disguised under funds for employment of the unemployed. There are numerous indications in the last two months of increased activity in the German armaments industry. Reports have been received that twelve firms, which are not allowed to produce armaments, have received test orders for war material. Preparations are reported to have been made for the re-opening of eight former Government arsenals.

At Geneva the German attitude has stiffened considerably. . . . The increasing insolence of the Germans has brought discussion on effectives to a complete standstill. When material is discussed, there are strong indications that the demands for samples of military aeroplanes, tanks and heavy guns will be very large.

What then is to be our attitude? Are we to go forward as if nothing has happened? Can we afford to ignore what is going on behind the scenes in Germany? . . . the intensification of military preparations under the Hitler regime, coupled with the strident appeals to force of the Nazi leaders, not only means a secret German rearmament, but creates an entirely new situation. Admittedly, it would be a good thing to get Germany bound by a Convention, as a breakdown would mean that she would commence to rearm at once. On the other hand, there is little use in a Convention limiting effectives and material, if the preparations above indicated are to proceed unchecked, while the war like spirit is being openly roused to a fever heat against the Poles as the first objective, with France as the ultimate enemy. . . . No moment could be worse chosen than the present one to advocate drastic reductions in the armaments of France, the Little Entente and Poland. Moreover, the destruction of all heavy material and bombing machines belonging to the French and her Allies and to our own armed forces seems madness in the face of this direct German menace. . . .

If it is dangerous to go forward with disarmament, what then is to be done? There appears to be one bold solution. France, the United States and ourselves should address a stern warning to Germany that there can be no disarmament, no equality of status and no relaxation of the Treaty of Versailles unless a complete reversion of present military preparations and tendencies takes place in Germany. Admittedly this will provoke a crisis and the danger of war will be brought appreciably nearer. We should have to say that we shall insist upon the enforcement of the Treaty of Versailles, and in this insistence, with its hint of force in the background, presumably the United States would not join. But Germany knows that she cannot fight at present and we must call her bluff. She is powerless before the French army and our fleet. Hitler, for all his bombast, must give way. If such a step seems too forceful, the only alternative is to carry out some minimum measure of disarmament and to allow things to drift for another five years, by which time, unless there is a change of heart in Germany, war seems inevitable. German rearmament will by then be an accomplished fact and the material of the ex-Allies, which would take years of work and scores of millions of pounds to replace, may have been destroyed. This is an alternative which is unlikely to lead us anywhere. Strong combined action, however ... should prove decisive, even though the threat of military pressure might have to be maintained for years, calling for fresh monetary sacrifices, until Germany is brought to her senses. But even this heavy responsibility should be accepted rather than that we should allow all the sacrifices of the last war to be in vain and the world to go down in economic ruin. There is a mad dog abroad once more and we must resolutely combine either to ensure its destruction or at least its confinement until the disease has run its course.

III.5.c Extracts from Broadcast Speech by Hitler, 14 October 1933 (*DIA* 1933, p. 293).

... Germany cannot tolerate the deliberate degradation of the nation by the perpetuation of a discrimination which consists in withholding the rights which are granted as a matter of course to other nations ... the men who are at present the leaders of Germany have nothing in common with the traitors of November 1918. Like every decent Englishman and every decent Frenchman, we all had our duty to our fatherland and placed our lives at its service. We are not responsible for the war or for what occurred in it, but we feel responsible for what every honest man must do in the time of his country's distress and for what we have done. We have such infinite love for our people that we desire whole-heartedly an understanding with other nations, and whenever it is possible we shall try to attain it, but, as representatives of an honourable nation and as men of honour, it is impossible for us to be members of institutions under conditions which are only bearable to those who are devoid of a sense of honour. ...

Since it has been made clear to us from the declarations of the official representatives of certain great Powers that they were not prepared to consider real equality of rights for Germany at present, we have decided that it is impossible, in view of the indignity of her position, for Germany to continue to force her company upon other nations.

III.5.D The Russian newspaper *Izvestia* was quick to analyse the implications of Germany's withdrawal, in its edition of 16 October 1933,
pl. (1). Soon afterwards, Russia applied to join the League, and
Litvinov spelled out Russian fears in the League Assembly of
1934 (*L of Ns OJ*, 1934) (2).

(1) ... Germany has not only withdrawn from the League of Nations—
it has refused to participate in the further work of the Disarmament
Conference. In other words, German fascism declares to the entire
world that it has decided to take the path of preparation for war, the
essential condition for which is the increase of armaments. ... The
action of fascist Germany, confronted by the failure of its internal
policy and face to face with international isolation, is threatening
international peace with exceptionally dangerous adventures. The
seriousness of this danger will of course be recognised by everyone
who considers it his duty to struggle by all means for the preservation
of peaceful relations between peoples. The withdrawal of Germany
from the League of Nations is an alarm warning for partisans of peace
concerning the need to be on guard.

(2) ... The Soviet Government, following attentively all developments of international life, could not but observe the increasing activity
in the League of Nations of States interested in the preservation of
peace and their struggle against aggressive militarist elements. More, it
noted that these aggressive elements themselves were finding the
restrictions of the League embarrassing and trying to shake them off.
All this could not be without its influence on the attitude towards the
League of Nations of the Soviet Government, ever searching for
further means for the organisation of peace, for co-operation in which
we have been invited to come here.

One thing is quite clear for me, and that is that peace and security
cannot be organised on the shifting sands of verbal promises and
declarations. The nations are not to be soothed into a feeling of security
by assurance of peaceful intentions, however often they are repeated,
especially in those places where there are grounds for expecting aggression or where, only the day before, there have been talk and publications
about wars of conquest in all directions, for which both ideological and
material preparations are being made. We should establish that any
State is entitled to demand from its neighbours, near and remote,
guarantees for its security, and that such a demand is not be be considered as an expression of mistrust. Governments with a clear conscience and really free from all aggressive intentions, cannot refuse to
give, in place of declarations, more effective guarantees which would be
extended to themselves and give them also a feeling of complete
security.

IV

THE MANCHURIAN INCIDENT

JAPAN'S ATTACK ON Mukden in 1931 presented the League of Nations with its first major challenge, a challenge magnified by the geographical location of the disputed area, the near-anarchic conditions prevailing in that part of North China, and the general international situation. The repercussions of the 1929 slump were dominating the attentions of the world's statesmen, and had just brought about a dramatic change of Government in Great Britain. In the United States, a Presidential Election was pending; in Europe, France was obsessed by political events unfolding across her northern frontier. The timing could not have been more unpropitious for a major League initiative.

IV.1 THE OBSCURITY OF THE FACTS

In the immediate aftermath of the 'Mukden Incident', it was extremely difficult for European statesmen to sort out the intricacies of the dispute. Manchuria was known to be a lawless area, only nominally under the control of Chiang Kai Shek's National Government, and the Japanese had certain prescribed treaty rights, dating from the 1905 Treaty of Portsmouth, involving the use of troops to guard concession areas and particularly railways. Many European observers believed that the Japanese troops had been provoked by marauding Chinese war-lord troops and had acted in self-defence.

IV.1.A Appeal of the Chinese Government to the League Council, 21 September 1931 (*L of Ns OJ*, 1931).

Through statements made to it at its meeting on 19 September, by the representatives of China and Japan, the Council was advised of the fact that a serious situation had been created in Manchuria. In his statement at that meeting, the representative of China declared that the information which he then had, indicated that the situation had been created through no fault upon the part of the Chinese. Since 19 September, the undersigned has received from his Government information which discloses a situation of greater gravity than had appeared by the first report, and which revealed that, beginning from ten o'clock of the night of 18 September, regular troops of Japanese soldiers, without provocation of any kind, opened rifle and artillery fire upon Chinese soldiers at or near the city of Mukden, bombarded the arsenal and barracks of the Chinese soldiers, set fire to the ammunition depot, disarmed the Chinese troops in Changhun, Kwanchengtse, and other places, and later took military occupation of the cities of Mukden and Antung and other places and of public buildings therein, and are now in such occupation. Lines of communication have also been seized by Japanese troops.

To these acts of violence the Chinese soldiers and populace, acting under instructions from the Chinese Government, have made no resistance, and have refrained from conduct which might in any way aggravate the situation.

In view of the foregoing facts, the Republic of China, a member of the League of Nations, asserts that a situation has arisen which calls for action under the terms of Article 11 of the Covenant. I am, therefore, instructed by my Government to request that, in pursuance of authority given to it by Article 11 of the Covenant, the Council take immediate steps to prevent the further development of a situation endangering the peace of nations; to re-establish this *status quo ante*; and to determine the amounts and character of such reparations as may be found due to the Republic of China.

I will add that the Government of China is fully prepared to act in conformity with whatever recommendations it may receive from the Council, and to abide by whatever decisions the League of Nations may adopt in the premises.

IV.1.B Statement by the Japanese Government, 24 September 1931
        (*L of Ns OJ*, 1931).

1. The Japanese Government has constantly been exercising honest endeavours, in pursuance of its settled policy, to foster friendly relations between Japan and China, and to promote the common prosperity and well-being of the two countries. Unfortunately, the conduct of officials and individuals of China for some years past has been such that our national sentiment has frequently been irritated. In particular, unpleasant incidents have taken place one after another in the regions of Manchuria and Mongolia, in which Japan is interested in an especial degree, until the impression has gained strength in the minds of the Japanese people that Japan's fair and friendly attitude is not being reciprocated by China in a like spirit. Amidst the atmosphere of perturbation and anxiety thus created, a detachment of Chinese troops destroyed the tracks of the South Manchuria Railway in the vicinity of Mukden and attacked our railway guards at midnight on 18 September; a clash between the Japanese and Chinese troops then took place.

2. The situation became critical, as the number of Japanese guards

stationed along the entire railway did not exceed 10,400, while there were in juxtaposition some 220,000 Chinese soldiers. Moreover, hundreds of thousands of Japanese residents were placed in jeopardy. In order to forestall an imminent disaster, the Japanese army had to act swiftly. The Chinese soldiers garrisoned in the neighbouring localities were disarmed, and the duty of maintaining peace and order was left in the hands of the local Chinese organisations under the supervision of Japanese troops.

3. These measures having been taken, our soldiers were mostly withdrawn within the railway zone. There still remain some detachments in Mukden and Kirin and a small number of men in a few other places, but nowhere does a state of military occupation as such exist. The reports that the Japanese authorities have seized the customs of the saltgabelle office at Yingkou, or that they have taken control of the Chinese railways between Ssupingkai and Chengchiatun or between Mukden and Sinmintun are entirely untrue, nor has the story of our troops having ever been sent north of Changchun or into Chientao any foundation in fact.

4. The Japanese Government, at the special Cabinet meeting of 19 September, took the decision that all possible efforts should be made to prevent an aggravation of the situation, and instructions to that effect were given to the Commander of the Manchurian Garrison. It is true that a detachment was dispatched from Changchun to Kirin on 21 September, but it was not with a view to military occupation. It was sent only for the purpose of removing the menace to the South Manchuria Railway on its flank. As soon as that object has been attained, our detachment will be entirely withdrawn. It may be added that, while a mixed brigade of 4,000 men was sent from Korea to join the Manchurian Garrison, the total number of men in the Garrison at present still remains within the limit set by treaty, and that fact cannot therefore be regarded as having in any way added to the seriousness of the international situation.

5. It may be superfluous to repeat that the Japanese Government harbours no territorial designs in Manchuria. What we desire is that Japanese subjects shall be enabled safely to engage in various peaceful pursuits, and be given the opportunity of participating in the development of that land by means of capital and labour. It is the proper duty of a Government to protect the rights and interests legitimately enjoyed by the nation or individuals. The endeavours of the Japanese Government to guard the South Manchuria Railway against wanton attacks should be viewed in no other light. The Japanese Government, true to its established policy, is prepared to co-operate with the Chinese Government in order to prevent the present incident from developing into a disastrous situation between the two countries, and to work out

such constructive plans as will once and for all eradicate causes of future friction. The Japanese Government would be more than gratified if the present difficulty could be brought to a solution which will give a new turn to the mutual relations of the two countries.

IV.1.c Memorandum by Sir John Simon, prepared for circulation to the Cabinet, on the Manchurian situation, 23 November 1931 (*DBFP* Series II, vol. VIII, no. 769).

... There has been an unsolved Sino-Japanese problem in Manchuria for over twenty years—ever since the Japanese succeeded to Russian rights in that region after the Russo-Japanese war [of 1904–5]. The Chinese have never willingly accepted the Japanese position in Manchuria. In recent years their resistance—for the most part passive—has taken on a more active character. There have been frequent incidents and great friction eventually culminating in the affair of 18 September last. The Japanese military force guarding the zone of the South Manchuria Railway, alleging an attack by Chinese troops on the railway line just north of Mukden, carried out what was evidently a carefully prepared *coup* and proceeded systematically to drive out the Chinese authorities and establish their own authorities instead. On 21 September China appealed to the Council of the League, then in session at Geneva, under Article 11 of the Covenant. On 30 September the Council adopted unanimously a Resolution in which it took note of the Japanese representative's statement that his Government would continue as rapidly as possible the withdrawal of its troops, which had already been begun, into the railway zone in proportion as the safety of the lives and property of Japanese nationals was effectively assured and that his Government hoped to carry out this intention in full as speedily as may be. The Japanese Government, however, failed to carry out the assurances given to the Council which therefore met again at Geneva from 13–24 October. The Japanese representative now adopted the attitude that a preliminary agreement, binding China to recognise Japan's treaty rights in Manchuria, was an essential element of security and must be a condition precedent to evacuation. The other members of the Council on the other hand maintained that evacuation must be a condition precedent to the negotiations for a settlement of the questions in dispute between the parties. On 24 October, therefore, the Council adopted a draft Resolution by thirteen votes to 1 (the Japanese alone voting against) calling upon Japan to evacuate within three weeks, namely by 16 November, the date fixed for the next meeting of the Council. Owing to the want of unanimity, this resolution had no juristic effect. Japanese military operations in execution of the programme above described have continued during this session of the Council as during the last. The Japanese representative has been persuaded to propose that a

League Commission should visit Manchuria and China, but it is very doubtful whether agreement can be reached as to the terms of reference of this Commission. The Chinese delegate has indicated that he does not reject, in principle, the suggestion of a Commission, but that its appointment should not furnish a pretext for delay in Japanese evacuation. If the appointment of such a Commission could be secured by general consent of the members of the Council, it would undoubtedly be able to supply much useful information on points which are at present obscure or disputed between the contesting parties.

There is a widespread feeling, which I believe to be justified, that although Japan has undoubtedly acted in a way contrary to the principles of the Covenant by taking the law into her own hands, she has a real grievance against China and the merits of the matter are complicated by a further consideration. This is not a case in which the armed forces of one country have crossed the frontiers of another in circumstances where they had no previous right to be on the other's soil. Japan owns the South Manchurian Railway and has been entitled throughout to have a body of Japanese guards upon the strip of land through which the railway runs. Japan's case is that, having her armed guards lawfully there, she was compelled by the failure of China to provide reasonable protection for Japanese lives and property in Manchuria in the face of attacks of Chinese bandits, and of an attack upon the line itself, to move Japanese forces forward and to occupy points in Manchuria which are beyond the line of the railway. This has grown by degrees into what is in effect an organised occupation, leading in its turn to serious fighting and bombing. But Japan continues to insist that she has no territorial ambitions in Manchuria—an expression, it will be observed, which does not necessarily imply that she is not thinking of some sort of protectorate, at any rate in Southern Manchuria. In spite of Japan's protests to the contrary, there can of course be no real doubt that she is pursuing the course of putting pressure on China by means of this occupation for the purpose of securing that the Japanese claims against China in that region may be met, e.g. the stopping of cut-throat competition with the South Manchurian Railway, which Japan asserts is already promised to her by a Protocol of 1905 and the reaffirmation by China of the rights which Japan claims to have secured by a Treaty of 1915. . . .

It may well be that the Chinese Delegate will put into effect the threat which he has often uttered, and appeal to the Council under Article 15 of the Covenant. . .

Under the Article the Council must make an investigation and could decide, independently of the parties, to send out a Commission of Enquiry. It has hitherto been desired to avoid the application of Article 15 on the ground that it introduces a more menacing atmosphere. In fact, it seems difficult to see how the position is in that respect changed.

Indeed, it might give a respite of six to nine months during which passion may cool. But M. Briand's own conversations with me show that he is personally anxious to keep all discussion within Article 11.

IV.2 LEAGUE COUNCIL HESITATIONS

The problems facing the League were greatly increased by growing evidence that the Japanese army in Manchuria had acted on its own initiative in an attempt to undermine civilian rule and prepare the way for a military coup d'etat in Japan. Agreements reached between the League Council and the Japanese Government could not be enforced; the Kwantung Army was determined to disobey all civilian commands in order to weaken and discredit the Japanese Government as much as possible. The leading members of the League, and the United States, were thus concerned to do nothing which would further weaken the Japanese Government and strengthen the position of the military faction.

IV.2.A The British Ambassador in Tokyo, Sir F. Lindley to the Marquess of Reading, 1 October 1931 (*DBFP* Series II, vol. VIII, no. 550.

. . . Whether [the Mukden Incident] was a genuine attempt of ill-disciplined Chinese troops to interfere with the line or whether it was engineered by the Japanese will probably never be known for certain. In any case, it was the excuse for a momentous decision. The perplexities which have made Japanese policy in China so vacillating of late years . . . were suddenly brought to an end. The defence of Manchurian interests had triumphed over commercial considerations in China as a whole.

If one looks for a sound reason for this sudden decision—a reason sufficient to convince a Cabinet of sensible civilians—it is difficult to find; though popular exasperation at Chinese tactics, especially in Manchuria, had been growing steadily and had reached a dangerous point. . . . My own feeling is that it was due less to such serious Sino-Japanese differences regarding competing railways, treatment of Korean immigrants, export duties on Fushun coal and double customs duties at Dairen than to anti-Japanese propaganda and Chinese truculence. . . . But, in any case, there was no sign on 17 September that a crisis had been reached. . . .

The Military party have never been in doubt that South Manchuria is worth any volume of actual or potential trade. It was conquered from Russia in an heroic campaign which opened the province to Japanese enterprise and penetration. Full advantage has been taken of the opportunities offered; and the vast immigration of Chinese from the tortured provinces further south has testified to the benefits conferred by the presence of a few thousand Japanese troops. For two months and more preceding 18 September, General Minami, the Minister of War, did all in his power to rouse popular opinion on the subject of Manchuria....

Such are the considerations which have led most of my colleagues and myself to believe that this Manchurian adventure is due, not to any well-weighed Cabinet decision, but to the army on its own initiative. And this conclusion is strengthened by the course of events after 18 September. The first Cabinet Council sat for eight hours; and it was followed by others almost as long. The officials at the Gaimusho [Japanese Ministry of Foreign Affairs] were in a state of quite evident anxiety and perplexity; and I think it is certain that they, at any rate, had no inkling of what was in the wind. It is possible, though not I think probable, that the War Office were also in the dark; and that when the explosion occurred the local commander, sure of the support of his chiefs, put into immediate force a plan which had been long perfected down to the last detail for such an emergency.

Faced with an accomplished fact and an international crisis, Baron Shidehara and his civilian colleagues were bound to accept the position and take the responsibility for what had occurred. Ministers would probably have felt so bound in any country. In Japan they were doubly bound by every dictate of Japanese honour. And the exasperation they may have felt at having their hands forced was soon mitigated by the popularity of their action. There was not a dissentient voice in the press; and the Prefectural Elections, fought on purely party lines a week ago, brought to the Minseito party a measure of success beyond their most sanguine hopes.

Thus we have a Government and a people united in the defence of what they believe to be the most vital interest of their country. The Government, at least, realise that hardly less vital interests have, for a time at least, been sacrificed owing to the decision taken; and they must be expected to strain every nerve to reap results in Manchuria which will compensate for their losses in China proper ... the Japanese [have] not yet assimilated the ideas of international relations which have guided British policy since the war. When their vital interests are threatened, as they believe them to be now, they will be guided solely by regard for those interests; and they will only tolerate intervention from the League of Nations or from any other quarter if they believe it dangerous to those same interests not to do so....

It must not be assumed ... that Japan is indifferent to opinion at Geneva. This is far from being the case. But when it comes to a choice between deference to that opinion and her vital interests she will choose the latter. In the present instance she does not believe that it is as vital for her future to stand well with the League as to defend herself in

Manchuria. When it comes to intervention from the side of the United States or from Russia, she is less sure of herself. That she would not seriously risk a war with either is, I think, certain. And I am inclined to believe that she would yield further to pressure from Washington than from Geneva, even with no possible threat of war in the background.

If the Military party are so dominant and the temper of the country such as described above, there may well be anxiety as to the future course of Japanese policy. Without attempting to prophecy, it is useful to bear certain aspects of the position in mind. The Military party, though we believe they forced the issue, lost their full control of events as soon as the military movements of the opening days of the crisis came to an end. Automatically the Cabinet, as a whole, re-asserted its authority when it was no longer possible to urge local military necessity as an excuse for action. The further despatch of troops and the contemplated occupation of fresh points were vetoed, and the total number of the forces in Manchuria was kept below the Treaty limit of fifteen thousand. Troops were even withdrawn in part or in whole from a good many points outside the Railway zone. In short, a policy of prudence and moderation quickly succeeded the military outburst. This is not surprising when one considers that the League of Nations, the United States and Soviet Russia all had their eyes directed on Manchuria.

. . . The Japanese Government have given solemn assurances, both to the League and to Washington, that they have no territorial ambitions whatever. These assurances can, we believe here, be accepted as completely genuine. . . . Baron Shidehara . . . informed me that the strictest orders had been given both to the Japanese military and civilians in South Manchuria not to meddle in Chinese politics. That individual military officers have so meddled in the past is hardly to be doubted. And, if reports from Peking are to be credited, they have even contemplated setting up a Manchurian Dynasty entirely independent of the rest of China. Though it seems incredible that the Japanese Government can have sanctioned these antics, it is certain that the Chinese believe that the Japanese Government intend to set up in the Three Eastern Provinces some Government which will be subservient to themselves and more or less independent of Nanking. My own view is that the Japanese Government will proceed with the greatest caution. Their interest seems to lie in allowing things to sort themselves for the time being. They require a settled Government and are not likely to compromise the formation of such a Government by premature pressure. . . .

IV.2.B Mr Osborne (Washington) to the Marquess of Reading, 24 September 1931 (*DBFP* Series II, vol. VIII, no. 524).

Mr Castle sent for me this morning to explain United States attitude in Manchurian affair which they want you to understand.

They are determined to back the League's action whole-heartedly. But they are very conscious of one factor which they apprehend may not be fully appreciated at Geneva namely conflict between military and civil elements in Japan. If action taken at Geneva is such as to enable military party to arouse national feeling and enlist national support the task of pacification of civil party represented by the Prime Minister and the Minister for Foreign Affairs will be greatly complicated. United States Government feel strongly that full account should be taken of this consideration and generally of oriental mentality. But subject to this precaution they will co-operate in every possible way.

IV.3 THE LIMITS OF AMERICAN CO-OPERATION

The world's two leading non-League members, the United States and Russia, were far more intimately concerned with events in Manchuria, and far more able to influence them through diplomatic, economic or military pressure, than any League member except Britain. Unfortunately, neither Government was prepared to co-operate fully with the League of Nations in helping to settle the dispute. The United States Government was only prepared to act through the 1928 Kellogg-Briand Pact and the 1922 Nine-Power Washington Treaty, and favoured a policy of concerted international protest. The United States Secretary of State, Stimson, told the British Foreign Secretary Simon in April 1932 that 'nothing beyond protest could be done' but 'if suitable occasions were chosen, the accumulated effect on public opinion was considerable and this would in the end influence Japan.' (*DBFP* Series II, vol. X, no. 228.)

IV.3.A Statement by the American Representative to the League Council, 16 October 1931 (*L of Ns OJ*, 1931; US State Department Press Release, no. 107, 17 October 1931).

In this moment of deep international concern, I thank you for your invitation to sit in [on] your deliberations and to participate in your discussions in so far as the Pact of Paris, to which my country is a party, is concerned.

The Government of the United States of America has been following with the closest attention the proceedings before the Council for the settlement of the dispute at present unhappily existing between China and Japan. My Government does not seek to intrude with respect to such measures as you may propose under the Covenant of the League of Nations, and is not in a position to participate with the Members of the Council in the formulation of any action envisaged under that instrument, for the composing of differences existing between two of its members. It has already conveyed to you its sympathetic appreciation of your efforts and its whole-hearted accord with the objective you have in view; and it has expressed the hope that the tried machinery of the League may in this case as on previous occasions, be successful in bringing this dispute to a conclusion satisfactory to both parties. Moreover, acting independently and through diplomatic channels, my Government has already signified its moral support of your efforts in this capacity to bring about a peaceful solution of the unfortunate controversy in Manchuria.

In your deliberations as to the application of the machinery of the Covenant of the League of Nations, I repeat, we can, of course, take no part. But the Pact of Paris, bearing as it does the signature of the President of this meeting [Briand] together with that of our former Secretary of State as joint proponents, represents to this extent in America an effective means of marshalling the public opinion of the world behind the use of pacific means only, in the solution of controversies between nations. We feel not only that this public opinion is a most potent force in the domestic affairs of every nation, but that it is of constantly growing importance and influence in the mutual relations of the members of the family of nations.

The timely exercise of the power of such opinion may be effective to prevent a breach of international peace of world-wide consequences. We assume that this may be the reason why the consideration of the relationship between the provisions of the Pact of Paris and the present situation has been brought forward in this body; and the purpose which has moved my Government to accept your invitation is that we may most enthusiastically and effectively take common counsel with you on this subject.

IV.3.B   British Ambassador at Washington, Sir R. Lindsay, to Sir John Simon, 31 December 1931, outlining American attitude towards the Manchurian dispute (*DBFP* Series II, vol. IX, no. 42).

Even before the Chinese Government appealed, on 21 September, to the Council of the League of Nations under Article 11 of the Covenant against the Japanese occupation of Mukden and certain other towns in Manchuria, and the seizure by Japanese troops of important Manchurian railways, the United States Government had been quietly urging moderation on both disputants. The League Council's resolution of 22 September afforded a convenient opportunity for more overt action, and Mr Stimson wasted no time in proclaiming the 'whole-hearted sympathy' of the United States Government with the Council's attitude as expressed therein, and in despatching notes to Japan and

China on similar lines to those sent by the President of the Council as regards abstention from acts which might prejudice a pacific settlement. Even at this stage, however, a certain divergence of method was to be observed, for while the Council spoke of seeking 'means to allow the two countries to proceed immediately to the withdrawal of the respective troops without compromising the safety of the lives or property of their nationals,' Mr Stimson merely expressed the hope that they would 'so dispose respectively of their armed forces as to satisfy the requirements of international law and international agreements'.

The Council's resolution of 30 September called forth no special expression of the American viewpoint, but on the eve of their meeting on 13 October the members of the Council received through the Secretary-General a message in which Mr Stimson, after stating his belief that 'our co-operation in this difficult matter should proceed along the course which has been followed ever since the first outbreak of the trouble,' and noting the fact that 'the Covenant of the League of Nations provides permanent and already tested machinery for handling such issues as between States members of the League,' went on to say that 'as the disputants have made commitments to the Council, it is most desirable that the League in no way relax its vigilance and in no way fail to assert all the pressure and authority within its competence towards regulating the action of China and Japan in the premises. On its part the American Government, acting independently through its diplomatic representatives will endeavour to reinforce what the League does and will make clear, that it has a keen interest in the matter and is not oblivious to the obligations which the disputants have assumed to their fellow signatories in the Pact of Paris as well as in the Nine-Power Pact should a time arise when it would seem advisable to bring forward those obligations. By this course we avoid any danger of embarrassing the League in the course to which it is now committed.'

It thus appeared that the United States Government intended to take simultaneous, but independent action in invoking the Pact of Paris. It was feared at Geneva that unless some closer form of American co-operation could be secured, the case would come before two tribunals —the signatories of the Pact and the Council of the League—and that the Japanese Government might be able to play off one against the other and escape between the two. Accordingly, an arrangement was concerted over the protests of the Japanese delegate, whereby the American representative at Geneva should be invited to 'sit at the Council table, so that he may be in a position to consider with the Council the relationship between the provisions of the Pact of Paris and the present unfortunate situation in Manchuria, and at the same time to follow the deliberations of the Council with regard to other aspects of the problem with which it is now confronted.' . . . In accepting this invitation on 16 October, Mr Prentiss Gilbert, the United States Consul at Geneva, delivered a carefully-worded statement elaborating the instructions which he had received from his Government. . . .

On the following day (17 October) Mr Gilbert called on the principal members of the Council to inform them that Mr Stimson had been somewhat disappointed that no steps had been taken formally to invoke the Pact of Paris, which was the ostensible reason for the appearance of a representative of the United States Government at the Council table. Suitable steps were taken, and on 19 October Mr Gilbert informed Lord Reading that he had received instructions from Mr Stimson to participate in no further secret sessions of the Council, and at the next public meeting to withdraw from the Council table, after making a statement to the effect that the object of his temporary association with the Council had been served by the invocation of the Pact of Paris. Lord Reading at once telephoned to Mr Stimson and represented the disastrous effects which the carrying out of these instructions might be expected to have on the prestige of the Council. After much discussion it was agreed that Mr Gilbert, while taking part in no further secret meetings of the Council, should continue for the time being to attend its public meetings, but should be seated at a separate table as an observer, rather than at the Council table.

On 20 October Mr Stimson sent for me and explained the difficulties which underlay his action. These had been twofold, namely, the tendency in the United States to revolt against too close co-operation with the League, and the fear of exacerbating sentiment in Japan, between which and the United States feeling is never too cordial. With regard to the former difficulty, Mr Stimson had to be able to represent at home that his co-operation was not so much with the League as with the Powers assembled at Geneva and that it was in the main based on the Pact of Paris and the Nine-Power Treaty rather than on the League Covenant. . . .

The United States Government was not associated in any way with the resolution adopted by the Council of the League . . . on 24 October, which called upon the Japanese Government to withdraw all its troops to the railway zone by the next meeting of the Council on 16 November, and recommended that when the evacuation was completed, direct negotiations should begin between Japan and China on all questions outstanding between them. Asked for his views on this resolution, the Under Secretary in special charge of Manchurian affairs informed me on 2 November that in view of the State Department the resolution made a mistake in fixing a definite date by which evacuation must be completed, and that they also thought it injudicious to insist that evacuation must precede negotiation as this attitude, in their opinion, must result in the indefinite postponement of the former. Meanwhile they proposed to make a representation to Tokyo in general support of the *spirit* of the Council's resolution. . . . Mr Stimson was inclined to recommend negotiations between China and Japan in the presence of neutrals, dropping questions of legal right and concentrating on practical methods of ending the controversy.

On 16 November officials of the State Department were concerned to deny . . . a report that the United States Government was no longer supporting the League over Manchuria, and that the Japanese Ambassador at Washington had been informed that the United States would not co-operate with the League in imposing sanctions against Japan. The officials stated that Mr Stimson hoped the use of sanctions could be avoided, but that in any event the United States Government could not commit itself in advance as to whether it would or would not support measures adopted by the League. . . .

Confused and irresolute as the attitude of the United States Government may have appeared to those unaccustomed to the limitations under which that government labours, a consistent thread of ideas may nevertheless be traced. . . . It cannot be too often recalled that the separation of executive and legislature under the American system of government engenders great weakness in the executive, which is constantly exposed to subsequent repudiation of its acts by an irresponsible legislature. Only in courses of policy which have been previously sanctioned either by long tradition or by the express approval of the legislature can the executive proceed without grave political risks. In the case of the Manchurian dispute, the United States Administration has to bear in mind that

1. Neither association nor even co-operation with the League of Nations has thus been sanctioned;

2. No specific support has ever been pledged on behalf of the American people to the territorial or administrative *status quo* anywhere save on the American continent, and, even there, only to a very limited extent;

3. A majority of American opinion would be opposed to participation in any economic boycott of Japan . . . ;

4. On the other hand the American Congress and people will generally support even the most vigorous action in pursuance of immediate, comprehensible and demonstrably American interests. Whether or not such action involves co-operation with other Powers is a matter of indifference once the decision to act in a particular way on grounds of American interest has been taken. . . .

Having regard to all these considerations, it will be seen that the actions of the United States Government in connection with the Manchurian crisis have hitherto not been other than the ineluctable conditions of American policy would lead one to expect; and its future actions in the matter may be expected to follow similar lines.

IV.4 THE RUSSIAN ANALYSIS OF THE SITUATION

The Russian Government was extremely concerned about the Manchurian crisis. Though fearful of a strong Japanese presence in North China close to her frontiers, the Russian Government, not at this time a member of the League, would only stand helplessly by and deride what was considered to be the weak and ineffective response of the League.

IV.4.A An analysis by *Izvestia* of the Manchurian Situation, 22 November 1931, pl. no. 321.

The situation in Manchuria is becoming more and more serious every day. On the day when the Council of the League of Nations met in Paris, Japan demonstrated its attitude to the resolution of the League, which called on it to withdraw Japanese troops from Manchuria, by advancing its troops further north and occupying Teitsihai.

How did the League of Nations react to this defiance of its decisions? It not only failed to take any measures against the further consolidation and widening of the Japanese occupation of Manchuria but on the contrary, met Japan fully half way. The League of Nations intends to send a commission to investigate the situation in Manchuria. Japan wishes to make this commission a kind of research institute to study the reasons for the civil war in China, the weakness of the central government, the attitude of China towards treaties, etc. There is no talk whatsoever of the withdrawal of Japanese troops. The Japanese delegate to the League, Yoshizawa, who agreed to a truce, has been disavowed by his government. This is understandable from the viewpoint of Japanese imperialism. Japan denies that military actions are actually taking place in Manchuria. Japan is only 'defending' its interests against illegal actions on the part of China. The League is unable to support firmly the stand that military actions are actually taking place in Manchuria, for if it accepted this viewpoint, it would have to ask who is the culprit and consequently would have to draw conclusions on the basis of its covenant. The imperialist powers, which many a time have signed treaties dealing with the partitioning of China, and which today act as masters on Chinese territory, are not in a position to come out against Japan without becoming involved in an argument among themselves. Therefore, each of the powers is only concerned as to how it can compensate itself for the increased influence of Japan in China.

IV.4.B HM Ambassador in Moscow to Simon, 25 October 1932 (*DBFP* Series II, vol. XI, no. 18).

I have the honour to report that the *Izvestyia* on 13 October published a long article by Karl Radek [Member of editorial panel of *Izvestiya*] on the findings of the League of Nations Commission to the Far East. Apart from this one article, there has been an almost complete absence of comment in the 'Izvestiya', which can alone be regarded as the mouthpiece of the government, and I understand that Karl Radek is, on this occasion, expressing the official view. . . .

The policy of the Soviet Government in the present Far Eastern crisis is clear enough and has been consistently pursued since the crisis arose. They regard the Japanese as guilty of a flagrant act of imperialist aggression. They are not themselves prepared to take positive action against Japan's act of aggression, and are not likely to be drawn into hostilities with Japan unless Japanese aggression should culminate in a threat to Soviet territory itself. Nor are they prepared to make common cause, diplomatic or military, with other Powers in resistance to Japanese action, for the reason, among others, that it is a point of principle with them to conduct their foreign policy on a bilateral basis with each foreign Power singly and to avoid international collaboration with current political affairs. Meanwhile, they are content to wait, in the conviction that the Japanese will not in the long run gain anything by their forward policy and that the Chinese will in their own good time make the Japanese position in Manchuria untenable, even if the Japanese are not weakened by a crisis at home.

This is not what Radek says, but it underlies his rather mischievious analysis of the situation. The Lytton report, he says, has no chance whatever of being put into effect. The aggressive attitude of Japan in Manchuria is due to her realisation that she is no match for the other imperialist powers in the matter of 'peaceful' financial competition in China, and to her fear that revolution in China will find those Powers unprepared to cope with it and will endanger even the interests of Japan if she does not act in time in the area which specially concerns her. . . . The predominant factor in the Far Eastern situation is, he says, the pressure brought by the United States upon Great Britain and France, supported by concessions in Europe and on the questions of debts and disarmament, to wean them away from Japan. The State Department have been successful in this to the extent that the Lytton Report rejected the major Japanese claim that Manchuria was 'self-created', and will serve to mobilise world-opinion against Japan. This will be its real and only function, for any settlement on the basis of its recommendations is impossible of achievement. Its compromise character is illustrated, for another thing, by the fact that it at one and the same time incites Japan against the USSR, and vainly tried to draw the USSR into an anti-Japanese combination. Meanwhile, he concludes, the high priests of the League of Nations, who are trying to frighten Japanese imperialism with the revolutionary danger from the USSR, are themselves pinning their hopes on a revolution in Japan to rid them of the Manchurian problem.

IV.5 LEAGUE ACTION AND JAPANESE REACTION

As the scope of the dispute widened, the Chinese Government appealed for League action under Articles 10 and 15 of the Covenant and asked for the dispute to be transferred from the Council to the Assembly. A League Commission was sent out to the Far East in early 1932 under the chairmanship of Lord Lytton to investigate the situation in North China and to draw up a report on the facts of the dispute. The Report was considered by the Council and the Assembly at the end of 1932 and was submitted to the Japanese and Chinese Governments for their observations. Meanwhile, under Japanese military pressure, Manchuria had declared itself independent of China in February 1932 and had proclaimed itself the new state of Manchukuo. The Japanese military authorities were tightening their control over the central Governmental machinery, and were not prepared to accept the recommendations formulated on the basis of the Lytton proposals and adopted by the Assembly in February 1933 by forty-two votes to the one of Japan, with only Siam abstaining. Instead, the Japanese Government announced its intention of withdrawing from the League, which it did in the course of 1933.

IV.5.A Extracts from the Lytton Commission Report, 4 September 1932 (*League Document*, 1932).

. . . The issues involved in this conflict are not as simple as they are often represented to be. They are, on the contrary, exceedingly complicated, and only an intimate knowledge of all the facts, as well as of their historical background, should entitle anyone to express a definite opinion upon them. This is not a case in which one country has declared war on another country without previously exhausting the opportunities for conciliation provided in the Covenant of the League of Nations. Neither is it a simple case of the violation of the frontier of one country by the armed forces of a neighbouring country, because in Manchuria there are many features without an exact parallel in other parts of the world.

The dispute has arisen between two States, both Members of the League, concerning a territory the size of France and Germany combined, in which both claim to have rights and interests, only some of which are clearly defined by international law; a territory which, although legally an integral part of China, had a sufficiently autonomous

character to carry on direct negotiations with Japan on the matters
which lay at the root of this conflict.

Japan controls a railway and a strip of territory running from the sea
right up into the heart of Manchuria, and she maintains for the protection of that property a force of about 10,000 soldiers, which she claims
the right by treaty to increase, if necessary, up to 15,000. She also
exercises the rights of jurisdiction over all her subjects in Manchuria
and maintains consular police throughout the country.

These facts must be considered by those who debate the issues. It is a
fact that, without declaration of war, a large area of what was indisputably
Chinese territory has been forcibly seized and occupied by the armed
forces of Japan and has, in consequence of this operation, been separated
from, and declared independent of, the rest of China. The steps by
which this was accomplished are claimed by Japan to have been consistent with the obligations of the Covenant of the League of Nations, the
Kellogg Pact, and the Nine-Power Treaty of Washington, all of which
were designed to prevent action of this kind. Moreover, the operation
which had only just begun when the matter was first brought to the
notice of the League was completed during the following months, and
is held by the Japanese Government to be consistent with the assurances
given by their representative at Geneva on 30 September and 10
December. The justification in this case has been that all the military
operations have been legitimate acts of self-defence, the right of which
is implicit in all the multilateral treaties mentioned above, and was not
taken away by any of the resolutions of the Council of the League.
Further, the administration which has been substituted for that of
China in the Three Provinces is justified on the ground that its establishment was the act of the local population, who, by a spontaneous
assertion of their independence, have severed all connection with China
and established their own Government. Such a genuine independence
movement, it is claimed, is not prohibited by any international treaty
or by any of the resolutions of the Council of the League of Nations, and
the fact of its having taken place has profoundly modified the application
of the Nine-Power Treaty, and entirely altered the whole character of
the problem being investigated by the League.

It is this plea of justification which makes this particular conflict at
once so complicated and so serious. It is not the function of our Commission to argue the issue, but we have tried to provide sufficient
material to enable the League of Nations to settle the dispute consistently with the honour, dignity, and national interest of both the con-
tending parties. Criticism alone will not accomplish this: there must
be practical efforts at conciliation....

. . . It must be clear from everything that we have already said that a
mere restoration of the *status quo ante* would be no solution. Since the

present conflict arose out of the conditions prevailing before last September, to restore these conditions would merely be to invite a repetition of the trouble. It would be to treat the whole question theoretically and to leave out of account the realities of the situation.

... the maintenance and recognition of the present regime in Manchuria would be equally unsatisfactory. Such a solution does not appear to us compatible with the fundamental principle of existing international obligations, nor with the good understanding between the two countries upon which peace in the Far East depends. It is opposed to the interests of China. It disregards the wishes of the people of Manchuria, and it is at least questionable whether it would ultimately serve the permanent interests of Japan.

About the feelings of the people of Manchuria towards the present regime there can really be no doubt; and China would not voluntarily accept as a lasting solution the complete separation of her Three Eastern Provinces. . . . The millions of Chinese farmers now settled permanently on the land have made Manchuria in many respects a simple extension of China south of the Wall. The Three Eastern Provinces have become almost as Chinese in race, culture, and national sentiment as the neighbouring Provinces of Hopei and Shantung, from which most of the immigrants came.

Apart from this, past experience has shown that those who control Manchuria have exercised a considerable influence on the affairs of the rest of China—at least of North China—and possess unquestionable strategic and political advantages. To cut off these provinces from the rest of China, either legally or actually, would be to create for the future a serious irredentist problem which would endanger peace by keeping alive the hostility of China and rendering probable the continued boycott of Japanese goods.

The Commission received from the Japanese Government a clear and valuable statement of the vital interests of their country in Manchuria. Without exaggerating the economic dependence of Japan on Manchuria . . . and certainly without suggesting that economic relationship entitles Japan to control the economic, still less the political, development of those provinces, we recognise the great importance of Manchuria in the economic development of Japan. Nor do we consider unreasonable her demands for the establishment of a stable Government which would be capable of maintaining the order necessary for the economic development of the country. But such conditions can only be securely and effectively guaranteed by an administration which is in conformity with the wishes of the population and which takes full account of their feelings and aspirations. And equally it is only in an atmosphere of external confidence and internal peace, very different from that now existing in the Far East that the capital which is necessary for the rapid economic development of Manchuria will be forth-coming....

It may, however, be less economic considerations than anxiety for her own security which has determined the actions and policy of Japan in Manchuria. It is specially in this connection that her statesmen and military authorities are accustomed to speak of Manchuria as 'the life-line of Japan'. One can sympathise with such anxieties and try to appreci-ate the actions and motives of those who have to bear the heavy respon-sibility of securing the defence of their country against all eventualities. While acknowledging the interest of Japan in preventing Manchuria from serving as a base of operations directed against her own territory, and even her wish to be able to take all appropriate military measures if in certain circumstances the frontiers of Manchuria should be crossed by the forces of a foreign Power, it may still be questioned whether the military occupation of Manchuria for an indefinite period, involving, as it must, a heavy financial burden, is really the most effective way of ensuring against this external danger; and whether, in the event of aggression having to be resisted in this way, the Japanese troops in Manchuria would not be seriously embarrassed if they were surrounded by a restive or rebellious population backed by a hostile China. It is surely in the interests of Japan to consider also other possible solutions of the problem of security, which would be more in keeping with the principles on which rest the present peace organisation of the world, and analogous to arrangements concluded by other great Powers in various parts of the world. She might even find it possible, with the sympathy and goodwill of the rest of the world, and at no cost to her-self, to obtain better security than she will obtain by the costly method she is at present adopting.

Apart from China and Japan, other Powers of the world have also important interests to defend in this Sino-Japanese conflict. We have already referred to existing multilateral treaties, and any real and lasting solution by agreement must be compatible with the stipulations of these fundamental agreements, on which is based the peace organisa-tion of the world. The considerations which actuated the representatives of the Powers at the Washington Conference are still valid. It is quite as much in the interests of the Powers now, as it was in 1922, to assist the reconstruction of China and to maintain her sovereignty and her territorial and administrative integrity as indispensable to the mainten-ance of peace. Any disintegration of China might lead, perhaps rapidly, to serious international rivalries, which would become all the more bitter if they should happen to coincide with rivalries between divergent social systems. Finally, the interests of peace are the same the world over. Any loss of confidence in the application of the principles of the

Covenant and of the Pact of Paris in any part of the world diminishes the value and efficacy of those principles everywhere.

The Commission has not been able to obtain direct information as to the extent of the interests of the USSR in Manchuria, nor to ascertain the views of the Government of the USSR on the Manchurian question. But, even without sources of direct information, it cannot overlook the part played by Russia in Manchuria, nor the important interests which the USSR have in that region as owners of the Chinese Eastern Railway and of the territory beyond its north and north-east frontiers. It is clear that any solution of the problem of Manchuria which ignored the important interests of the USSR would risk a future breach of the peace and would not be permanent.

. . . A satisfactory regime for the future might be evolved out of the present one without any violent change . . . we would . . . define the general principles to which any satisfactory solution should conform [as]. . . .

1. *Compatability with the interests of both China and Japan*
Both countries are Members of the League and each is entitled to claim the same consideration from the League. A solution from which both did not derive benefit would not be a gain to the cause of peace.

2. *Consideration for the interests of the USSR*
To make peace between two of the neighbouring countries without regard for the interests of the third would be neither just nor wise, nor in the interests of peace.

3. *Conformity with existing multilateral treaties*
Any solution should conform to the provisions of the Covenant of the League of Nations, the Pact of Paris, and the Nine-Power Treaty of Washington.

4. *Recognition of Japan's interests in Manchuria*
The rights and interests of Japan in Manchuria are facts which cannot be ignored, and any solution which failed to recognise them, and to take into account also the historical associations of Japan with that country, would not be satisfactory.

5. *The establishment of new treaty relations between China and Japan*
A re-statement of the respective rights, interests, and responsibilities of both countries in Manchuria in new treaties, which shall be part of the settlement by agreement, is desirable if future friction is to be avoided and mutual confidence and co-operation are to be restored.

6. *Effective provision for the settlement of future disputes*
As a corollary to the above, it is necessary that provision should be made for facilitating the prompt settlement of minor disputes as they arise.

7. *Manchurian autonomy*
The Government in Manchuria should be modified in such a way as to secure, consistently with the sovereignty and administrative integrity of China, a large measure of autonomy designed to meet the local conditions and special characteristics of the Three Provinces. The new civil regime must be so constituted and conducted as to satisfy the essential requirements of good government.

8. *Internal order and security against external aggression*
The internal order of the country should be secured by an effective local gendarmerie force, and security against external aggressions should be provided by the withdrawal of all armed forces other than gendarmerie, and by the conclusion of a treaty of non-aggression between the countries involved.

9. *Encouragement of an economic rapprochment between China and Japan*
For this purpose, a new commercial treaty between the two countries is desirable. Such a treaty should aim at placing on an equitable basis the commercial relations between the two countries and bringing them into conformity with their improved political relations.

10. *International co-operation in Chinese reconstruction*
Since the present political instability in China is an obstacle to friendship with Japan and an anxiety to the rest of the world (as the maintenance of peace in the Far East is a matter of international concern), and since the conditions enumerated above cannot be fulfilled without a strong Central Government in China, the final requisite for a satisfactory solution is temporary international co-operation in the internal reconstruction of China....

If the present situation could be modified in such a way as to satisfy these conditions and embody these ideas, China and Japan would have achieved a solution of their difficulties which might be made the starting-point of a new era of close understanding and political co-operation between them. If such a *rapprochement* is not secured, no solution, whatever its terms, can really be fruitful.

... We suggest ... that the Council of the League should invite the Governments of China and Japan to discuss a solution of their dispute on the lines indicated....

IV.5.B Foreign Office Memorandum, written by Mr Orde, on the Lytton Report, October 1932 (*DBFP* Series II, vol. X, no. 746).

The Report is, beyond question, an admirable survey of the whole situation and its background, and there is nothing of any substance, and practically nothing even of detail which I feel able to criticise.... There remains the general question of how the problem is to be handled.

From the practical point of view—that of reaching a settlement—the Report impresses me as being a valuable diplomatic document. I think it is true that to the thoughtful and impartial reader the Report goes far to exonerate Japan, although she must expect some blame for her methods of precipitating the crisis and for the exaggerated political aims which she has pursued. It is not certain that everyone will read the Report in this sense, but I think there is good ground for hoping that no one will be much inclined after reflection to consider Japan to deserve expulsion from the League or to oppose a settlement which gives her substantial satisfaction. Some blame will no doubt have to be meted out, but there is material in the Report for justifying blame to China on account of her general anti-foreign policy, her treatment of Koreans and of Japanese rights, her deliberate building of competitive railways in defiance of her somewhat informal but nevertheless pretty clearly established undertaking not to do so, and her lavish expenditure for this purpose of money which should properly have been devoted to paying off the Japanese loans with which some of the railways were built and, . . . to maintaining other railways in China, south of the Wall which, themselves mainly built with foreign money, were allowed to fall into decay and to default on their obligations.

There are indications that the Japanese, who are not anxious to leave the League, will accept a certain measure of reproof for their methods provided that their future is safeguarded. . . . The Chinese, we have good evidence to show, are not disposed to take too intransigent a line at Geneva, and realise that they must come to terms with Japan. . . .

There is thus considerable ground for hope that Japan will not be altogether unreasonable *vis-à-vis* the League and that China will be fairly reasonable, both with the League and with Japan. In some manner there will have ultimately to be negotiations between China and Japan. . . . Discussion between China and Japan, with or without outside assistance, is clearly the main objective, and on the Chinese side at least it should not be difficult to bring about. Japan may be more difficult to manage. The recognition of Manchukuo can hardly be openly retracted, and the Japanese Minister for Foreign Affairs recently declared that no solution would be tolerable which perpetuated any form of Chinese authority in Manchuria. This will make it difficult for Japan to agree to the retention of a nominal Chinese suzerainty, which is likely to be a Chinese essential in form, however little reality they may in the last resort require underneath it. . . .

I see little hope of anything being done in regard to the reconstruction of China, but I do not feel certain that it is necessary to a tolerably satisfactory solution of the Manchurian problem or in fact to the only sort of solution which seems to have a chance of being accepted by Japan. . . . It is true that without genuine reconstruction in China no solution of the Manchurian problem can be reached which involves any real voice in Manchurian affairs for China proper, but to me there seems no essential need for such a reconstruction as a prior condition if Chinese control is limited to a nominal suzerainty. This seems a possible and not unsatisfactory outcome.

IV.5.c British Ambassador in Tokyo to Sir John Simon, 13 October 1932, reporting reaction in Japan to publication of Lytton Commission report (*DBFP* Series II, vol. XI, no. 4).

... That the Japanese press would condemn the Report unanimously was inevitable, unless the Commission refrained from recording the most self-evident facts connected with the occupation of Manchuria. It was therefore no surprise to anyone when the newspapers of Japan burst into an universal chorus of dissatisfaction when the long awaited report finally became known ... the two points in the Report which have especially rankled were, as was to be expected, that declaring that the military measures taken by the Japanese in September 1931, were beyond the legitimate needs of self-defence; and that denying the Manchukuo State to be a manifestation of the spontaneous wishes of the people of Manchuria. That the Commission should come to these conclusions was, for every unbiased person, a foregone conclusion ... but the inevitability of the conclusions in no way renders them more palatable to the Japanese public—possibly the reverse. More justifiable criticisms of the Report which have also found constant expression are that a far too favourable view is taken of the present conditions and the future prospects of China, and that the suggested future government of the Three Eastern Provinces would prove quite unworkable in practice. Whether this latter contention is true or not, it should be noted that no voice from any quarter has been raised in favour of recognising the sovereignty of China over those Provinces, and that all those who have expressed any opinion are unanimous in their determination to uphold the complete sovereignty and independence of Manchukuo and the Treaty which has been signed between that so-called State and Japan.

Though it will be seen from the preceding paragraph that there is no prospect of any change of policy as regards Manchuria in the near future, it must not be supposed that a great deal of misgiving is not felt in the country regarding that policy. In the first place there is no doubt that those who direct Japanese policy and Japanese political thought, at any rate outside the Army, look with apprehension at the possible results of a breach with the League. It is not so much that they fear economic sanctions or war as that they shrink from the stigma which the solemnly expressed disapprobation of the League would inflict on Japan and they are apprehensive of the ultimate material results which may well follow sooner or later from Japanese isolation. In these circumstances it is not surprising that unusual efforts are being made to prepare the Japanese case for Geneva and that nothing will be neglected which can present that case in a favourable light and enable Japan to escape an open breach with the West. . . .

In spite of the opinion mentioned in the last paragraph, and although it appears probable that the verdict of the Lytton Report will, as the time goes on, exercise a growing influence on the more serious members of the community, it must not be supposed that the army has yet lost its grip on the direction of Japanese policy. There is at present no sign of this and it can scarcely be doubted that, should a crisis arise in the near future, the bulk of the population would back up a military policy through thick and thin. . . .

IV.5.D   Telegram from the Japanese Minister for Foreign Affairs to the Secretary-General of the League of Nations, regarding Japan's withdrawal from the League of Nations, March 1933 (*L of Ns OJ*, May, 1933).

The Japanese Government believe that the national policy of Japan, which has for its aim to ensure the peace of the Orient and thereby contribute to the cause of peace throughout the world, is identical in spirit with the mission of the League of Nations, which is to achieve international peace and security. It has always been with pleasure, therefore, that this country has for thirteen years past, as an original Member of the League, and a permanent member of its Council, extended a full measure of co-operation with her fellow-members towards the attainment of its high purpose. It is indeed a matter of historical fact that Japan has continuously participated in the various activities of the League with a zeal not inferior to that exhibited by any other nation. At the same time, it is, and has always been, the conviction of the Japanese Government that in order to render possible the maintenance of peace in various regions of the world, it is necessary in existing circumstances to allow the operation of the Covenant of the League to vary in accordance with the actual conditions prevailing in each of those regions. Only by acting on this just and equitable principle can the League fulfil its mission and increase its influence.

Acting on this conviction, the Japanese Government have, ever since the Sino-Japanese dispute was ; . . . submitted to the League, at meetings of the League, and on other occasions, continually set forward a consistent view. This was, that if the League was to settle the issue fairly and equitably, and to make a real contribution to the promotion of peace in the Orient, and thus enhance its prestige, it should acquire a complete grasp of the actual conditions in this quarter of the globe, and apply the Covenant of the League in accordance with these conditions. They have repeatedly emphasised and insisted upon the absolute necessity of taking into consideration the fact that China is not an organised State—that its internal conditions and external relations are characterised by extreme confusion and complexity, and by many abnormal and exceptional features—and that, accordingly, the general principles and usages of international law which govern the ordinary relations between nations are found to be considerably modified in their operation so far as China is concerned, resulting in the quite abnormal and unique practices which actually prevail in that country.

However, the majority of the Members of the League evinced in the course of its deliberations during the past seventeen months a failure either to grasp these realities or else to face them and take them into proper account. Moreover, it has frequently been made manifest in these deliberations that there exist serious differences of opinion between Japan and these Powers concerning the application and even the interpretation of various international engagements and obligations, including the Covenant of the League and the principles of international law. As a result, the Report adopted by the Assembly at the Special Session of 24 February last, entirely misapprehending the spirit of Japan, pervaded as it is by no other desire than the maintenance of peace in the Orient, contains gross errors both in the ascertainment of facts and in the conclusions deduced. In asserting that the action of the Japanese army at the time of the incident of 18 September, and subsequently, did not fall within the just limits of self-defence, the Report assigned no reasons and came to an arbitrary conclusion, and in ignoring alike the state of tension which preceded, and the various aggravations which succeeded, the incident—for all of which the full responsibility is incumbent upon China—the Report creates a source of fresh conflict in the political arena of the Orient. By refusing to acknowledge the actual circumstances that led to the foundation of Manchukuo, and by attempting to challenge the position taken up by Japan in recognising the new State, it cuts away the ground for the stabilisation of the Far Eastern situation. Nor can the terms laid down in its recommendations . . . ever be of any possible service in securing enduring peace in these regions.

The conclusion must be that, in seeking a solution of the question, the majority of the League have attached greater importance to upholding inapplicable formulae than to the real task of assuring peace, and higher value to the vindication of academic theses than to the eradication of the sources of future conflict. For these reasons, and because of the profound differences of opinion existing between Japan and the majority of the League in their interpretation of the Covenant and of other treaties, the Japanese Government have been led to realise the existence of an irreconcilable divergence of views, dividing Japan and the League on policies of peace, and especially as regards the fundamental principles to be followed in the establishment of a durable peace in the Far East. The Japanese Government, believing that in these circumstances there remains no room for further co-operation, hereby give notice, in accordance with the provisions of Article 1, Paragraph 3, of the Covenant, of the intention of Japan to withdraw from the League of Nations.

V

THE ABYSSINIAN AFFAIR

IN MANY RESPECTS, the Italian invasion of Abyssinia was the most clear-cut case of aggression which the League of Nations had to face in the inter-war period. But the League's handling of the crisis was complicated by its members' conception of their national interests and how best these could be served. While the British and French Governments, for various reasons, wanted to try to come to terms with Mussolini, smaller powers were eager to enforce rigidly the coercive provisions of the Covenant. The tragic outcome was the almost complete breakdown of the League's authority as a peace-keeping organisation, and the development of close relations between the Italian and German Governments.

V.1 ITALIAN AMBITIONS IN ABYSSINIA

Since seizing power in 1922, Mussolini had never concealed his ambition of wanting to extend Italy's colonial empire across the Mediterranean Sea. Abyssinia was a tempting prize, not only because it lay between the Italian colonies of Eritrea and Italian Somaliland, but because it was Abyssinian troops who had inflicted a humiliating check on Italian expansionist aims in Africa in 1896 at the Battle of Adowa. Since the mid-1920s, the Italian Government had stepped up Italian economic activities in the area, and after a skirmish with Abyssinian troops at a border outpost at Walwal in late 1934, full-scale military operations were worked out for the invasion of Abyssinia, to start not later than the Autumn of 1935.

V.1.A   General Emilio de Bono was appointed High Commissioner for East Africa by Mussolini, and was sent out there after the 1934 Walwal clash to prepare the way for an Italian invasion of Abyssinia. In 1937 he wrote of his experiences in a book *Anno XIIII : The Conquest of an Empire* (Cresset Press, 1937) from which these extracts are taken.

I had told the Duce my own opinion as regards the colonial future of our country. . . . Reduced to its simplest expression, the idea was this: In Libya, after the frontier problems had been adjusted with the two neighbouring European Powers, there was nothing more to be done, either in the political or in the military sense; all that had to be considered was the economic development of the Colony.

Hence the possibilities of our colonial future must be sought in East Africa, situated on one of the most important highways of international trade, with a hinterland which could be profitably exploited.

But our two colonies were being stifled; Somalia without harbours, and with a most unfortunate coast-line; Eritrea with one good harbour and a good roadstead at Massawa [which] had almost ceased to be a port with the building of the Khartoum and Port Sudan railways, to which almost the whole trade of the interior now found its way.

Apart from this, one had to consider the fact that the absolute lack of good lines of communication from west to east—that is, from Abyssinia to our coasts—nullified the possibilities of trade.

Hence, if the mother-country was to derive the desired advantage from her two colonies it would be necessary to abolish the vital inconveniences which I have indicated.

To this end a careful and decisive political action was required, subsidised by plenty of money to supply all the material necessities.

. . . Before determining the cardinal lines of the programme to be followed in respect of the preparations as a whole, it was necessary to decide, as a fundamental criterion, whether it was our intention to initiate operations by assuming a posture of defence, or whether we should take the offensive without more ado.

If we intended to assume the offensive the initiative would be wholly on our side, and at first sight it seemed that all that was needed was to fix the date for beginning operations. However, even in the case of an offensive war one must always allow for what the enemy can and will endeavour to do. Now the Abyssinians, under a feudal government, had the advantage of a comparatively rapid mobilisation, when one considers that a good part of our forces and *all* materials and munitions of war had to be sent from the Mother-Country, and would be retarded by having to pass through the Suez Canal.

No unusual movement of arms and troops could avoid passing through the canal, where, one may say, it would be exposed to the espionage of all the nations of Europe.

This being so, the incontestable advantages of our superiority in every military sense would be largely paralysed, since we should not be able to reckon on the factor of *surprise*, of capital importance in all military operations, and above all in an offensive war.

A very brief calculation, made under my direction in the Colonial Ministry, gave us the approximate strength of the forces required for an offensive war.

. . . It was the autumn of 1933. The Duce had spoken to no one of the coming operations in East Africa; *only he and I knew what* was going to happen and no indiscretion occurred by which the news could reach the public.

[After the incident at Walwal, de Bono was sent out to East Africa.]

The Duce's instructions were as follows: 'You leave with the olive-bough in your pocket; we shall see how the Wal-Wal affair turns out. If it suits us to accept the conditions offered us in consequence of the award you will inform the Emperor of your assumption of the post of High Commissioner, telling him that you have been sent to clear up any misunderstandings, and to collaborate in establishing friendly relations in the moral and material interests of the two States. In the meantime continue to make active preparations such as you would make in view of the more difficult and adverse outcome of the affair.

'If no solution of the incident is offered, or if it is not such as to satisfy us, we shall follow subsequent events *exclusively in accordance with our own standpoint.*'

About this time the conversations with Laval took place in Rome, which gave us reason to hope that if we did have to take action in East Africa France would put no obstacle in our way.

V.2   THE LEAGUE ROLE: THE FRENCH VIEW

French statesmen in the mid-1930s, though aware of the broad scope of Italian colonial aims, were obsessed by the bellicose activities of Hitler and wanted to enlist Italian help against German expansionist aims in Central and Eastern Europe. This was the purpose of the 1934 Stresa Conference between Italy, France and Great Britain, and there was a strong suspicion that at this Conference the British and French delegates had tacitly agreed to accept Italian colonial expansion in East Africa in return for close collaboration in Europe. Thus at Geneva Pierre Laval, the French Prime Minister, was concerned to stress the conciliatory aspects of the League machinery in settling the Italo-Abyssinian dispute rather than its potential coercive role, after the Abyssinian Government appealed to the League under Article II and then under Article 15.

V.2.A   Extracts from M. Laval's speech at Geneva, 13 September 1935
(*L of Ns OJ* Special Supplement, no. 138, pp. 65–6).

. . . France is loyal to the Covenant. She cannot fail to carry out her obligations. The League of Nations was born of the suffering of mankind. It was reared on the ruins, and conceived in order to prevent the return of war. The unreserved support we have given the League has been at once enthusiastic and considered. We place our hopes in the co-operation of all nations in the work of realising our ideal of peace.

Sometimes, at difficult moments, we have suffered real disappointments at Geneva; yet our faith has never wavered. With a perseverance which no difficulty has ever been able to discourage, the representatives of France have constantly sought to increase the moral authority of this supreme international institution. They were resolved, and they are still resolved, to make it stronger, to give it the means to act.

From the 1924 Protocol to the Conference for the Reduction and Limitation of Armaments, they have supported with the same zeal the doctrine of collective security. That doctrine is and will remain that of France.

The Covenant is our international law. How could we allow such a law to be weakened? To do so would be to deny our whole ideal, and it would be contrary to our interest to do so. France's policy rests entirely on the League. . . .

Any attack on the League would be an attack on our security. . . .

I speak on behalf of a country which does not fear war, but which hates it, a country which intends to remain strong, and which, rich in the highest military virtues, is inspired by a fierce desire for peace. We do not harbour prejudice against any nation. We desire peace for all through the collaboration of all. . . .

On 7 January last, M. Mussolini and I, acting not only in the interests of our two countries, but also in that of the peace of Europe, reached a final settlement of all our differences. Conscious of the immense value of the Franco-Italian friendship, I have left nothing undone to prevent any blow to the new policy happily established between France and Italy.

At Stresa, together with the delegates of the United Kingdom Government, we found the head of the Italian Government imbued with the same desire and the same will to serve the cause of peace. I know he is prepared to persevere in this collaboration. I need say no more to show how much importance I attach to the maintenance of such solidarity in the interests both of the European Community and of general peace.

I have spared no effort at conciliation. We all desire to reach an understanding, and in the supreme effort being made by the Council, I shall have the satisfaction of once more fulfilling my duty as the representative of a Member of the League, and that dictated to me by friendship.

I still hope that the Council may shortly be able to carry out its mission of conciliation. The task is doubtless a difficult one, but I still do not think it hopeless.

. . . we are studying every proposal likely to satisfy Italy's legitimate aspirations so far as is compatible with respect for the sovereignty of another State Member of the League.

V.2.B   Statement by Hoare in House of Commons, 22 October 1935
         (*Hansard*, 22 October 1935, cols. 17–33).

... In January of this year the French and Italian Governments came
to an agreement in Rome, part of which related to Abyssinia. Under this
agreement France disinterested herself economically in Abyssinia,
except for certain undertakings and except for a specified zone covering
the French railway from Djibouti to Addis Ababa. ...

As to the Stresa Conference, the facts are as follows: In March, that
is to say at the moment that the world was resounding with the declaration of German rearmament—Europe at that time was thinking of
nothing but the declaration of German rearmament—it was rightly felt
that the acute problems of the hour called for the closest consultation
and co-operation between France, Italy and the United Kingdom. At
the Conference at Stresa in April, steps were taken which it was hoped
would ensure the maintenance of this co-operation. It has lately been
suggested in certain quarters—may I say, by those whose wisdom comes
after the event?—that the Abyssinian question should have been included
in the agenda. It is not true that this subject was not mentioned there.
It was not, indeed, formally discussed at the Conference itself, which
had in fact little enough time to deal with the problems to which I have
referred, but it was discussed between members of the two delegations.
The Italian Government were then ... as before and after, in possession
of our views, and the hope of an amicable settlement between Italy
and Abyssinia was still strongly entertained, while the immediate and
all-important objective was to secure unity between France, Italy and
the United Kingdom in Europe. Indeed it was hoped that this object,
not lightly achieved, would be regarded as a precious inducement to do
nothing which might imperil it. It seemed legitimate to suppose that the
resultant collaboration between the three Governments would facilitate
the solution not only of purely European questions, but of all important
political issues in which all three were jointly interested. The fact that
these hopes have not materialised does not mean that they should not
have been entertained. They were, and should have been, entertained
by every reasonable man.

V.2.C   A report from *The Times* correspondent in Paris, carried on 31
         August 1935.

... Two reasons have been put forward to explain M. Laval's un-
doubted fear of losing Italian friendship. The first is a belief (expressed
with obstinacy by a section of the Press) that during his visit to Rome he
gave Signor Mussolini *carte blanche* in Abyssinia on behalf of France.
M. Laval's flat denial that he agreed to anything more than economic
expansion has already been reported. The second is that he has formed

the view that Great Britain is not strong enough to embark on any practical attempt to enforce the provisions of the Covenant. He has had enough encouragement from a part of his own Press, and perhaps even more from across the Channel, to think so. On the other hand, his technical advisers, and particularly his naval experts, have certainly told him a very different tale.

In any event, there is no doubt that the principal consideration which inclines M. Laval to caution is the one which obsesses the whole of France today—the fear of starting a general conflagration in Europe. For it can be said with assurance that Signor Mussolini's attempt to convince the Government of this country that he will treat military sanctions, or even a blockade, as an act of war has come dangerously near to success.

The French dilemma has not two horns but many. The League apart, it is held here there are two possibilities, both equally unpleasant. If Signor Mussolini is not putting up a gigantic bluff and sanctions are imposed, he will go to war. If he did there is not the slightest doubt that France would be found on the side of Great Britain, and there is no fear here of the ultimate result, provided that the conflict could be kept, in the current phrase 'circumscribed', but nobody believes that it could be so restricted. If, on the other hand, Italy is forced to withdraw from the Abyssinian venture, few people in France have the slightest doubt that a combination with Germany and possibly others would instantly follow, and the whole of Europe would be in an upheaval which could have only one end.

Against these arguments are the certain enfeeblement, and perhaps the destruction, of the League and the alienation of British sentiment and support if a transparent breach of the Covenant goes unchallenged. With all this before him M. Laval will not be lightly driven into irrevocable action. . . .

V.3 THE LEAGUE ROLE: THE BRITISH GOVERNMENT'S DILEMMA

British Government Ministers were well aware of the possibility that the French Government might not co-operate in a strong League stand against Italy. They also wanted to conciliate Mussolini and enlist his support against German ambitions in Europe, and did not consider that Italian expansion in East Africa would threaten Britain's position as the predominant naval power in the Mediterranean. At the same time, however, a General Election was pending and Baldwin, ever sensitive to the currents of public feeling, was aware that a strong British stand on the principle of collective League action against Mussolini would command strong electoral support. Thus the British Government pursued a dual policy of conciliation of Italy's legitimate aspirations and coercive action through the League machinery which had the effect of seriously undermining the authority of the League.

V.3.A   Extract from statement of Eden, Minister for League of Nations Affairs, in the House of Commons, 1 July 1935 (*Hansard*, 1 July 1935, cols. 1525–6).

I now turn to the dispute between Italy and Abyssinia, in regard to which I had conversations with Signor Mussolini on 24–5 June. I expressed to Signor Mussolini the grave concern of His Majesty's Government at the turn which events were taking between Italy and Abyssinia. Our motives were neither egoistic nor dictated by our interests in Africa, but by our membership of the League of Nations. I said that British foreign policy was founded upon the League. His Majesty's Government could not, therefore, remain indifferent to events which might profoundly affect the League's future. Upon this issue public opinion in this country felt very strongly. It was only through collective security that in our judgement peace could be preserved, and only through the League that Great Britain could play her full part in Europe. It was for this reason that His Majesty's Government had been anxiously studying whether there was any constructive contribution which they could make in order to promote a solution.

I then described to Signor Mussolini the kind of contribution which His Majesty's Government had in mind and which I was authorised to make to him as a tentative suggestion. This suggestion was broadly speaking as follows:

To obtain a final settlement of the dispute between Italy and Abyssinia, His Majesty's Government would be prepared to offer to Abyssinia a strip of territory in British Somaliland giving Abyssinia access to the sea. This proposal was intended to facilitate such territorial and economic concessions by Abyssinia to Italy as might have been involved in an agreed settlement. His Majesty's Government would ask for no concession in return for this arrangement save grazing rights for their tribes in such territory as might be ceded to Italy. This suggestion was not lightly made, and only the gravity of the situation could justify the cession of British territory without equivalent return.

I much regret that this suggestion did not commend itself to Signor Mussolini, who was unable to accept it as the basis for a solution of the dispute.

V.3.B   Hoare in the House of Commons, 11 July 1935 (*Hansard*, 11 July 1935, cols. 516–18).

. . . we have always understood and well understand Italy's desire for overseas expansion. Indeed, we have in the past done our best to show our sympathy with Italian aspirations in a practical way. In 1925 we ceded Jubaland to Italy, and in the present negotiations we showed our willingness to endeavour to ensure for Italy some territorial satisfaction by a reasonable and legitimate arrangement with Abyssinia. . . . Let no one therefore in Italy, in view of these outward and visible signs of our sympathy, suggest that we are unsympathetic to Italian aspirations.

We admit the need for Italian expansion. We admit again the justice of some of the criticisms that have been made against the Abyssinian Government. But are the facts that Italy needs expansion and that complaints are made against the Abyssinian Government sufficient cause for plunging into a war? We have surely found in the past that it is possible to adjust demands and differences of this kind without recourse to war, and I am not prepared even now to abandon any chance that may present itself for averting what I believe will be a calamity, whether it be through the machinery of the 1906 Treaty, or whether it be through the machinery of the League, or whether it be through both. Today, I cannot say more than that we are working on these lines. In the meanwhile, let Hon. Members dismiss from their minds the rumours, altogether without foundation, that we have asked the French Government to join in a blockade of Italy and that we ourselves are preparing some isolated form of coercion against the country which has been our friend since the Risorgimento. We stand for peace, and we will not abandon any reasonable chance that may offer itself for helping to prevent a disastrous war.

V.3.c   Cabinet discussions on the Abyssinian question (Cab. 23/82, PRO).

Meeting on 3 July 1935.

An invasion of Abyssinia would . . . raise the issues envisaged by Article 16 of the Covenant, which involved collective, but not individual, commitment for the signatories. If those obligations were ignored or evaded, a heavy blow would be struck at the whole of the Pacts and agreements on which the post-war system of Europe had been built up. It would amount to an admission that the attempt to give the League coercive powers was a mistake—an admission that would have serious effects in increasing the existing confusion abroad, as well as on public opinion at home.

The responsibility of the Powers on which the burden of fulfilling Article 16 would fall was recognised to be a heavy one, since it involved not only the present dispute and relations with Italy, but also the whole of the existing international system. If France was prepared to honour its obligations, other nations would probably follow. Without French co-operation the application of Article 16 was out of the question, and as yet the attitude of France was uncertain. . . .

The Cabinet were reminded that previous investigation of economic sanctions had shown that (since they involved blockade) they were almost bound to lead to hostilities.

Conference of Ministers, 21 August 1935.

The Prime Minister inquired whether Sir Samuel Hoare had any information regarding Germany's intentions.

[Hoare] The Prime Minister's question raised the whole problem of how far the non-Member States would participate in economic sanctions. The non-Member States which it was necessary to consider were the United States, Germany, Japan and Brazil.

His view was that these States might conceivably be induced to take part in economic sanctions. The chances of their doing so were . . . improved by the latest investigations of the Foreign Office, which had disclosed the possibility of applying economic sanctions in two separate stages. While there could be no hope of non-Member States participating in a second and more stringent stage, there was no reason why they should not participate in a first stage—i.e. in sanctions involving no belligerent action. Such measures might be negative, not positive. For example, States participating might simply refuse to accept imports from Italy. If the greater part of the world went even as far as that the effect on Italy might be considerable. . . .

The Lord President of the Council enquired whether Sir Samuel Hoare had had in mind that the step of refusing to export to Italy might be reserved for the second stage.

[Hoare] was inclined to think that this might be wise . . . the Chancellor of the Exchequer and the Home Secretary raised the question whether Sir Samuel Hoare's suggestion that economic sanctions might be divisible into two or more stages of increasing stringency, was consonent with the actual terms of Article 16. . . .

[Eden] . . . the answer to these doubts was to be found in the Resolutions regarding the interpretation of Article 16 which the League of Nations Assembly adopted in 1921 [see Appendix II] . . . on the whole there was no reason to doubt that they could be treated as rules of guidance recommended by the Council and to the Members of the League. It was in the light of certain specific Recommendations, among those just referred to, that the Foreign Office experts had advised that the application of economic sanctions by stages was legitimate.

A further material consideration was that at the time when the League Covenant had been framed the expectation had been that membership of the League would be universal. At present this was far from being the case and they were entitled to interpret Article 16 in the light of that fact. . . .

[Hoare] . . . had been left with the impression that there would be a wave of public opinion against the Government if it repudiated its obligations under Article 16—that was to say, its obligations under the principle of collective responsibility, on the assumption that France would go as far as we were prepared to do. It was abundantly clear that the only safe line for His Majesty's Government was to try out the regular League of Nations procedure.

The Lord President of the Council said that he recognised to the full the advantages of proceeding by stages in the matter of economic sanctions. It must be admitted, however, that a piecemeal procedure would be correspondingly slow in producing effects and he would not be surprised if, in the meantime, the Italians managed to pull off a great initial success. It might be difficult to commend the piecemeal procedure to public opinion in the countries co-operating in the sanctions. . . .

The Chancellor of the Exchequer thought that we might find ourselves in considerable difficulties even if the United States and Japan, for example, were induced to prohibit trade with Italy. The possibility would still remain that the activities of German shipping might render the sanction meaningless; in such a situation we should have to be very careful if we were not to land ourselves in war with both Germany and Italy.

The Minister for League Affairs hoped that in practice economic sanctions would not be begun until a committee of the League Council had carefully worked out the methods of their application—that is, until it had ascertained definitely what attitude the non-Member States were going to adopt.

[Hoare] . . . such an investigation by experts might very probably lead to a decision not to impose economic sanctions. . . .

The Lord President of the Council said that if Italy proceeded to extremes, it would be a great shock to British public opinion if no outward action were taken by His Majesty's Government. He had been encouraged by the present discussion to hope that it would be possible to discover a completely pacific method of applying economic sanctions against Italian trade.

V.3.D   Hoare's 'strong speech' at the League Assembly, 11 September 1935 (*L of Ns OJ* Special Supplement 138, pp. 43–6).

. . . Collective security, by which is meant the organisation of peace and the prevention of war by collective means, is, in its perfect form, not a simple but a complex conception. It means much more than what are commonly called sanctions. It means, not merely Article 16, but the whole Covenant. It assumes a scrupulous respect for all treaty obligations. Its foundation is the series of fundamental obligations, freely accepted by Members of the League, to submit any dispute likely to lead to war to peaceful methods of settlement according to the procedure provided by the Covenant, and not to resort to war for the settlement of disputes in violation of the Covenant.

The two principal conditions in which the system of collective security is designed to operate are, first, that the Members of the League shall have reduced their armaments to the lowest point consistent with national safety and the enforcement by common action of international obligations; and, secondly, that the possibility is open, through the machinery of the League, for the modification, by consent and by peaceful means, of international conditions whose continuance might be a danger to peace. Finally, to complete the system, there is the obligation to take collective action to bring war to an end in the event of any resort to war in disregard of the Covenant obligations. Underlying these obligations was the expectation that this system would be subscribed to by the universal world of sovereign States, or by far the greatest part of it.

This whole system is an inspiring conception; indeed, it is one of the most inspiring in the history of mankind. Its realisation could not be easy, even in the most favourable circumstances. I need not labour to show how unfavourable the circumstances have become or how much more grievous is the burden which lies upon faithful Members of the League to preserve what has been won in the struggle for the organisation of peace.

For what is the position?

In spite of the obligation of the Covenant by which Members of the League undertook to govern their conduct in accordance with a new international ethic, the spirit of war . . . has raised its head in more places than one. From fear of war, the over-optimistic examples in limitation and reduction of armaments by certain countries, and in particular by my own, have not been followed; and now, from the growing fear of war, the armaments of most countries, and last of all of my own country, are increasing. So far, we have found it impossible to make progress with this part of the League's programme.

Side by side with this disappointment, there is a natural reluctance voluntarily to contemplate the possibility of changes in the existing position; and yet elasticity, where elasticity is required, is also a part of security. A vicious circle of insecurity has been set up.

Lastly, the League has from the outset lacked the membership of certain powerful nations and has since lost the membership of others. This lack of universality inevitably introduces an element of uncertainty as to how far we can count on world-wide support in the work of organising and maintaining peace. There are too many empty chairs at our table. We want no more.

These, then, are the conditions in which we find ourselves. The obligations of the Covenant remain, their burden upon us has been increased manifold. But one thing is certain. If the burden is to be borne, it must be borne collectively. If risks for peace are to be run, they must be run by all. The security of the many cannot be ensured solely by the efforts of a few, however powerful they may be. On behalf of His Majesty's Government in the United Kingdom, I can say that, in spite of these difficulties, that Government will be second to none in its intention to fulfil, within the measure of its capacity, the obligations which the Covenant lays upon it. ...

... In conformity with its precise and explicit obligations, the League stands, and my country stands with it, for the collective maintenance of the Covenant in its entirety, and particularly for steady and collective resistance to all acts of unprovoked aggression. The attitude of the British nation in the last few weeks has clearly demonstrated the fact that this is no variable and unreliable sentiment, but a principle of international conduct to which they and their Government hold with firm, enduring, and universal persistence.

V.3.E   Extract from the National Government Manifesto, prepared for the 1935 General Election. (*The Times*, 28 October 1935.)

The League of Nations will remain, as heretofore, the keystone of British foreign policy. The prevention of war and the establishment of settled peace in the world must always be the most vital interest of the British people, and the League is the instrument which has been framed and to which we look for the attainment of these objects. We shall therefore continue to do all in our power to uphold the Covenant and to maintain and increase the efficiency of the League. In the present unhappy dispute between Italy and Abyssinia there will be no wavering in the policy we have hitherto pursued. We shall take no action in isolation, but we shall be prepared faithfully to take our part in any collective action decided upon by the League and shared in by its members. We shall endeavour to further any discussions which may offer the hope of a just and fair settlement, provided that it be within the framework of the League and acceptable to the three parties to the dispute—Italy, Abyssinia, and the League itself.

Peace is not only the first interest of the British people; it is the object to which all their hopes and efforts are directed. Our attitude to the League is dictated by the conviction that collective security by collective action can alone save us from a return to the old system which resulted in the Great War. ...

V.4   SANCTIONS

At the prompting of the British Government, the League adopted a policy of mild economic sanctions against Italy with the intention of making them progressively more stringent. There were difficulties from the start, however, stemming from the ambiguity of the Rules of Guidance adopted by the League Assembly in 1921 to serve as an interpretive guide to Article 16 in the light of the non-universality of the League. [See Appendix II.] With the United States, Japan and Germany out of the League, the British and French Governments were aware that the effectiveness of economic sanctions was likely to be limited, unless their co-operation could be assured. Only from the United States was this assurance likely to be forthcoming. Furthermore, Austria and Hungary declared their inability to participate even at this level of activity. As to stringent economic sanctions on such vital war commodities as oil, or progression towards military sanctions, neither the British nor the French Governments were prepared to risk the implications which might arise from the imposition of such measures.

V.4.A Resolutions adopted by the Committee of the League of Nations, set up to co-ordinate the measures which members might prepare to take under Article 16, between 11 October and 19 October 1935 (*L of Ns OJ* Special Supplement, no. 145, pp. 14–27).

Proposal I, adopted by the Co-ordination Committee on 11 October 1935.

EXPORT OF ARMS, AMMUNITION, AND IMPLEMENTS OF WAR

With a view to facilitating for the Governments of the Members of the League of Nations the execution of their obligations under Article 16 of the Covenant, the following measures should be taken forthwith:

1. The Governments of the Members of the League of Nations which are enforcing at the moment measures to prohibit or restrict the exportation, re-exportation, or transit of arms, munitions, and implements of war to Ethiopia will annul these measures immediately.

2. The Governments of the Members of the League of Nations will prohibit immediately the exportation, re-exportation, or transit to Italy or Italian possessions of arms, munitions, and implements of war enumerated in the attached list.

3. The Governments of the Members of the League of Nations will take such steps as may be necessary to secure that arms, munitions, and implements of war enumerated in the attached list, exported to countries other than Italy, will not be re-exported directly or indirectly to Italy or to Italian possessions. . . .

Proposal II adopted by the Co-ordination Committee on 14 October 1935.

Financial Measures

With a view to facilitating for the Governments of the Members of the League of Nations the execution of their obligations under Article 16 of the Covenant, the following measures should be taken forthwith:

The Governments of the Members of the League of Nations will forthwith take all measures necessary to render impossible the following operations:

1. All loans to or for the Italian Government and all subscriptions to loans issued in Italy or elsewhere by or for the Italian Government.

2. All banking or other credits to or for the Italian Government and any further execution by advance, overdraft, or otherwise of existing contracts to lend directly or indirectly to the Italian Government;

3. All loans to or for any public authority, person, or corporation in Italian territory and all subscriptions to such loans issued in Italy or elsewhere.

4. All banking or other credits to or for any public authority, person, or corporation in Italian territory and any further execution by advance, overdraft, or otherwise of existing contracts to lend directly or indirectly to such authority, person or corporation.

5. All issues of shares or other capital flotations for any public authority, person or corporation in Italian territory and all subscriptions to such issues of shares or capital flotations in Italy or elsewhere.

6. The Governments will take all measures necessary to render impossible the transactions mentioned in paragraphs 1–5 whether effected directly or through intermediaries of whatsoever nationality.

The Governments are invited to put in operation at once such of the measures recommended as can be enforced without fresh legislation, and to take all practicable steps to secure that the measures recommended are completely put into operation by 31 October 1935. Any Governments which find it impossible to secure the requisite legislation by that date are requested to inform the Committee, through the Secretary General, of the date by which they expect to be able to do so.

Each Government is requested to inform the Committee, through the Secretary General of the League, within the shortest possible time of the measures which it has taken in conformity with the above provisions.

Proposal III, adopted by the Co-ordination Committee on 19 October 1935.

Prohibition of Importation of Italian Goods

With a view to facilitating for the Governments of the Members of the League of Nations the execution of their obligations under Article 16 of the Covenant, the following measures should be taken:

1. The Governments of the Members of the League of Nations will prohibit the importation into their territories of all goods (other than gold or silver bullion and coin) consigned from or grown, produced, or manufactured in Italy or Italian possessions, from whatever place arriving.

2. Goods grown or produced in Italy or Italian possessions which have been subjected to some process in another country, and goods manufactured partly in Italy or Italian possessions and partly in another country will be considered as falling within the scope of the prohibition unless 25 per cent or more of the value of the goods at the time when they left the place from which they were last consigned is attributable to processes undergone since the goods last left Italy or Italian possessions;

3. Goods, the subject of existing contracts, will not be excepted from the prohibition.

4. Goods *en route* at the time of imposition of the prohibition will be excepted from its operation. In giving effect to this provision Governments may, for convenience of administration, fix an appropriate date, having regard to the normal time necessary for transport from Italy, after which goods will become subject to the prohibition.

5. Personal belongings of travellers from Italy or Italian possessions may also be excepted from its operation.

Having regard to the importance of collective and, so far as possible, simultaneous action in regard to the measures recommended, each Government is requested to inform the Co-ordination Committee, through the Secretary General, as soon as possible, and not later than 28 October, of the date on which it could be ready to bring these measures into operation. The Co-ordination Committee will meet on 31 October for the purpose of fixing, in the light of the replies received, the date of the coming into force of the said measures.

Proposal IV, adopted by the Co-ordination Committee on 19 October 1935.

EMBARGO ON CERTAIN EXPORTS TO ITALY

With a view to facilitating for the Governments of the Members of the League of Nations the execution of their obligations under Article 16 of the Covenant, the following measures should be taken:

1. The Governments of the Members of the League of Nations will extend the application of paragraph 2 of Proposal No. I of the Co-ordination Committee to the following articles as regards their exportation and re-exportation to Italy and Italian possessions, which will accordingly be prohibited:

(a) horses, mules, donkeys, camels, and all other transport animals;

(b) rubber;

(c) bauxite, aluminium and alumina (aluminium oxide), iron ore, and scrap iron;

(d) chromium, manganese, nickel, titanium, tungsten, vanadium, their ores and ferro-alloys (and also ferro-molybdenum, ferro-silicon, ferro-silico-manganese, and ferro-silico-manganese aluminium); tin and tin-ore.

List (c) above includes all crude forms of the minerals and metals mentioned and their ores, scrap and alloys.

2. The Governments of the Members of the League of Nations will take such steps as may be necessary to secure that the articles mentioned in paragraph 1 above exported to countries other than Italy or Italian possessions will not be re-exported directly or indirectly to Italy or Italian possessions.

3. The measures provided for in paragraphs 1 and 2 above are to apply to contracts in course of execution.

4. Goods *en route* at the time of imposition of the prohibition will be excepted from its operation. In giving effect to this provision Governments may, for convenience of administration, fix an appropriate date, having regard to the normal time necessary for transport to Italy or Italian possessions, after which goods will become subject to the prohibition.

Having regard to the importance of collective, and so far as possible, simultaneous action in regard to the measures recommended, each Government is requested to inform the Co-ordination Committee, through the Secretary-General, as soon as possible, and not later than 28 October, of the date on which it could be ready to bring these measures into operation. . . .

Proposal V, adopted by the Co-ordination Committee on 19 October 1935.

ORGANISATION OF MUTUAL SUPPORT

The Co-ordination Committee draws the special attention of all Governments to their obligations under paragraph 3 of Article 16 of the Covenant, according to which the Members of the League undertake mutually to support one another in the application of the economic and financial measures taken under this article.

1. With a view to carrying these obligations into effect the Governments of the Members of the League of Nations will:

(a) Adopt immediately measures to ensure that no action taken as a result of Article 16 will deprive any country applying sanctions of such advantages as the commercial agreements concluded by the participating States with Italy afforded it through the operation of the most-favoured-nation clause;

(b) take appropriate steps with a view to replacing, within the limits of the requirements of their respective countries, imports from Italy by the import of similar products from the participating States;

(c) be willing, after the application of economic sanctions, to enter into negotiations with any participating country which has sustained a loss, with a view to increasing the sale of goods so as to offset any loss of Italian markets which the application of sanctions may have involved;

(d) in cases in which they have suffered no loss in respect of any given commodity, abstain from demanding the application of any most-favoured-nation clause in the base of any privileges granted under paragraphs (b) and (c) in respect of that commodity.

2. With the above objects, the Governments will ... study, in particular, the possibility of adopting within the limits of their existing obligations ... the following measures:

(a) the increase by all appropriate measures of their imports in favour of such countries as may have suffered loss of Italian markets on account of the application of sanctions;

(b) in order to facilitate this increase, the taking into consideration of the obligations of mutual support and of the advantages which the trade of certain States Members of the League of Nations, not participating in the sanctions, would obtain from the application of these sanctions, in order to reduce by every appropriate means and to an equitable degree imports coming from these countries;

(c) the promotion, by all means in their power, of business relations between firms interested in the sale of goods in Italian markets which have been lost owing to the application of sanctions and firms normally importing such goods;

(d) assisting generally in the organisation of the international marketing of goods with a view to offsetting any loss of Italian markets which the application of sanctions may have involved.

They will also examine, under the same conditions, the possibility of financial or other measures to supplement the commercial measures in so far as these latter may not ensure sufficient international mutual support.

Proposal IV (a) adopted by the Committee of Eighteen on 6 November 1935.

EMBARGO ON CERTAIN EXPORTS TO ITALY

... It is expedient that the measures of embargo provided for in Proposal IV should be extended to the following articles as soon as the conditions necessary to render this extension effective have been realised:

Petroleum and its derivatives, by-products, and residues;

Pig-iron; iron and steel (including alloy steels), cast, forged, rolled, drawn, stamped, or pressed;

Coal (including anthracite and lignite), coke and their agglomerates, as well as fuels derived therefrom.

If the replies received by the Committee to the present proposal and the information at its disposal warrant it, the Committee of Eighteen will propose to Governments a date for bringing into force the measures mentioned above.

V.4.B   Speech by M. de Velics, Hungarian representative at the League of Nations Sixteenth Assembly, 9 October 1935 (*L of Ns OJ* Special Supplement, no. 138, p. 101).

The proposal to apply sanctions against Italy places Hungary in a particularly difficult and delicate situation. I do not intend to mention the painful feelings experienced by Hungary at this moment when measures are to be applied against a country which is united to her by age-long traditions of friendship, which has on many occasions given proof of its friendship for my country and to which, at this very hour, I wish to express my country's gratitude.

... I desire to refer briefly to the question of the principle of sanctions as it affects the Hungarian Government. The League of Nations, as an institution, and the Covenant of the League were created and exist for one sole purpose: the maintenance of peace. The maintenance of peace means an effort to eliminate all the causes that might lead to war. Obviously the lives of the various nations cannot be confined for ever within a static and immovable framework; they must develop according to the rule of nature itself, which is a rule of perpetual change. It is a fundamental duty of the League to see that these movements shall take place under proper conditions, after the ground has been prepared and made ready by the League itself.

I wonder whether, in the present case, all means have been employed and exhausted with a view to achieving the purpose to which I have just referred.

I wonder whether the present case is really one in which to apply sanctions, which are reserved as a last resort against manifest bad faith. It is not for the Hungarian Government to answer that question.

I will merely therefore define the views of the Hungarian Government on the question now under discussion, seeing that it is proposed to appoint a committee to draw up a plan for the application of sanctions against Italy. As regards economic sanctions, Hungary is in a very special position. In numerous reports and resolutions of the League of Nations concerning Article 16 of the Covenant, it has been laid down that account must be taken of the special conditions and requirements of certain countries and that certain forms of economic action might produce very harmful effects on the very countries which adopt them and might, indeed, involve these countries in serious danger. Consequently, I think that it would be more in keeping with the League's aims to allow Members of the League some degree of latitude. Nobody can be better aware than the Council, which has for years been supervising the finances of Hungary, of the economic and financial difficulties experienced by my country. The exclusion of Italy from Hungary's restricted and limited trade outlets would completely upset our economic and financial equilibrium, which has hitherto been preserved at great cost, largely by means of exports to Italy.

For these reasons, and for the further reason that my Government has not had an opportunity of examining conscientiously, and with the necessary care, the facts and documents on which such serious resolutions might with full certainty be based, the Hungarian delegation is unable to associate itself with the conclusions mentioned in the President's communications.

V.4.C Statement by President Roosevelt, 30 October 1935 (US State Department, Press Releases, no. 318, 2 November 1935).

In dealing with the conflict between Ethiopia and Italy, I have carried into effect the will and intent of the neutrality resolution recently enacted by Congress [31 August 1935, adopted by Congress on 24 August 1935]. We have prohibited all shipments of arms, ammunition, and implements of war to the belligerent governments . . . we have warned American citizens against transactions of any character with either of the belligerent nations except at their own risk.

This Government is determined not to become involved in the controversy and is anxious for the restoration and maintenance of peace.

However, in the course of war, tempting trade opportunities may be offered to our people to supply materials which would prolong the war. I do not believe that the American people will wish for abnormally increased profits that temporarily might be secured by greatly extending our trade in such materials; nor would they wish the struggles on the battlefield to be prolonged because of profits accruing to a comparatively small number of American citizens.

Accordingly, the American Government is keeping informed as to all shipments consigned for export to both belligerents.

V.4.D Extracts from the reply of the US Secretary of State to the Note of 21 October from the Chairman of the Co-ordination Committee (US State Department, Press Releases, no. 318, 2 November 1935).

... In regard to your statement that the Governments represented on the Co-ordination Committee would welcome any communication which any non-member State may deem it proper to make to you, or notifications of any action which it may be taking in the circumstances, it is, of course, well known that the Government and people of the United States are deeply interested in the prevention of war, and hence in the sanctity of treaties and promotion of peace in every part of the world; that as a corollary to their abhorrence of war with the human sufferings, the impoverishment of States and peoples, business dislocation and embittered feelings engendered by warfare, we are by tradition strong proponents of the principle that all differences between members of the family of nations should be settled by pacific means. ...

As regards the situation now unhappily existing between Ethiopia and Italy, I may point out that the Government of the United States put forth every practicable effort to aid in the preservation of peace, through conferences, official acts, diplomatic communications, and public statements, and emphasised particularly the principles of the Pact of Paris and the high legal and moral obligations of the signatories thereto. This Government repeatedly expressed its anxiety and the hope that the controversy would be resolved without resort to armed conflict and the conviction of the entire nation that failure to arrive at a peaceful settlement of the dispute and the subsequent outbreak of hostilities would be a world calamity.

When, however, it was found that hostilities actually existed between Ethiopia and Italy, this Government, acting on its own initiative, promptly announced a number of basic measures primarily to avoid being drawn into the war, and which also would not be without effect in discouraging war. ...

These steps have been taken for the purpose of dealing with this specific controversy and the special circumstances presented.

The course thus pursued in advance of action by other Governments, most of which are parties to one or more of the peace pacts to which I have referred, represents the independent and affirmative policy of the Government of the United States and indicates its purpose not to be drawn into the war and its desire not to contribute to a prolongation of the war.

Realising that war adversely affects every country, that it may seriously endanger the economic welfare of each, causes untold human misery, and even threatens the existence of civilisation, the United States, in keeping with the letter and spirit of the Pact of Paris and other peace obligations, undertakes at all times not only to exercise its moral influence in favour of peace throughout the world, but to contribute in every practicable way within the limitations of our foreign policy, to that end. It views with sympathetic interest the individual or concerted efforts of other nations to preserve peace or to localise and shorten the duration of war.

V.4.E   Statement by the Right Hon. Sir Samuel Hoare, Foreign Secretary, 22 October 1935, in House of Commons (*Hansard*, 22 October 1935, cols. 17–33).

. . . However much we may hope from the League, can any of us expect that an organ as complex as this can establish its position in the world in the space of a few years and without the long period of growth that has been needed for almost every other great institution in the world?

There have been hesitations and uncertainties at Geneva. Who would have expected otherwise, with more than fifty States discussing a totally new problem in the world, and in face of one of the greatest difficulties which have confronted us in our generation? I go so far as to say that it is a good thing that there have been these hesitations and doubts, that they at least show that the member States are taking the League seriously and are thinking, each for himself, of the League in the form of a complete organisation affecting his particular State. My wonder is not that the League has worked slowly or that it has worked with hesitation, but, in face of these difficulties, that it has worked at all.

Here was a controversy . . . affecting particularly one of the great Powers of the League, and affecting indirectly other great Powers. Here was a controversy that concerned a part of Africa with which scarcely any of the member States had any connection at all. What wonder, in view of these unprecedented conditions, that there should have been doubts and hesitations, and that it should have taken days, and it may be weeks, to arrive at agreed action. None the less, in spite of these difficulties, agreed action has been taken and collective action has been approved.

. . . if the purposes of the Covenant are to be fulfilled, all the Members of the League must play their part. . . . His Majesty's Government are prepared to play their part to the full, but on the clear understanding that the part that they play is a joint part, and that the risks and responsibilities incurred are accepted and shared by the other Members of the League. As it is, a large measure of agreement has been reached. It has been reached first of all on the merits of the dispute—a unique event in the history of the world, a verdict by more than fifty sovereign States upon the merits of the controversy. Secondly, it has been reached upon the arms embargo, the withdrawal of credit, and, subject to the considered views of the various Governments, certain methods of economic pressure.

No doubt any action of this kind is open to a double line of criticism.

There are those who say that action of this kind will be ineffective and futile, and there are those who say that it will lead directly to military sanctions and to war. I disagree with both lines of criticism. I do not believe that economic pressure of this kind will, in the circumstances, be ineffective. I believe, on the other hand, that if it is collectively applied and the States that are not members of the League do not attempt to frustrate it—and I have no reason to think that they will frustrate it—it will definitely shorten the duration of the war. The House will have observed the kind of economic pressure that is being considered at Geneva: an embargo on munitions and certain key commodities, an embargo on credit, and an embargo on Italian exports. So far as the British Government are concerned, we have had actual experience of the effect of action of this kind in the past, and it is well worth noting that we have not found it ineffective. . . . But if action of this kind is to be effective it must, in the first place, be really collective. Member States must take their share of the risks, the inconveniences, and the losses. And, in the second place, all member States must co-operate to resist an attack upon any one State for the action that it has taken to defend the Covenant.

. . . I will pass from the question of economic pressure to the question of so-called military sanctions. This is clearly a delicate matter, and much harm has been done by ignorant talk on this subject. I will say frankly that, in my view, the pre-condition for the enforcement of such sanctions, namely, collective agreement at Geneva, has never existed. Military sanctions, like economic sanctions, can only be applied collectively, and so far as we are concerned we have made it clear from the beginning of the controversy that though we are prepared to take our full share as a loyal Member of the League, we are only prepared to take our share in collective action. I emphasise the word 'collective', as it is the essence and soul of the League. Only by this essence can the League live—not by ringing bells or blowing whistles for policemen from outside. We are not prepared, and we do not intend, to act alone. Further, from the beginning of the present deliberations at Geneva until now, there has been no discussion of military sanctions, and no such measures, therefore, have formed any part of our policy. I make the statement with special emphasis, as there have been misconceptions both at home and abroad regarding the matter of sanctions. The action that we have been considering, which we believe it to be our solemn obligation to consider, is not military but economic. The distinction is that between a boycott and a war. Nobody in this House can believe that anybody in Europe desires a war. . . .

. . . We have tried to avoid recriminations and we have tried, in particular, to avoid any action or the discussion of any action that was impracticable in present conditions and might yet extend the duration, the danger, and the disaster of the war. . . . The League, let us remember, is a great instrument of peace. Let the critics remember this fact when they say that we ought to block up the Suez Canal and cut the Italian communications. (*Interruption.*)

Do my Hon. Friends opposite mean that we should do this alone? I hear one still small voice in response to that question. If they do mean that we should take this action alone, what becomes of collective action? What is the good of talking of measures of this kind that may set a spark to very inflammable material, when we know that there is no collective agreement behind them upon which we can base our action? No wise man will wish to throw a spark into this inflammable material by threats that cannot be collectively carried out or, if they were carried out, would turn the Abyssinian into a European war. The economic pressure that is now proposed is intended not to expand but to limit the war; not to extend its duration but to shorten it. In the meanwhile, not a day or week should pass without the Members of the League showing their readiness to find an honourable settlement of this unhappy controversy. I take this opportunity of emphasising this need to search for some means of an honourable settlement within the framework of the League.

V.5   THE HOARE-LAVAL PACT

While economic sanctions were being put into operation the French Prime Minister M. Laval was becoming desperately anxious to effect a settlement of the dispute which would placate Mussolini. The spectre of oil sanctions also spurred the British Government into intensifying their search for a compromise acceptable to all parties. In early December, Sir Samuel Hoare, travelling through Paris on his way to Switzerland for a rest after a strenuous period of overwork, was pressurised by Laval into accepting a peace settlement subsequently referred to as the Hoare-Laval Pact. While it might have satisfied Mussolini, it could certainly never have been acceptable to the Abyssinians, and when its details were revealed to the British public it caused such an outcry that the British Government was forced to disavow both it and Sir Samuel Hoare, thus alienating Italy and France.

V.5.A   Outline of an Agreed Settlement of the Italo-Ethiopian Conflict, 10 December 1935 (*L of Ns OJ*, January 1936, pp. 40–1).

I. Exchange of Territories

The Governments of the United Kingdom and France agree to recommend to His Majesty the Emperor of Ethiopia the acceptance of the following exchanges of territory between Ethiopia and Italy.

1. Tigre: Cession to Italy of Eastern Tigre, approximately limited on the south by the River Gheva and on the west by a line running from north to south, passing between Aksum (on the Ethiopian side) and Adowa (on the Italian side).

2. Rectification of frontiers between the Danakil country and Eritrea, leaving to the south of the boundary line Aussa and the extent of Eritrean territory necessary to give Ethiopia an outlet to the sea to be defined below.

3. Rectification of frontiers between the Ogaden and Italian Somaliland. Starting from the tri-junction point between the frontiers of Ethiopia, Kenya, and Italian Somaliland, the new Italo-Ethiopian frontier would follow a general north-easterly direction, cutting the Webi Shebeli at Iddidole, leaving Gorahai to the east, Warandab to the west, and meeting the frontier of British Somaliland where it intersects the 45th meridian.

The rights of the tribes of British Somaliland to the use of grazing areas and wells situated in the territories granted to Italy by this delimitation should be guaranteed.

4. Ethiopia will receive an outlet to the sea with full sovereign rights. It seems that this outlet should be formed preferably by the cession, to which Italy would agree, of the port of Assab and of a strip of territory giving access to this port along the frontier of French Somaliland.

The United Kingdom and French Governments will endeavour to obtain from the Ethiopian Government guarantees for the fulfilment of the obligations which devolve upon them regarding slavery and arms traffic in the territories acquired by them.

II. Zone of Economic Expansion and Settlement

The United Kingdom and French Governments will use their influence at Addis Ababa and at Geneva to the end that the formation in Southern Ethiopia of a zone of economic expansion and settlement reserved to Italy should be accepted by His Majesty the Emperor and approved by the League of Nations.

The limits of this zone would be: on the east, the rectified frontier between Ethiopia and Italian Somaliland; on the north, the eighth parallel; on the west, the thirty-fifth meridian; on the south, the frontier between Ethiopia and Kenya.

Within this zone, which would form an integral part of Ethiopia, Italy would enjoy exclusive economic rights which might be administered by a privileged company or by any other like organisation, to which would be recognised—subject to the acquired rights of natives and foreigners—the right of ownership of unoccupied territories, the monopoly of the exploitation of mines, forests, etc. This organisation would be obliged to contribute to the economic equipment of the country and to devote a portion of its revenue to expenditure of a social character for the benefit of the native population.

The control of the Ethiopian administration in the zone would be exercised under the sovereignty of the Emperor, by the services of the scheme of assistance drawn up by the League of Nations. Italy would take a preponderating, but not an exclusive, share in these services, which would be under the direct control of one of the principal advisers attached to the Central Government. The principal adviser in question, who might be of Italian nationality, would be the assistant, for the affairs in question, of the Chief Adviser delegated by the League of Nations to assist the Emperor. The Chief Adviser would not be a subject of one of the Powers bordering on Ethiopia.

The services of the scheme of assistance, in the capital as well as in the reserved zone, would regard it as one of their essential duties to ensure the safety of Italian subjects and the free development of their enterprises.

The Government of the United Kingdom and the French Government will willingly endeavour to ensure that this organisation, the details of which must be elaborated by the League of Nations, fully safeguards the interests of Italy in this region.

V.5.B   Extracts from the note of the Abyssinian Government to the Secretary-General of the League of Nations, 12 December 1935 (*L of Ns OJ*, January 1936, pp. 41–2).

By order of my Government, I have the honour to request you to communicate the following declaration to the President of the Assembly, the President of the Council, and all the Members of the League of Nations:

1. The Imperial Ethiopian Government has received, from two Members of the League of Nations, communication of a proposal for putting an end to the war of aggression undertaken against Ethiopia by the Italian Government....

3. ... In the present circumstances, it is the Ethiopian Government's imperative duty to do nothing which can contribute towards creating a precedent prejudicial to any of the States Members of the League of Nations. Each of these States would be entitled to reproach the Ethiopian Government with having deprived it of the means of discussing publicly before the Assembly, which is the sovereign guardian of all the clauses of the Covenant, a problem which is vital to the future of the League of Nations and to the security of each of the States Members.

4. As the Ethiopian Government understands it, the proposal submitted to it consists, as far as it is concerned, in the following settlement:

Ethiopia, the victim of an act of aggression which has been

formally recognised as such by the Council and by the Assembly, is invited:

(a) to cede to its Italian aggressor, in a more or less disguised form and under the pretext of a fallacious exchange of territories, about half of its national territory, in order to enable the aggressor country to settle part of its population there;

to agree that the League of Nations should confer upon its aggressor, in a disguised form, control over the other half of its territory pending future annexation.

5. Before replying to this proposal, the Ethiopian Government urgently asks that the Assembly of the League of Nations be convened immediately in order that, by a full and free public debate, conducted frankly in the face of the world, free from all pressure, direct or indirect, every member State should be enabled to express its opinion on the true practical significance of the proposals submitted to Ethiopia and on the general problem of the conditions which are indispensable if a settlement between the victim of a properly established act of aggression and the aggressor Government is not in practice to result in destroying the League of Nations by bringing final ruin upon the system of guaranteed collective security provided for by the Covenant.

The Ethiopian Government, taught by cruel experience, declares itself firmly opposed to all secret negotiations.

V.5.c   Personal explanation by Hoare to the House of Commons, 19 December 1935 on the day after his resignation was announced, of his part in the Hoare-Laval negotiations and settlement (*Hansard*, 19 December 1935, cols. 2003–12).

It must have been clear to every Hon. Member that the threat of war and the outbreak of war had raised very difficult questions between ourselves and France. It must have been obvious to every Hon. Member that a great body of opinion in France was intensely nervous of a breach with Italy, was intensely nervous of anything that was likely to weaken French defence. In view of those facts, I did everything in my power to make a settlement possible, and while loyally continuing a policy of sanctions and coercive action. . . . I never allowed a day to pass without attempting by some means or another to find a peaceful settlement to this hateful controversy. That was the position after the Election. We were engaged upon our double task of taking our full share in collective action and also with that other task imposed upon us by the League itself of trying to find a basis of settlement of this unfortunate dispute, and particularly was I concentrating upon the second of those two tasks in view of the situation that I saw inevitably developing before me in the immediate future.

In both these fields, in both the field of collective action and also in the field of peaceful negotiations, we reached a turning point about a fortnight ago. The turning point came sooner than many of us expected. Perhaps it came as a result of the sanctions that had already been imposed and the collective front that, I am glad to say, had been created at Geneva. In any case, about a fortnight ago it was clear that a new situation was about to be created by the question of the oil embargo. It seemed clear that, supposing an oil embargo were to be imposed and that the non-Member States took an effective part in it, the oil embargo might have such an effect upon the hostilities as to force their termination. Just because of the effectiveness of the oil sanction, provided that the non-Member States had a full part in it, the situation immediately became more dangerous from the point of view of Italian resistance. From all sides we received reports that no responsible government could disregard that Italy would regard the oil embargo as a military sanction or an act involving war against her. Let me make our position quite clear. We had no fear as a nation whatever of any Italian threats. If the Italians attacked us we should retaliate, and, judging from our past history, we should retaliate with full success. What was in our mind was something very different, that an isolated attack of this kind launched upon one Power, without . . . the full support of the other Powers, would, it seemed to me, almost inevitably lead to the dissolution of the League.

It was in these circumstances ten days ago that I went to Paris. I did not want to go to Paris. I was in urgent need of a period of rest, but, apart from that fact, I disliked intensely the practice of the Foreign Minister leaving this country and conducting negotiations in a foreign capital. None the less, I was pressed on all sides to go, and I was pressed in such a way as to make refusal impossible. It was in an atmosphere of threatened war that the conversations began, and it was in an atmosphere in which the majority of the Member States—indeed, I would say the totality of the Member States—appeared to be opposed to military action. It was a moment of great urgency. Within five days the question of the oil embargo was to come up at Geneva, and I did not feel myself justified in proposing any postponement of the embargo, unless it could be shown to the League that negotiations had actually started. It was a moment when, while most member States had taken a part in the economic sanctions, no Member State except ourselves had taken any military precautions.

Lastly, it was a moment when it seemed to me that Anglo-French co-operation was essential if there was to be no breach at Geneva and if the sanctions when functioning were not to be destroyed. For two days M. Laval and I discussed the basis of a possible negotiation. We were not discussing terms to be imposed upon the belligerents. We were discussing proposals that might bring the two parties into the same room and that might make subsequent negotiation possible. The

proposals that emerged from those discussions were not French proposals or British proposals in the sense that we liked them. Neither
M. Laval nor I liked many features of them. But that basis did seem to
us to be the only basis upon which it was even remotely likely that we
could at least start a peace discussion. It was certainly the minimum
basis upon which the French Government were prepared to proceed,
and this minimum was only reached after two days of strenuous discussion. So far as I myself was concerned it seemed to me to be so
important to start a negotiation, even if it had to be on this basis, that,
much as I disliked some features of the scheme, I could not withhold
my provisional assent. I felt that the issues were so grave and the dangers
of the continuance of the war were so serious that it was worth making an
attempt and that it was essential to maintain Anglo-French solidarity.
It was in this spirit and this spirit alone that we agreed to the suggestions. . . .

What were the suggestions that we put forward to the belligerents
and the League? I am aware that many of my friends have said to me,
'Say nothing about the proposals. They are dead. The world is against
them.' I could not accept that advice in justice either to myself or, what
is much more important, in justice to the gravity of the issues that are
raised by it. I would venture . . . to ask the indulgence of the House for
two or three minutes whilst in my own words I give a description, I
hope a not controversial description, of the actual proposals, for I am
anxious to have these proposals on the records of the House in order
that it can be seen what in actual practice were the proposals that led to
my resignation.

There were three classes of proposals: the first for international supervision; the second for territorial exchanges; and the third for opportunities for Italian economic expansion and settlement. These were the
three principles of the Report of the Committee of Five, and it is
important to remind the House that whilst Signor Mussolini refused to
accept them the Emperor accepted them in principle when the threat
of war was hanging over him. Secondly, it should also be remembered
that not long ago the Emperor himself showed his great desire for an
outlet to the sea by offering to exchange for it the vast region of Ogaden.
The Paris proposals substituted for Ogaden a part of the Tigre province
that is now in Italian occupation and in which the Abyssinian chieftains
seem to have gone over to the Italian side, but they would have meant the
Italian evacuation of certain of the occupied territories, including the
sacred town of Aksum. Secondly, they suggested a strip of Danakil and
Ogaden territory of limited area. This territory is entirely desert.

As to the port, let me make it quite clear that the proposal was for an
effective outlet, with a wide corridor in full sovereignty for Abyssinia, at
Assab, and no stipulation was discussed concerning any restriction upon

it as to the building of a railway. The Zeila alternative was only included as an alternative if both sides preferred it. As to the South, a large area was to be set aside for Italian economic development and expansion. This area is non-Amharic. It represents comparatively recent conquest by Abyssinia; it is sparsely populated, slave-raiding has devastated it in some parts, while slave-ownership is prevalent over the whole area, as indeed over the whole country. Here, however, let me make it as clear as I can that there was to be no transfer of sovereignty, and that the Administration, while continuing to be Abyssinian, was to be under the guidance and control of the League Plan of Assistance. . . . At the same time, as was bound to be the case in an area in which Italians were to settle and Italian capital was to be sunk, officials of Italian nationality would take a predominant part in the local control, but that local control would be subject to the League Plan of Assistance. . . . In no sense was the area to be a transferred territory, nor, so far as the League supervision was concerned, was it to be differentiated from the rest of Abyssinia.

I am aware that this part of the scheme has met with the fiercest criticism. I would, however, remind Hon. Members firstly, that a free hand was left to the League to fill in this chapter as it willed; and, secondly, that from all parts of the House we have heard demands for Italian colonial expansion. . . . I would also remind Hon. Members that by various instruments, more particularly the 1906 Treaty as regards the French and ourselves, and the 1925 exchange of Notes between ourselves and Italy, we have recognised Italian economic interests over a much wider area of Abyssinia than that comprised in this southern zone, whilst only recently we have made it clear that so far as we ourselves are concerned we have no other economic interest in the country than those centred in the waters of Lake Tsana and the Blue Nile.

These proposals are immensely less favourable to Italy than the demand that Signor Mussolini made to my right Hon. Friend the Minister for League of Nations Affairs last summer. They are immensely less favourable to Italy than the demands that Signor Mussolini has subsequently made. In the summer Signor Mussolini said that in any settlement without war he would require to annex all those parts of Abyssinia which did not form part of Abyssinia proper but which had been conquered by Abyssinia, and to control Abyssinia proper. The parts of Abyssinia which Italy then wished to annex are far greater than the cessions contemplated in the Paris proposals. Moreover, Signor Mussolini made it also clear that if he had to go to war to secure his ends his aim would be to wipe out the name of Abyssinia from the map. I venture to make those observations to meet the charge that is made against me that I have approved of terms more favourable than those which Signor Mussolini demands himself. I have spoken of the Italian side of the controversy, but let no Hon. Member think that throughout these difficult months I have not equally been thinking of the Abyssinian side of the controversy. I will tell Hon. Members what has constantly been in my mind. I have been terrified with the thought . . . that we might lead Abyssinia on to think that the League could do more than it can do, that in the end we should find a terrible moment of disillusionment in which it might be that Abyssinia would be destroyed altogether as an independent State. I have been terrified at that position, and I could not help thinking of the past in which, more than once in our history, we have given, and rightly given, all our sympathies to some threatened or down-trodden race, but because we had been unable to implement and give effect to those sympathies all that we had done was to encourage them, with the result that in the end their fate was worse than it would have been without our sympathy. . . .

The fact is that there are only two ways of ending a war—either peace by negotiation or peace by surrender. . . . If it is to be a peace by surrender, it will mean the complete collapse of one or other of the belligerents. My own view . . . is that I believe the end of the war will come by peace by negotiation. I believe that it will not come by peace by complete surrender either of one side or the other. . . the present peace negotiations have failed, but the problem of settlement still remains. Failure makes the position more difficult and dangerous than it was before. This fact I had constantly in mind in my talks in Paris. I knew that if the negotiations proved to be impossible the situation must inevitably become more acute. The situation has become more acute. . . .

V.6 THE LESSONS OF LEAGUE FAILURE

The attempt to buy off Mussolini through the Hoare-Laval Pact exposed the unwillingness of France and Britain to intensify economic sanctions and risk a serious clash with Italy. Economic sanctions dragged on until the middle of 1936, but with little effect; by May 1936, Mussolini had annexed Abyssinia and declared it part of the Italian Empire. The credibility of the League as a coercive organisation was completely destroyed, and even more importantly, the will of its members to work together was greatly weakened. Distrust between Britain and France contributed to the lack of concerted opposition to Hitler's re-occupation of the Rhineland in March 1936. After this successful coup, it was a case of each nation protecting its own interests as best it could, and discounting the possibilities of a common front against either Mussolini or Hitler. Meanwhile, French and British attempts to keep Mussolini out of Hitler's orbit failed. Thus the Abyssinian crisis shattered the League as a peace-keeping body, and paved the way for Hitler's domination of Europe.

V.6.A Extract from a speech made by the Rt. Hon. Neville Chamberlain, 10 June 1936, to the 1900 Club, as reported in *The Times*, 11 June 1936.

. . . I would like to make a few observations upon events of the last twelve months and their effect upon the League of Nations and the policy of collective security to which we have given so whole-hearted support with such disappointing results. The policy of collective security seemed to us, and I think it seemed to the people of the country as a whole, an attractive alternative to the old system of alliances and balance of power which nevertheless was unsuccessful in preventing the greatest war in history.

The circumstances in which the dispute between Italy and Abyssinia began appeared to offer an opportunity for the exercise of that policy which could hardly be more favourable for its success. The aggression was patent and flagrant, and there was hardly any country to which it appeared that a policy of sanctions could be exercised with a greater chance of success than upon Italy. There is no use for us to shut our eyes to realities. The fact remains that the policy of collective security based on sanctions has been tried out, as indeed we were bound to try it out unless we were prepared to repudiate our obligations and say, without having tried it, that the whole system of the League and the Covenant was a sham and a fraud. That policy has been tried out and it has failed to prevent war, failed to stop war, failed to save the victim of the aggression. I am not blaming anyone for the failure. I merely record it now because I think it is time that we reviewed the history of these events and sought to draw what lessons and conclusions we can from those events.

I want to put to you one or two conclusions which, it seems to me, may fairly be drawn. There are some people who do not desire to draw any conclusions at all. I see, for instance, the other day that the president of the League of Nations Union issued a circular to its members in which he said that the issue hung in the balance and urged them to commence a campaign of pressure upon members of Parliament and members of the Government with the idea that if we were to pursue the policy of sanctions and even to intensify it, it was still possible to preserve the independence of Abyssinia.

That seems to me the very midsummer of madness. If we were to pursue it it would only lead to further misfortunes which would divert our minds as practical men from seeking other and better solutions. There is no reason why, because the policy of collective security in the circumstances in which it was tried has failed, we should therefore abandon the idea of the League and give up the ideals for which the League stands. But if we have retained any vestige of common sense, surely we must admit that we have tried to impose upon the League a task which it was beyond its powers to fulfil.

That then is the first conclusion which, as it seems to me, is to be drawn from what has happened. Surely it is time that the nations who compose the League should review the situation and should decide so to limit the functions of the League in future that they may accord with its real powers. If that policy were to be pursued and were to be courageously carried out, I believe that it might go far to restore the prestige of the League and the moral influence which it ought to exert in the world. But if the League be limited in that sort of way it must be admitted that it could no longer be relied upon by itself to secure the peace of the world.

That leads me to the second conclusion which I wish to suggest to your minds. Is it not apparent that the policy of sanctions involves, I do not say war, but a risk of war? Is it not apparent that that risk must increase in proportion to the effectiveness of the sanctions and also by reason of the incompleteness of the League? Is it not also apparent from what has happened that in the presence of such a risk nations cannot be relied upon to proceed to the last extremity of war unless their vital interests are threatened?

That being so, does it not suggest that it might be wise to explore the possibilities of localising the danger spots of the world and trying to find a more practical method of securing peace by means of regional arrangements which could be approved by the League, but which should be guaranteed only by those nations whose interests were vitally connected with those danger zones? I put these to you merely as provisional conclusions.

V.6.B   Mr te Water, of South Africa, in the Sixteenth League Assembly, 1 July 1936 (L of Ns OJ, 1936).

. . . The authority of the League of Nations is about to come to naught.

My Government, whom I have the honour to represent, desires me to say here that this renunciation by the most powerful Members of the League of the collective decision most solemnly taken by us all, under the obligation by which we declared ourselves bound, can alone be interpreted as surrender by them of the authority of the League—a surrender of the high trust and ideals of world peace entrusted to each member nation of this institution. I am to declare that this surrender, if it is agreed upon by the nations, cannot be interpreted as impotence to safeguard that trust, but as a simple denial of their ability to bear the sacrifices necessary for the fulfilment of their obligations.

The Union of South Africa cannot, without protest, subscribe to a declaration to the world which, in their profound belief, will shatter for generations all international confidence and all hope of realising world peace. For it is idle to suppose that, by a process of reconstruction thereafter, the League can survive as an instrument of world influence and peace. . . .

And so I beg to announce the decision of my Government that it is still prepared to maintain the collective action legitimately agreed upon by the resolution of this Assembly of the League of Nations on 10 October 1935.

We offer this course, which, in our deep conviction, will alone maintain the League of Nations as an instrument of security for its Members. We commend it to this Assembly even at this eleventh hour as the only way which will ensure salvation to the nations.

V.6.c M. Litvinov at the Sixteenth Assembly of the League, 1 July 1936 (*L of Ns OJ*, 1936).

We have met here to complete a page in the history of the League of Nations, a page in the history of international life which it will be impossible for us to read without a feeling of bitterness. We have to liquidate a course of action which was begun in fulfilment of our obligations as Members of the League to guarantee the independence of one of our fellow Members, but which was not carried to its conclusion. Each of us must feel his measure of responsibility and of blame, which is not identical for all, and which depends, not only on what each of us did in fact, but also on the measure of our readiness to support every common action required by the circumstances.

In saying this, I have to declare that the Government I represent here, from the very beginning of the Italo-Ethiopian conflict, took up a perfectly clear and firm position, arising by no means from its own interests or its relations with the belligerents, but solely from its conception of the principle of collective security, of international solidarity, of the Covenant of the League, and of the obligations imposed upon it by that Covenant. . . .

However, sooner than might have been expected, the moment came when the necessity for reconsidering the measures adopted at Geneva, from the angle of their serving any useful purpose, became absolutely clear. That moment was when the resistance of the valiant Ethiopian troops was broken, when the Emperor and Government of Ethiopia left their territory, and when a considerable portion of their territory was occupied by the Italian army. It appeared then indubitable that by economic sanctions alone it would be impossible to drive the Italian army out of Ethiopia and restore the independence of that country, and that such an objective could only be attained by more serious sanctions, including those of a military nature.

Such measures could only be considered if one or several States could be found which, in virtue of their geographical position and special interests, would agree to bear the main brunt of a military encounter. Such States were not to be found among us; and, even if they had been found, the other States, before deciding on any particular degree of co-operation in serious measures, would require guarantees that similar co-operation could also be counted upon in other cases of opposing the aggressor. Such guarantees were all the more necessary because some actions and statements of one European State, whose aggressive intentions leave no room for doubt—indeed, are openly proclaimed by that State itself—indicated an accelerated rate of preparations for aggression in more than one direction. The attitude of some countries to these actions, and the lenient treatment accorded to their authors, shook the belief that those guarantees which I have just mentioned could be immediately secured. In view of these circumstances, I came to the conclusion, even during the May session of the Council of the League, that the further application of economic sanctions was useless, and that it was impossible to afford any practical aid to Ethiopia in this way. It seems that this conclusion was reached by nearly all Members of the League. . . .

I assert that Article 16 equipped the League of Nations with such powerful weapons that, in the event of their being fully applied, every aggression can be broken. Moreover, the very conviction that they may be applied may rob the aggressor of his zeal to put his criminal intentions into practice. The melancholy experience of the Italo-Ethiopian conflict does not contradict this assertion: on the contrary. In this particular case, whether because this was the first experiment in the application of collective measures; whether because some considered that this case had particular characteristics; whether because it coincided with the preparations elsewhere for aggression on a much larger scale, to which Europe had to devote special attention; whether for these or other reasons, it is a fact that, not only was the whole terrible mechanism of Article 16 not brought into play, but from the very outset there was a manifest striving to confine the action taken to the barest minimum. Even economic sanctions were limited in their scope and their function, and even in this limited scope sanctions were not applied by all Members of the League.

Four Members of the League, from the very beginning, refused to apply any sanctions whatsoever. One Member of the League bordering on Italy refused to apply the most effective sanction—namely, the prohibition of imports from Italy; while, of those countries which raised no objections in principle to sanctions, many did not in actual fact apply several of them, pleading constitutional difficulties, the necessity of 'study', etc. Thus, even the embargo on arms was not applied by seven Members of the League, financial measures by eight countries, prohibition of exports to Italy by ten countries, and prohibition of imports from Italy by thirteen countries—i.e. 25 per cent of the total membership of the League. It may be said that the Latin-American countries, with a few exceptions, did not apply in practice the more effective sanctions at all. I am not in any way making this a reproach against any one; I am simply illustrating the point I have been making. . . .

Given all these restrictions, sanctions could have been effective only in the event of their more prolonged application side by side with the military resistance of Ethiopia herself. The latter, however, was broken down much sooner than our most authoritative sources of information anticipated.

In such circumstances it may be said that Members of the League of Nations, for one reason or another, refrained from bringing Article 16 completely into play. But it does not follow from this that Article 16 itself is a failure.

Some are inclined to attribute the failure of League action to the absence from it of some countries, or its insufficiently universal character. We see, however, that not every Member of the League took part in sanctions. There is no reason to believe that sanctions would have been endorsed by those States which left the League, since they rejected the very foundations of the League, and particularly the presence of Articles 10 and 16 in the Covenant. Their membership of the League would only have facilitated the still further disorganisation of our ranks, and would have acted rather as a demoralising factor than otherwise.

V.6.D Speech by Litvinov at the Eighteenth League of Nations Assembly, 21 September 1938, on League Policy and the Czechoslovakian crisis (*L of Ns OJ*, Supplement 183, p. 75).

There are inside and outside the League two tendencies, two conceptions of how best to preserve peace. There exists an opinion that when some State announces a foreign policy based on aggression, on violation of other people's frontiers, on the violent annexation of other people's possessions, on the enslavement of other nations, on domination over entire continents, the League of Nations has not only the right, but also the duty of declaring, loudly and clearly, that it has been set up to preserve universal peace; that it will not permit the realisation of such a programme; and that it will fight that programme by every means at its disposal. Within the framework of such declarations, individual Members of the League can and must constitute special groups for the joint defence of individual sectors of the threatened peace front.

It is presumed that States which openly denounce the principles underlying the League Covenant and the Briand-Kellogg Pact, which extol aggression and ridicule international obligations, are inaccessible to persuasion and argument—save the argument of force—and that there is no room for bargaining or compromise with them. They can be restrained from carrying their evil designs into effect only by a demonstration of the force which they will encounter, should they make the attempt.

Naturally, at the least attempt to carry out aggression in practice, there should be brought into play in appropriate measure, and according to the capacities of each Member of the League, the collective action provided by Article 16 of the Covenant . . . the aggressor should be met with the programme laid down by the League Covenant, resolutely, consistently and without hesitation. Then the aggressor himself will not be led into temptation, and peace will be preserved by peaceful means. There is, however, another conception, which recommends as the height of human wisdom, under cover of imaginary pacificism, that the aggressor be treated with consideration, and his vanity be not wounded. It recommends that conversations and negotiations be carried on with him, that he be assured that no collective action will be undertaken against him, and no groups or *blocs* formed against him—even though he himself enters into aggressive *blocs* with other aggressors—that compromise agreements be concluded with him, and breaches of those very agreements overlooked; that his demands, even the most illegal, be fulfilled; that journeys be undertaken, if necessary, to receive his dictates and ultimatums; that the vital interests of one State or another be sacrificed to him; and that, if possible, no question of his activity be raised at the League of Nations—because the aggressor does not like that, takes offence, sulks. Unfortunately, this is just the policy that so far has been pursued towards the aggressors; and it has had as its consequence three wars, and threatens to bring down on us a fourth. Four nations have already been sacrificed, and a fifth is next on the list. . . .

At the moment when the mines are being laid to blow up the organisation on which were fixed the great hopes of our generation and which stamped a definite character on the international relations of our epoch; at a moment when . . decisions are being taken outside the League which recall to us the international transactions of pre-war days, and which are bound to overturn all present conceptions of international morality and treaty obligations; at a moment when there is being drawn up a further list of sacrifices to the god of aggression, and a line is being drawn under the annals of all post-war international history, with the sole conclusion that nothing succeeds like aggression—at such a moment, every State must define its role and its responsibilities before its contemporaries and before history. That is why I must plainly declare here that the Soviet Government bears no responsibility whatsoever for the events now taking place, and for the fatal consequences which may inexorably ensue.

VI

THE LEAGUE'S SOCIAL
AND HUMANITARIAN ACTIVITIES

THE LEAGUE OF NATIONS undoubtedly achieved its greatest success in the field of social and humanitarian activities. It served to co-ordinate the work of the many *ad hoc* organisations which had sprung up around the turn of the century to deal with new scientific and technological advances. League supporters in 1919 also hoped that its efforts to come to grips with such long-term international problems as control of epidemics and conditions of labour would promote human happiness and thus indirectly contribute to the preservation of international peace. While the League failed to prevent the outbreak of a major war in 1939, its efforts in the fields of health, international labour legislation, refugee settlement and international administration (in such areas as the Saar and Danzig) were invaluable, and pointed the way forward to the intensification of such international co-operation.

VI.1.A Extract from the section of the Report of the British Delegates to the Third League Assembly in 1922 dealing with the activities of the Fifth League Assembly Committee on Social and General Questions (British Government White Paper, Cmd. 1807).

Opium

The traffic in opium and other dangerous drugs was the first subject considered by the Fifth Committee, which had before it the report of the Opium Advisory Committee on its work during the past year. It was agreed to urge all Governments to adopt the system of import and export certificates for opium and its derivatives without delay, to invite the United States of America to be represented on the Opium Advisory Committee, and to ask Governments to make returns as soon as possible of the amounts of opium and similar drugs per 100,000 inhabitants estimated to be required by each country for internal consumption. . . .

Russian Refugees

A report on his work and the present position of the refugees was submitted by Dr Nansen, who emphasised the necessity of Governments giving passport facilities to refugees who had no papers to establish their identity and no money to pay for passport fees. Without passports they could not move to places where work was awaiting them. He also urged Governments, if possible, to make their Labour Exchanges available for finding employment for refugees.

Refugees from the Near East

The capture of Smyrna by the Turkish troops occurred during the course of the Assembly, and immediately gave prominence to the problem of relieving the thousands of refugees threatened with massacre or starvation in Asia Minor. The Fifth Committee recommended the grant of 100,000 fr. from the vote for 'unforeseen expenditure' in order to enable the League's machinery actually in existence at Constantinople for dealing with the Russian refugees to be used for the refugees from the Near East. . . .

Traffic in Women and Children

. . . Discussion started on the report of the League's Advisory Committee about its work of the past year which showed in detail the efforts made by the Governments to combat the traffic. Central authorities had been set up in many countries in order to exchange rapidly and directly with each other any information as the traffic which came to their knowledge. It was now proposed that these central authorities should keep in touch with the Secretariat, which would be the means of providing an international centre to receive and distribute information. Both Germany and the United States of America had been invited to sit on the Advisory Committee.

VI.1.B   The state of Austria's economic difficulties in the aftermath of the first world war was one of the earliest problems facing the League of Nations. Balfour outlined the League approach to Austria's difficulties at the Twenty-fifth Plenary Meeting of the Third Assembly, 30 September 1922 (*L of Ns OJ*, 1922).

. . . The problem which we have to face is one of very great difficulty. Two things are plain. Austria cannot get on without some pecuniary assistance from other nations, or . . . without some assistance from sources outside herself. Austria cannot get on without such assistance, and yet such assistance can never be given her, and never will be given her, as long as she is in the hopeless condition of national bankruptcy with which she is now faced.

This problem was the one that presented itself to the Council and to the Austrian Committee of the Council. We felt that there could be no loans to Austria without the reform of Austria, while at the same time there could be no reform of Austria without loans to Austria. Austria could not recover left to herself by her own efforts, and yet who was going to help her? Who was going to lend her money unless there was clear proof that she was herself going to put an end to the state of things which had brought her to her present unhappy condition?

No loans without reform; no reform without loans. Those were the two principles which we had to consider and which we had, if possible, to reconcile.

... Let me take, first, loans and then reforms. ... No one will lend to Austria unless Austria can produce not only what are called good securities for the loan but some clear prospect that the State will be henceforth governed on those sound financial principles on which alone the permanent stability of the State depends, a stability without which no wise lender is going to risk his money.

If it is clear that the private lender will not come forward in the existing condition of Austria and lend money simply upon Austrian securities, what is the remedy? There is but one remedy and that is that other nations should supply the guarantees, furnishing that basis of credit which Austria herself is incapable of supplying. ...

Four nations have each agreed that, speaking very broadly, they will take 20 per cent each of the total loan required to enable Austria to pay her way during the two years which our financial advisors tell us must elapse before an equilibrium is arrived at in the Austrian Budget....

... The four together ... may be expected to guarantee 80 per cent of the total requirements of Austria. That leaves 20 per cent undealt with. I am glad to say that we know already that some other nations are prepared to contribute towards the 20 per cent, and I have great hopes that the whole of the 20 per cent may be fully guaranteed when the nations which have money to lend, or are able to guarantee, see the whole scope and value of the plan which we propose. ...

I come now to the second—the most important, and in many respects the most novel—part of the plan that we are carrying into effect. The second part ... dealt with Austrian reforms. ... That the reforms are required no Austrian and no observer of Austrian affairs is likely for one moment to deny. Large sums have been contributed to Austria from outside during the last two disastrous years, but they have, under the existing system, no more than sufficed to enable the Austrian Government to get on somehow or another from day to day. They do not contain in themselves the smallest element of permanence; they are unable in the slightest degree to contribute to the permanent establishment of Austrian credit.

Now what are the conditions which, in our view, are required for this scheme of reform? In the first place, we are of opinion that, since it is inevitable that there shall be some external influence acting in co-operation with the Austrian Government, it shall be made quite clear, first to the Austrian people and then to the world at large, that no interested motive presides over the action of any of the guaranteeing Powers, and that we are all mutually engaged one to the other, to the League of Nations and in the face of the world at large, that no interference with Austrian sovereignty, no interference with Austrian economic or financial independence, shall be regarded as tolerable or possible under the new system. We have therefore prepared a very carefully drawn protocol which contains this declaration on the part of the great guaranteeing Powers . . . that they have no selfish ends to pursue in connection with this great effort at reform.

. . . Valuable as I regard this protocol . . . I attach even more value to the fact that it will be signed under the auspices of this League. That is the great guarantee against separate interests being allowed to prevail over international interests.

I think every Austrian citizen may rest assured that, while undoubtedly there must be, under the guidance of the League and through the machinery which is going to be provided, a control exercised over the financial policy of Austria, that can only end in benefit to his country, and that when at the end of two years Austria finds herself again a solvent nation, she will be so without having lost one shadow or title of any of that sovereignty or that supremacy over her own affairs which we all desire, and, indeed, are bound, as Members of the League of Nations, to preserve.

. . . If . . . we are successful in bringing this great work to an issue, the benefits which we shall confer upon others will not be confined to the limits of the Austrian Republic; they will spread far and wide over the whole of Europe, and, through Europe, over the world; and we shall have done something really important, really material, and really lasting to remove from ourselves the charge that we are unable to deal with the economic difficulties of the world, and to remove from the world the heavy burden which those difficulties are now inflicting upon it.

VI.1.c   Extracts from the Report by the British Delegate to the Twenty-seventh Session of the League Council, 1923, Lord Cecil (British Government White Paper, Cmd. 2018).

Austria

The Council received the Tenth and Eleventh Reports of the Commissioner-General appointed by the League, Dr Zimmerman. These reports showed that good progress had been made in every Department towards the carrying out of the programme of reforms and the balance of the budget upon which the League scheme had been founded, and in virtue of which the reconstruction loan had been raised on the foreign market. In particular, Dr Zimmerman reported that the figures for foreign trade showed a further increase in Austrian exports; that the number of unemployed had fallen to 80,000, the lowest figure registered for a long time; that the cost of living was lower than in September 1922 before the League scheme came into operation, in spite of the fact that a start had been made with the revision of house rents; that there was a considerable increase in the agricultural area under cultivation and in the crops obtained; and that Savings Bank deposits now amounted to a gold value of 32–4 million crowns, which is more than fourteen times higher than they were a year ago. . . .

Greece

It will be recalled that at its twenty-fifth session in July the Council definitely approved a scheme for raising an international loan on the money markets of the world for the settlement of refugees in Greece. This scheme involved the appointment by the Council of a Settlement Commission to whom the Greek Government were to make over a large quantity of land upon which the refugees could be settled. This land, together with the revenues which should be derived therefrom, was to be held by the Commission as the first and principal security for the loan to be raised.

. . . The Greek Government had taken all the action which was required of it in order to promote the establishment of the Settlement Commission and the consequent raising of the loan. The Greek Government had also made provisional arrangements for raising on the market the first part of the money required. The Council accordingly had appointed the Settlement Commission. . . .

At its twenty-seventh session the Council received a report that all the Members of the Commission had accepted their nomination, that the Commission had met in Athens in November, and that it was now engaged in making plans for the practical work of settlement and for utilising to the best advantage the money which had been already raised. . . .

Hungary

The Council was called upon to consider important proposals for the financial reconstruction of Hungary. The problem was in many ways similar to the problem of Austria. . . .

Minorities

The Minorities Sub-Committee of the Council held a number of meetings and considered various complaints which had been made on behalf of

Minorities, alleging the violation of their Treaty rights, which are placed under the guarantee of the League. . . .

The Sub-Committee were also asked by the Council to consider an important question concerning German Minorities in Poland, with which the Council has dealt at most of its meetings during the past two years. It concerns the expropriation of certain German settlers whose properties the Polish Government has . . . been taking over. . . .

In the discussion of these Minority questions the British representative took occasion to explain the great importance which the British Government attaches to the strict maintenance of the system of minority protection laid down by the Peace Treaties and other subsequent treaties and declarations. The system is one under which the personal and political rights of many millions of people in Europe are secured, and its strict observance is a matter which directly affects the peace of Europe as a whole.

Mandates

The Council had to consider the report of the third Session of the Permanent Mandates Commission, the duty of which, under Article 22 of the Covenant, is to receive and examine the annual reports of the Mandatory Powers and to advise the Council on all matters relating to the observance of Mandates. . . .

The Mandates Commission had received reports concerning all the mandated areas in Central Africa, South West Africa and the Pacific. It had considered these reports in great detail during a session which lasted for almost five weeks. . . .

On many different subjects, and particularly with regard to the liquor traffic, financial and economic administration, the prevalence of disease, and military recruitment, the Mandates Commission made valuable suggestions which the Council duly transmitted to the Mandatory Powers.

VI.1.D Report by the British Government delegates to the Minister of Labour, on the International Labour Conference held in May and June of 1925 (British Government White Paper, Cmd. 2465).

WORKMEN'S COMPENSATION FOR INDUSTRIAL ACCIDENTS

. . . by the provisions of the convention, States undertake to ensure that workmen who suffer personal injury due to an industrial accident or the dependents of such workmen shall be compensated on terms not less favourable than those provided in the convention. . . . No minimum scale of compensation is specified, but the convention deals with the method of payment, the waiting period in cases of incapacity and the payment of additional compensation in cases where the injured workman must have the constant help of another person. It also deals with the provision of medical aid and such surgical and pharmaceutical aid as is recognised to be necessary, and the supply and normal renewal of artificial limbs and surgical appliances. Lastly, the convention requires States to make such provision as having regard to the national circumstances they deem most suitable for ensuring in all circumstances the payment of the compensation in the event of the insolvency of the employer or insurer....

WORKMEN'S COMPENSATION FOR OCCUPATIONAL DISEASES

... by the terms of the draft convention States undertake to provide that compensation shall be payable to workmen incapacitated by occupational diseases, or in the case of death to their dependents, in accordance with the general principles of the national legislation relating to compensation for industrial accidents. It is specially provided that the rates of compensation may not be less than those prescribed in the national legislation for industrial accidents, but subject to this, each State is at liberty to apply such legislation with any adaptations and modifications it deems expedient....

GENERAL PRINCIPLES OF SOCIAL INSURANCE

... The Committee held fourteen meetings and presented a report which included the resolution . . . requesting the Governing Body of the International Labour Office to place the question of general and sickness insurance for workers on the agenda of an early session of the Conference, if possible that of 1927, and on the agenda of the same or succeeding sessions, the question of invalidity, old age, and widows' and orphans' insurance. It will be seen that the report also sets out, for the guidance of the International Labour Office certain points concerning which it should collect and distribute information in relation to social insurance.

... OTHER BUSINESS

... Some reference should perhaps be made to the debate on the Hours Convention adopted by the first Labour Conference [at Washington, 1919].

... Mr Tschoffen (Belgian Government) claimed that in Belgium the eight-hour law was applied scrupulously. Belgium intended to maintain that law and was ready to ratify the Hours convention; but it could not take such action in isolation. If the great industrial nations which were competitors of Belgium in the world's market would adopt a similar attitude, there would be no further need for a debate on the question of ratification.

Mr Betterton, speaking on behalf of the British Government, referred to the difficulties in the way of ratification with which Great Britain was confronted. . . . He pointed out that in Great Britain the principle of the forty-eight-hour week had long ago been recognised and that the Government viewed with concern the possibility of a retrograde movement on the part of the chief industrial powers towards longer hours of labour. They intended thoroughly to explore every means of avoiding a movement of this kind and were prepared to enter into consultation with this end in view. . . .

Dr Reig (German Government) said that the German Ministry of Labour was at present engaged in examining the final effects of a Bill regulating hours of work and everything was being done to draft provisions which would be in conformity with those of the Washington convention. . . .

Mr Pfister (Swiss Government) referred to the fact that the ratifications of the Hours convention by Austria and Italy had been made conditional on its ratification by certain other named countries including Switzerland. In these circumstances, Mr Pfister thought it necessary to point out that though Switzerland had a law providing for a forty-eight-hour week in industry, this law did not cover small industrial undertakings or the railways. Any attempt to bring small undertakings—especially those in the country—under the Act would meet with the opposition of the majority not only in Parliament but among the people. Switzerland believed that international conventions when ratified should be strictly observed and for the reasons which he had given it had so far been impossible for Switzerland to ratify the eight-hour convention.

M. Durafour (French Government) referred to the possibility of the meeting of certain industrial powers which had not yet ratified the convention with a view to arriving at an agreement as to simultaneous ratification. . . .

The Government, employers' and workers' delegates of India all took part in the discussion and referred particularly to the disadvantageous position in which India found herself owing to the failure of Japan to ratify the convention. . . .

In the course of the debate on the Director's report, certain speakers referred to the alleged absence of freedom of association for workers in certain countries. As in previous years there were complaints by workers' representatives that ratification of a convention did not necessarily mean that the law of the ratifying country was adapted and administered to give effect to its terms. . . .

VII

EPILOGUE: THE LEAGUE IS DEAD LONG LIVE THE UNITED NATIONS!

DESPITE THE OUTBREAK of the second world war, the allies in that war were determined to lay the foundations for a successor organisation to the League which would help to re-establish international harmony after the conclusion of the war. The 1939 Bruce Report had already foreshadowed ways in which the League's social and economic activities could be expanded, and it became the blueprint for United Nations organisation in these fields. The organisation and scope of the United Nations' political activities were based on what were perceived to be both the strong points and shortcomings of League experience, and were cast in the same mould. The necessity for inter-state co-operation to power the new international organisation was a basic characteristic inherited from the League. In most respects, indeed, the United Nations was the recognisable offspring of League experience.

VII.1.A Extracts from the Report of the Bruce Committee set up at the suggestion of the Secretary-General in 1939 to study and report to the League Assembly on the appropriate measures of organisation which would ensure the development and expansion of the League's machinery for dealing with technical problems.

The experience of the last twenty years has shown the growing extent to which the progress of civilisation is dependent upon economic and human values. State policies are determined in increasing measure by such social and economic aims as the prevention of unemployment, the prevention of wide fluctuations in economic activity, the provision of better housing, the suppression and cure of disease. These matters, which affect the daily lives of every man, woman and child, are among the principal pre-occupations of statesmen and politicians in all countries, whatever their political structure.

Modern experience has also shown with increasing clearness that none of these problems can be entirely solved by purely national action. The need for the interchange of experience and the co-ordination of action between national authorities has been proved useful and necessary time after time in every section of the economic and social fields. To meet this need, the League has built up a mechanism of international co-operation, which is rendering invaluable service to the world as a whole.

The League is not and never has been an institution concerned solely with the prevention of war. Its economic and humanitarian work, which is now an essential element in the promotion of peaceful civilisation, has always constituted a large part of its activities. . . . From that work every nation has benefited, whether a Member of the League or not, and to that work, officially or unofficially, non-member States or their nationals have largely contributed.

There has never been a time when international action for the promotion of economic and social welfare was more vitally necessary than it is at the present moment. The work of the League in these fields has developed and changed its nature in recent years, and the changes that have taken place necessitate, as we see it, a careful consideration of the means by which the mechanism of international collaboration can be rendered at once more efficient and more easily available to all.

There are two tendencies in the world today which render the need for Governmental co-operation in economic and social questions more urgent than heretofore, and at the same time give greater opportunities for the success of such co-operation.

The world, for all its political severance, is growing daily closer knit; its means of communication daily more rapid; its instruments for the spread of knowledge daily more efficient. At the same time, the constituent parts of the world, for all their diversity of political outlook, are growing in many respects more similar; agricultural States are becoming rapidly industrialised, industrial States are stimulating their agriculture. Nothing is more striking in this connection, or more characteristic, than the swift industrial development of the great Asiatic countries.

These changes inevitably give rise to new problems that can only be solved by joint effort. Thus, trade and personal contacts are facilitated, but simultaneously economic depressions become more widespread; and, were there any relaxation of control, human and animal diseases would spread more widely and more rapidly. Neither the economic nor the physical contagion—nor, indeed, the moral—can be checked by national action alone, except by recourse to almost complete isolation. . . . The fact that the form of economic structure in all countries is tending to become more similar means at once that the problems with which all Governments are faced also acquire greater similarity, and that the opportunities of each country to gain from the experience of others are increased. Countries of the world today are, on account of the rapidity of the changes to which we have alluded, in greater need than before of the aid which can be afforded by others, and are more capable of rendering that aid. It is only by joint discussion of the nature of the new problems which these changes present, by exchange of experience, and by co-ordination of national policies, that the adaptations essential to progress can be effected.

The growing similarity in the structure of the various countries and in the difficulties for which they must find solutions, is calculated to induce Governments to pool their experiences and thus enable them to help one another. All are concerned with the maintenance and the improvement of the economic welfare of their citizens—with their nutrition, housing and health conditions. And all these questions are subject to scientific treatment. What is required therefore, and what is being accomplished, is a joint and intensive study of those common problems on which the security of all nations and all classes of the population depends.

There are other reasons of a worldwide character which emphasise the necessity for a rapid development and expansion of the League's work in these fields.

It is by international discussion, and by the association in the work of independent experts, that Governments can best safeguard themselves against the danger of being pressed by one sectional interest or another to assist it at the expense of the general well-being.

Again, there is a continual growth in the material and intellectual demands which men make on life. Owing to the Press, and still more, the radio and the cinema, men and women all over the world are becoming keenly aware of the wide gap between the actual and the potential conditions of their lives. They know that, by a better use of the scientific and productive resources of the world, those conditions could be improved out of all knowledge; and they are impatient to hear that some real and concerted effort is being made to raise the standard of their lives nearer to what it might become.

Similarly, some countries feel that the standard of their economic well-being is below what it might be and what other countries with similar natural conditions have attained. It is only by international discussion and co-operation that these differences, where they exist, can be overcome, or, where they are rather imagined than real, can be appreciated in their true light; and it is essential to ensure that the machinery of the League is ready to promote such discussion and co-operation wherever the conditions make it possible. . . .

The League's resources enable it in the most economical possible way:
   (a) to collect and sift evidence drawn from all over the world;
   (b) to obtain the services of the best experts in the world working without reward for the good of the cause;
   (c) to arrange meetings between experts working in the same fields,

enabling them to discuss their pre-occupations, their successes, their failures;

(d) to provide the essential links between the experts and those responsible for policy;

(e) to provide constant and automatic opportunities for statesmen to meet and discuss their policy;

(f) to provide thereby means for better understanding of the aims and policies of different nations;

(g) to provide machinery for the conclusion of international conventions.

Finally, and perhaps most important of all, Governments which desire expert advice or help can get this, not from outside or as a favour, but from an institution which they themselves maintain and on whose services they have a right to call.

. . . the time has come when the Assembly should undertake a revision of the existing organisation of its economic and social work, in order to cope more effectively with the great developments which have taken place since 1920. . . .

In making the proposal which follows, our first aim has been to increase the efficiency of the work as a whole, and in particular:

1. To bring all this part of the work of the League under the supervision of an agency which should be both effective and representative;

2. To meet the fact that the development in the nature of the work results in a growing inter-connection between the activities of the different organisations, and that therefore a co-ordinating direction is more and more required.

3. To add fresh efficiency and vigour to the work itself, a result which may naturally be expected to follow if public knowledge in regard to it can be increased and if it becomes the primary interest of the directing organs. . . .

4. To give States not members of the League the opportunity of the fullest possible co-operation in the work itself as well as in its direction and supervision.

We suggest, therefore, that the Assembly should set up a new organism, to be known as the Central Committee for Economic and Social Questions, to which should be entrusted the direction and supervision of the work of the League Committees dealing with economic and social questions. . . .

VII.1.B Speech made by Lord Cecil at the final session of the League
          Assembly, 9 April 1946 (*L of Ns OJ*, 1946).

. . . It is common nowadays to speak of the failure of the League. Is it true that all our efforts for those twenty years have been thrown away? . . . The work of the League is purely and unmistakably printed on the social, economic and humanitarian life of the world. But above all that, a great advance was made in the international organisation of peace. There was indeed nothing new in the idea; for ages past at the conclusion of great wars men had asked whether something could not be done to stop the senseless slaughter of men and the destruction of their works, because one State had quarrelled with another. But nothing practical was accomplished. . . . At last, by the Covenant, a definite scheme was set up. It was not, indeed, a full-fledged federation of the world—far from it—but it was more than the pious aspiration for peace embodied in those partial alliances which had closed many great struggles. For the first time an organisation was constructed, in essence universal, not to protect the national interest of this or that country . . . but to abolish war. We saw a new world centre, imperfect materially, but enshrining great hopes, an Assembly representing some fifty peace-loving nations, a Council, an international civil service, a World Court of International Justice, so often before planned but never created, an International Labour Office to promote better conditions for the workers. And very soon there followed that great apparatus of committees and conferences striving for an improved civilisation, better international co-operation, a larger redress of grievances and the protection of the helpless and oppressed.

Truly this was a splendid programme, the very conception of which was worth all the efforts which it cost . . . but, as we know, it failed in the essential condition of its existence—namely, the preservation of peace—and so, rightly or wrongly, it has been decided to bury it and start afresh. That does not mean that the work of twenty years goes for nothing, far from it. All the main ideas I have briefly sketched . . . remain. True, there is a new organisation: it is founded on a Charter and not on a Covenant. The Charter contains various provisions and in one respect it is certainly an improvement. It recognises more clearly than did the Covenant that, in the last resort, peace must be enforced. That . . . was no doubt implicit in the League. . . . However, in the condition of public opinion when the League was founded, this was necessarily kept in the background. It is only right to recognise that the French representatives from the earliest times never ceased to urge greater clearness and definiteness in this. And now their opinions have prevailed and the negotiators of San Francisco used much ingenuity to provide for greater force to resist and crush aggression. They have given to the five Great Powers special rights and, more important, special responsibilities in this respect. . . . It is true that the support of the Great Powers is essential to peace and it is no less true that there can be no formidable war unless a Great Power takes part in it.

. . . But for the great experiment of the League, the United Nations could never have come into existence. The fundamental principles of

the Charter and the Covenant are the same and it is gratifying to some
of us that, after the violent controversies that have raged for the last
quarter of a century, it is now generally accepted that peace can be
secured only by international co-operation, broadly on the lines agreed
to in 1920.

Why, then, did it fail? . . . its failure was not due to any weakness in
the terms of the Covenant. To my mind it is plain beyond the possibility
of doubt that it failed solely because the Member States did not
genuinely accept the obligation to use and support its provisions. That
was due to several causes. Speaking of my own country, I must admit
that the general current of official opinion was either neutral or hostile.
I suspect that was also true in other countries. There were other causes,
but that alone was enough to prevent success. It was not so much that
the principles of the League were rejected. Few people hated it. Most
people desired peace. But Governments seemed to think that all they
need do was to give a general and somewhat tepid approval to its work
and, if that was not enough, it did not very much matter. . . . Inter-war
opinion greatly underrated both the danger of the international situation
and the difficulty of applying efficient remedies.

I wonder if that is sufficiently realised even now . . . the old view that
national safety depends on national preparation seems still very powerful, in spite of our experience of the results of the two wars and the
certainty that scientific discoveries, atomic and other, will make any
future wars infinitely more disastrous than those we have endured.

Believe me, there is no safety except in peace, and peace cannot be
maintained merely and solely by national armaments, however necessary
they may be, by each nation seeking safety for itself. Let us, then boldly
state that aggression . . . is an international crime, that it is the duty of
every peace-loving State to resist it, and to employ whatever force may
be necessary to crush it, that the machinery of the Charter, no less than
of the Covenant, is sufficient for this purpose if it is properly used, and
that every well-disposed citizen of every State should be ready to undergo any sacrifice in order to maintain peace.

. . . The League is dead: Long live the United Nations!

VII.1.c Speeech by M. Paul-Boncour, of France, at the last League
       Assembly, 10 April 1946 (*L of Ns OJ*: Assembly Records, 1946).

. . . It is not the League which has failed. It is not its principles which
have been found wanting. It is the nations which have neglected it. It is
the Governments which have abandoned it.

. . . The League of Nations was not a deceit. It lived vividly in the
heart and spirit of countless multitudes. It laboured. It leaves behind it
lasting works. Some fully succeeded and the new Organisation will
merely have to carry them on. This applies to its efforts in the field of

intellectual co-operation, public health, transit, social questions and rural life. It was closely associated with the work of Nansen on behalf of refugees. It took a leading part in those great migrations between Greece and Turkey which took place in all directions. Finally, it played a decisive role in the financial and monetary reconstruction of countries ravaged by the first world war....

Other works did not succeed. But the materials are there and the new Organisation will be able to use them for the necessary constructive tasks which it will have to undertake. This applies to disarmament. The new Organisation will . . . be very happy to find the records of our efforts and to consult our archives on the inevitable day when it is compelled to grapple once again with that problem. For the international armed force which is the great innovation, the most definite gain of the Charter of the United Nations, will remain a deceit unless there is a general and controlled reduction of armaments so that no State can retain forces capable of holding in check international force.

. . . Our balance sheet does not show only losses. I spoke to you just now about the positive achievements and successes of the League of Nations in matters of more or less incidental character; but in the essential task of maintaining peace it succeeded during a number of years. It succeeded as long as Governments, and particularly the Governments of the Great Powers, put their faith in it and animated and fortified it by their will and as long as the possibility could always be more or less perceived in the background that their force would be put at the service of its decisions.

During a number of years, in the period following the peace treaties, when Europe, disorganised by the war, was seeking to achieve consistence and to establish her frontiers, the League of Nations settled various grave disputes: Memel, the Aaland Islands, Upper Silesia and the dispute between Greece and Bulgaria—all of them involving areas which might have become battlefields if the League of Nations had not settled the disputes in their initial stages. It is, indeed, the very success which it achieved that caused the disputes to be minimised and that makes us forget all that it accomplished in this connection.

For years it prevented the dispute between Poland and Lithuania from degenerating into war; for years it prevented Germany from seizing Danzig, which was always coveted by her but whose independence was essential to the free access of Poland to the sea; for years it prevented Balkan rivalries from degenerating into war in connection with Albania, the Dobrudja and all those problems constantly surging up in countries where the constant racial alluvium has sometimes made frontiers uncertain.

No, no. Our balance sheet does not show only losses. It showed a deficit on the day when, imperialism having again broken loose in the

world . . . there were offered as the first victim to the myth of appeasement those precepts of the Covenant the application of which would . . .
have been the essential condition of a peace honourable for all.

I refer to the case of Manchuria. The League of Nations did nothing
but utter verbal protests against the action of Japan in attacking an
ancient country with a civilisation much older than ours. . . .

Manchuria was far off. Ethiopia, and still more Italy, was nearer. In
that case sanctions—or at any rate economic sanctions—were decided
on, but . . . they were slow-motion sanctions, imposed by driblets. We
recoiled before the only two sanctions which would have been effective
—the cutting-off of oil supplies and the closing of the Suez Canal. We
did enough to irritate Italy and to embarrass her, but not enough to
prevent her from accomplishing her conquest.

Then came the massive rearmament of Germany in 1935. Alas! The
nations concerned did no more than refer the dispute to the League of
Nations under the most lenient article of the Covenant, Article 11,
which gave the friendly right to call attention to situations likely to
engender international difficulties.

Then there was the re-occupation of the Rhineland. . . .

Then there was Albania, seized by Fascist Italy one Easter morning,
and then Austria, seized by Germany during a ministerial crisis in
France. Not only did the League of Nations remain inert, but, in
September 1938, its first Committee took the decision to strike Austria
off the list of nations adhering to the League.

The powerlessness of this Organisation to protect States which were
victims of aggression became so evident that in the two last great acts
of the drama—of which one, the abandonment of Czechoslovakia at
Munich, paved the way for the catastrophe and the other, the invasion
of Poland by Germany, unleashed it—the victims themselves did not
think of appealing to the League of Nations.

My dear colleagues, if I draw this sombre picture, it is not to engage
in vain recriminations over the past, still less to make my *mea culpa* at
the cost of others. I do not forget that certain French Governments
had their share in these backslidings. It is, on the contrary, to emphasise
my hope that the realisation of these errors and the determination to
repair them which finds expression in the Charter of the United Nations
will in the future preserve us from such mistakes. . . .

VII.1.D Speech by M. Beelaerts van Blokland (Holland) at last session of
        League Assembly, 10 April 1946.

. . . If we ask ourselves what were the causes of . . . failure, there are
three which in my opinion should be regarded as fundamental.

First of all, there was the lack of universality. That was one of the
defects which largely contributed to the League's failure. The absence

of one of the Great Powers, whose then President has rightly been described as the founder of the League of Nations, from the outset hampered the activities of the institution and handicapped its development, depriving it of that self-confidence which was so necessary in the solution of the grave problems with which the young organisation was confronted.

Secondly, I would mention as a defect in organisation the exaggerated equality between great and small Powers. In connection with the maintainance of peace and international security, the Great Powers were not given a position corresponding to their greater material means and the greater responsibilities devolving upon them. That, however, was not due to a defect in the Covenant. The authors of the Covenant fully realised the dangers of an exaggerated equalisation, as is shown by the composition of the Council in its original form. But the Members themselves, successive Assemblies, in short Governments, by repeatedly increasing the number of non-permanent Members of the Council distorted that body and prevented it from playing the political part assigned to it by the Covenant.

Lastly, I would indicate as one of the principal defects of the League of Nations the lack of solidarity among its Members. Any international organisation is bound to fail if it is not sustained by a common spirit, a common ideology and mutual confidence between the parties composing it . . . we can only pray God that this may show itself in the new Organisation with much greater force than in the League.

FINAL COMMENTS

THE DOCUMENTS IN this volume have illustrated the many facets of League activity and have revealed the complexities of the organisation. How best can the achievements of the League be measured and its failures analysed? Since the League was equipped to play many different roles, a meaningful assessment of its record can only be arrived at by examining its performance in each role.

As an international body meeting at regular intervals, with its own permanent secretariat and headquarters, the League was a qualified success. In its early years it was somewhat overshadowed by inter-allied conferences at such places as Genoa and Cannes, and by organisations such as the Conference of Ambassadors and the Inter-Allied Commission of Control,[1] but by the mid-1920s it was at the centre of international activity, drawing powerful non-members like the United States and Russia into its orbit. Between 1926 and 1929, the presence at League meetings of the British, French and German foreign secretaries, Chamberlain, Briand and Stresemann respectively, and their desire to use the League machinery to smooth out differences and secure friendly relations between their countries, made Geneva the focus of diplomatic activity. However, the slump of 1929 cast a dark shadow over the League, which was lengthened by the Manchurian crisis of 1931. Caught in severe economic and political cross-currents, nations cast about for well-worn national precedents to guide their policies instead of looking to Geneva to the possibility of internationally concerted action. The arrival of Hitler to the pinnacle of power in Germany worsened the situation for the League. It was in his interest to weaken any existing international body which could conceivably check his expansionist designs, and he did not find it difficult to undermine members' faith in the League's disarmament machinery at the League Disarmament Conference of 1931–3. Mussolini completed the destruction of the League by exposing the inadequacies of the League as a peace-keeping body, and after the conquest of Abyssinia and Hitler's re-occupation of the Rhineland, Geneva ceased to count as an international centre of any importance.

[1] The Inter-Allied Commission of Control was a body set up by the allies after the war to supervise the disarmament of Germany and ensure that German armament levels conformed to the limits laid down in the Versailles peace treaty.

Austria was struck off the list of League members in 1938 after its forcible incorporation into the German Reich and Czechoslovakia did not even bother to appeal to the League for assistance against Hitler. She turned instead to Britain and France, the League's leading members, who by this time were carrying out their policies as if the League no longer existed.

Three or four good years, and treble that number of bad ones does not seem to be a striking testimony to the success of the League as an institutionalised international conference. Yet in this role the League undertook some important tasks which it discharged efficiently and impartially. It administered two potential trouble-spots, the Saar until 1935 and Danzig until 1939 with some degree of success, and undertook the division of Upper Silesia in 1922 after Britain and France had failed to agree on an acceptable formula. It supervised mandates and minority provisions, not as effectively as many would have wished, but with more benefit to the subject peoples than they would have gained in the absence of the League. It built up an international secretariat without precedent in its cosmopolitan composition, efficiency and ability to work together for the common good, whose expertise was drawn on in all sorts of diverse ways in different fields of international activity between the wars. The fact that the allies in the second world war were determined to establish a successor to the League shows that they felt it had performed a more than useful function as an international meeting place.

What of the League as a guarantee scheme for members' territorial integrity and political independence? We have already seen, from our examination of this scheme in the introduction, that because of the way it was worded, the scheme was a non-starter. In this role the League was a complete failure, but the concept as it stood was unworkable, particularly in the turbulent aftermath of the first world war. Britain and her Dominions, especially Canada, were determined to thwart this side of the League's activities and found no difficulty in doing so. Instead they tried to promote the League as an agency through which international change could be peacefully regulated as international conditions fluctuated. But France and her eastern allies, who saw this side of the League's activities as a means of rehabilitating Germany at their expense, set their faces firmly against any such League initiative, and were able to prevent the League from functioning successfully in the sphere of peaceful change. This was not due in any way to a deficiency in the League's constitution or machinery, apart from the unanimity provision, but was the result of embittered Anglo-French relations. Had the membership of the League been more inclusive and had France received the assurances of support she sought in the early 1920s, the League might well have been allowed to regulate international change and might have pioneered a course of immense importance for international peace and stability.

However, the League was more successful in another field of preventive action. Its members were empowered to bring any issues which were felt to be endangering the peace of the world before the League for investigation and settlement by the relevant League bodies. This mechanism was widely employed by League members throughout the existence of the League. Britain used it to bring about the settlement of the Aland Islands dispute between Sweden and Finland in 1920,[2] and it was employed to bring to the League Council the question of the ownership of Vilna, hotly contested between Poland and Lithuania. On this occasion the League Council was unable to work out an acceptable compromise, but it was more successful over the Mosul area, claimed by both Turkey and Britain's mandate Iraq, and awarded to the latter by the League. Briand invoked this article to bring to the notice of the League the invasion of Greece by Bulgarian troops in 1925, a crisis which the League was able to resolve speedily and satisfactorily.[3] Both China in 1931 and Abyssinia in 1935 made their first appeals to the League under this head before going on to invoke Article 15 at a later date. The reason why the article was so popular was that it was flexible in operation and did not involve any threat of sanctions. It gave the various League bodies room for manoeuvre without tying them down to any specific modes of settlement.

When contentious issues were raised before they became acute, the League was often able to suggest acceptable solutions and see them implemented as in the case of the Aland Islands and the Mosul dispute. However, in cases where disputes had already reached the stage of armed conflict, the League was not very successful in imposing its will on the combatants, with a few notable exceptions. It was able in many cases to bring about a cessation of hostilities but was not equipped with enough powers to force the stronger party when in the wrong to withdraw, and redress the wrongs done to the weaker party. In the Corfu dispute of 1923, the force of League Assembly opposition to Mussolini's occupation of Corfu was undoubtedly a major factor in inducing Mussolini to evacuate the island, but not before he had secured an enormous Greek indemnity for the alleged crime committed against an innocent Italian official.[4] In the Manchurian affair, the League was able to order the cessation of hostilities between Japan and China, but was powerless to remove Japanese troops from Manchuria or to enforce the Lytton Commission proposals in East Asia. Only a combined Anglo-American naval blockade would have been effective, and the likelihood

[2] See James Barros, *The Aland Islands Question.*
[3] See James Barros, *The League of Nations and the Great Powers.*
[4] See James Barros, *The Corfu Incident of 1923.*

of its formation was remote. In the Abyssinian dispute, the threat of forceful action by League members was employed but without enthusiasm or serious intent on the part of its leading members. Why was the League not more successful in settling disputes which had already broken out? It was not equipped with its own forces, as the French had wished, and was not empowered to call upon members' armed forces to carry out its decisions. It could advise members on what actions to take, but had no authority to enforce its suggestions. When two or more powerful League members agreed on a course of action, as in the Greek-Bulgarian dispute of 1925, they could force less powerful members to follow suit and help them to settle the crisis along certain lines.[5] But if major powers disagreed over how best to deal with a dispute, as Britain and France invariably did, their disagreement could, and frequently did, paralyse the League. In the Polish-Lithuanian dispute over Vilna, the French delegates deliberately immobilised the League while their ally Poland, the stronger party in the dispute, consolidated its position. In the Manchurian incident, France made it clear that she was unwilling to participate in any major League initiatives outside Europe. In the Corfu and Abyssinian crises, France was reluctant to alienate Mussolini, while Britain was more prepared to call his bluff. It was not surprising that the record of the League in the field of peaceful settlement was rather dismal. Had Britain and France been able to resolve their differences, the story might well have been different, but once again friction between the leading members of the League undermined its authority.

The same lack of co-operation can be seen in the field of disarmament, though here other difficulties of a technical nature also intruded. France was unwilling to reduce her armaments unless she secured a cast-iron guarantee of speedy assistance against external aggression; Britain, while favouring armament limitation on economic grounds, was not willing to pay the price for French co-operation. In Eastern Europe, Poland and Czechoslovakia feared attack from east and west and refused to co-operate in schemes of disarmament unless and until the League machinery for combatting aggression was strengthened. Though the League was specifically charged with the task of effecting a reduction of members' armaments, it was not until 1926 that a Preparatory Commission was set up to work out a draft convention for disarmament. Meanwhile, those members of the League who, because of economic difficulties or moral attitudes, wished to reduce their levels of armaments went ahead and did so unilaterally or through bi-lateral agreements with other countries. Denmark undertook a drastic reduction of her armed forces in the early 1920s, and Britain cut down the size of her army and reduced her cruiser and battleship strength in negotiations

[5] See James Barros, *The League of Nations and the Great Powers.*

with the United States and Japan at Washington in 1922 and at London in 1930.[6]

With the onset of the great depression, League members were no nearer to agreement on what sort of disarmament scheme to operate or whether to operate a scheme at all. British statesmen argued that if League members did not disarm, Germany, forcibly disarmed by the terms of the Treaty of Versailles, should be allowed to rearm. French leaders protested that the German authorities had not abided by the Versailles restrictions but had encouraged large-scale evasion of the treaty provisions, with the help of Russia. They pointed to Russo-German collaboration in the Preparatory Commission for Disarmament, and said that France could not possibly reduce her armed strength until Germany gave more positive proofs of her good will and intention to abide by the 1919 peace settlement. Thus the League Disarmament Conference, convened twelve years after the establishment of the League, was threatened with failure from the start, even before the appearance of Hitler in 1933.

Yet the League's total failure as a disarmament agency was not due solely to its members' intransigence and short-sightedness. There were genuine difficulties to resolve and technical problems of great magnitude to face. What proof could there be that a member nation was adhering to the armament levels laid down by the League? No League member was prepared to allow League investigators to inspect their armament factories and military establishments, so what evidence would there be of members' good faith? How far could League members disarm and still be able to provide forces for League peace-keeping operations? And how were countries with large navies and small armies to be combined in one scheme with countries possessing large armies and negligible navies? How could a battleship be equated with a battalion, and what constituted the armed strength of a country—its actual fighting forces and military installations, or its overall manpower and mineral resources which could be converted to military use in times of crisis? These were the sort of questions debated endlessly at Geneva, that are with us still. Today, when the dangers of stockpiling weapons are enormously greater than they were fifty years ago, and when the need for armament control is more urgent, agreement over armament limitation is progressing painfully slowly. It is hardly surprising, then, that the League's achievements in the field of disarmament were so negligible. Certainly statesmen were, and still are, pitifully short-sighted. But since states exist primarily to secure the safety and well-being of their citizens, statesmen are bound to find it extremely difficult to place international obligations above more tangible national needs, especially when they feel that such obligations may endanger national security.

[1] See Rolland Chaput, *Disarmament in British Foreign Policy*.

Not surprisingly the League's achievements were greatest in the fields in which the benefits to its members were most immediately apparent. In the combating of infectious diseases, co-ordination of relief operations and drawing-up of agreed codes of practice for the employment of labour, the League improved old procedures and pioneered new ones. It was active in promoting co-operation between its members over a wide area of humanitarian and scientific activities, as well as in initiating its own investigations and inquiries. Its work with refugees, its rehabilitation of Austria and Hungary and its efforts to combat slavery, drug-smuggling and disease, while not spectacular, were of enormous benefit to millions of people. So successful was the League in this sphere of its activities that an expansion of its social and economic functions was advocated by a League committee in 1939. The Social and Economic Council of the United Nations was modelled on the machinery suggested by the Bruce Committee just before the second world war.

So to label the League a failure is to simplify an extremely complex issue. Certainly the League failed to guarantee the territorial integrity and political independence of its members, failed to promote an internationally-agreed disarmament scheme, and failed to stop a major war from breaking out in Asia in 1937 and in Europe in 1939. Yet it prevented some disputes from breaking out, settled others that had erupted into armed conflict, and carried out humanitarian activities and scientific investigations of great international importance.

Would the League have been more successful if the United States had been a member? The answer to this question has invariably been an unequivocal 'yes'. Certainly the presence of the United States within the League organisation would have given France a feeling of greater security and might have facilitated French co-operation in such League activities as treaty revision and disarmament which she discouraged as much as possible in the absence of the United States. Attempts to strengthen the League machinery would have been unnecessary. Britain might have been more prepared to co-operate with France in peace enforcement procedures, and an American presence at Geneva might have encouraged Britain and France to work out a concerted policy towards Germany and to admit her to the League before 1926. On the other hand, American participation in the League's activities might have had a less desirable outcome. The reluctance of American leaders to commit their country to war with a European state would undoubtedly have hampered League attempts to deal with an aggressor; in the Manchurian incident, American statesmen were adamant that no sanctions should be employed against Japan apart from the force of international public opinion, and in the Abyssinian affair, America might well have discouraged the use of sanctions against Mussolini had she been in the League, especially if a Presidential election had been pending.

Furthermore, had the United States been a member of the League, its constitution with its delicate balance between President and Congress could well have had a serious effect on the working of the League. Austen Chamberlain, in a letter to Lord Stonehaven in 1926, commented that before he went to Geneva he considered the absence of the United States from the League as its greatest danger, and their entry as the greatest object to be sought. But after his experience at Geneva he wondered how the League could include in its number a United States representative who could not bind his country to observe any particular decision. He pointed out that in America the executive often had no majority in Parliament and the participation of a member in the work of the League Council who could not on a critical occasion give a decision on behalf of his Government because the views of that Government were not binding unless approved by the Senate might well bring the whole proceedings of the Council to nullity and destroy the usefulness and influence of the League.[7] By the end of 1926 he felt that 'it is better for them and us that in their present state they should not join the League'. So it is by no means certain that the League would have functioned more effectively with American participation.

The same is true of Russian and German membership. Their participation in League activities from the date of its establishment would probably have been beneficial in the long run, but might have resulted in a Russo-German attempt to undermine the working of the League. The two countries, after all, worked closely together during the Geneva disarmament negotiations, not always conspicuously in the cause of a successful League disarmament programme. Thus the absence of leading world Powers from Geneva was not necessarily the major cause of League weakness. More important was undoubtedly the national egotism which drove leaders to place the objectives of their own country above the interests of the developing world community.

Members tried to tailor the functions of the League to fit their own particular requirements. France wanted to use the League solely as a protective mechanism in the event of German aggression, and tried to harness the League's activities to this end. Germany desired to use the League as a platform for airing grievances and as a means of getting them redressed. Britain aimed to use the League to stabilise international relations and facilitate the peaceful settlement of disputes in order to preserve intact with as little effort as possible her far-flung empire, and to encourage the revival of world trade. When the Russian Government branded the League in the 1920s as an instrument of repression directed at upholding the exalted position of the victorious allies and holding

[7] FO 800/259.

down the defeated nations, and at leading a crusade of capitalism against the socialist workers of Russia, they could not have been further from the truth. It is true that the French wanted to keep the Germans weak by any means possible, and were allied to eastern European countries who regarded Bolshevik Russia as one of their foremost enemies, and it is equally true that some British Governments of the inter-war years were anti-Bolshevik, but it was highly improbable that League members would agree on a concerted anti-Russian crusade or on a combined effort to uphold the *status quo*. France and Poland might have favoured these courses of action, but Britain, the Scandinavian countries, and Germany from 1926, were quite able and willing to thwart them and push other lines of action. In the 1930s, when the Russian Government joined the League and tried to organise it into an anti-Hitler alliance, Litvinov, their representative at Geneva, discovered just how difficult it was to orientate the League in any one direction, with so many members trying to pursue different objectives through the League.

Yet at the same time, the League was able to exploit the self-interest of its members to a certain extent. In the strong glare of Geneva publicity, nations were cautious about putting themselves too openly in the wrong, and tried to be seen to be acting in a reasonable and law-abiding way. League mechanisms served to maximise members' desire for inter-state co-operation and collaboration, and constant close contact with their counterparts from other nations encouraged statesmen to make concessions and friendly gestures. Foreign Office League of Nations files of the early 1920s are full of instances of Balfour exceeeding his instructions at Geneva, and coming to an accommodation on various matters with French and other delegates, much to the annoyance of Foreign Office officials who felt that he was jeopardising Britain's interests. When called to task on his return, Balfour invariably justified his action on the grounds that other delegates were making concessions and generous gestures, and he was reluctant to stand in the way of agreement on important issues and put Britain in a bad light. Austen Chamberlain, during his spell of duty as Britain's representative at Geneva, testified to the spirit of friendship and amity at Geneva which facilitated agreement and compromise amongst member nations.

Unfortunately the famous 'Geneva spirit' was not strong enough to overcome nations' deepest prejudices and what were considered to be essential interests, especially in time of depression and crisis. Only a handful of idealists believed that the basic interest of every League member was to build up a strong world community of states, and that national objectives must be subordinated to that overriding necessity. Statesmen, who prided themselves on being realists, stressed the need to construct a world order very cautiously from the bricks of national strength and self-sufficiency, their traditional touchstones. They were not prepared to take risks or make short-term sacrifices for intangible long-term benefits.

Yet even this limited vision could be harnessed to the cause of international understanding. There were times when the Geneva atmosphere and the conviction or sincerity of fellow delegates encouraged statesmen to swallow their doubts and be persuaded to be more daring than they had intended. It would be interesting to have detailed studies of the circumstances in which mutual concessions facilitated international agreement and of the reasons why, in some crises, statesmen refused to venture beyond certain defined national standpoints. With the source material now available, it should be possible to document in depth the factors which shaped League members' attitudes and policies in the various crises which the League tried to resolve. As yet, we have no satisfactory study of the Manchurian and Abyssinian conflicts,[8] let alone of less contentious issues like the ownership of Mosul, Memel and Vilna. And before we have a definitive study of the League, it will be necessary to trace the considerations which underlay the policies of Britain, France, Italy, Germany and other leading League members towards the League, and the extent to which they co-operated in such League activities as disarmament, the supervision of mandates and minorities, and the promotion of economic and financial accord. Such detailed investigations will not only add a much-neglected extra dimension to inter-war international history but will also furnish valuable insights into the possibilities and limitations of international bodies organised on a similar basis to the League of Nations.

   [8] Since writing this, a thorough study of the Manchurian dispute, utilising all the available documentary material, has been published. See Thorne, Christopher: *The Limits of Foreign Policy: The League, the West and the Far Eastern Crisis of 1931–33*

APPENDIX I

THE COVENANT OF
THE LEAGUE OF NATIONS

THE HIGH CONTRACTING PARTIES
In order to promote international co-operation and to achieve international peace and security:
   by the acceptance of obligations not to resort to war;
   by the prescription of open, just and honourable relations between nations;
   by the firm establishment of the understandings of international law as the actual rule of conduct among Governments;
   and by the maintenance of justice and a scrupulous respect for all treaty obligations in the dealings of organised peoples with one another.
Agree to this Covenant of the League of Nations.

Article 1

1. The original Members of the League of Nations shall be those of the Signatories which are named in the Annex to this Covenant and also such of those other States named in the Annex as shall accede without reservation to this Covenant. . . .

2. Any fully self-governing State, Dominion or Colony not named in the Annex may become a Member of the League if its admission is agreed to by two-thirds of the Assembly, provided that it shall give effective guarantees of its sincere intention to observe its international obligations, and shall accept such regulations as may be prescribed by the League in regard to its military, naval and air forces and armaments.

3. Any Member of the League may, after two years' notice of its intention so to do, withdraw from the League, provided that all its international obligations and all its obligations under this Covenant shall have been fulfilled at the time of its withdrawal.

Article 2

The action of the League under this Covenant shall be effected through the instrumentality of an Assembly and of a Council, with a permanent Secretariat.

Article 3

1. The Assembly shall consist of Representatives of the Members of the League.

2. The Assembly shall meet at stated intervals and from time to time as occasion may require at the Seat of the League or at such other place as may be decided upon.

3. The Assembly may deal at its meetings with any matter within the sphere of action of the League or affecting the peace of the world.

4. At meetings of the Assembly, each Member of the League shall have one vote, and may have not more than three Representatives.

Article 4

1. The Council shall consist of Representatives of the Principal Allied and Associated Powers, together with Representatives of four other Members of the League. These four Members of the League shall be selected by the Assembly from time to time in its discretion. Until the appointment of the Representatives of the four Members of the League first elected by the Assembly, Representatives of Belgium, Brazil, Spain and Greece shall be members of the Council.

2. With the approval of the majority of the Assembly, the Council may name additional Members of the League whose Representatives shall always be Members of the Council; the Council with like approval may increase the number of Members of the League to be selected by the Assembly for representation on the Council.

3. The Council shall meet from time to time as occasion may require, and at least once a year, at the Seat of the League, or at such other place as may be decided upon.

4. The Council may deal at its meetings with any matter within the sphere of action of the League or affecting the peace of the world.

5. Any Member of the League not represented on the Council shall be invited to send a Representative to sit as a member at any meeting of the Council during the consideration of matters specially affecting the interests of that Member of the League.

6. At meetings of the Council, each Member of the League represented on the Council shall have one vote, and may have not more than one Representative.

Article 5

1. Except where otherwise expressly provided in this Covenant or by the terms of the present Treaty, decisions at any meeting of the Assembly

or of the Council shall require the agreement of all the Members of the League represented at the meeting.

2. All matters of procedure at meetings of the Assembly or of the Council, including the appointment of Committees to investigate particular matters, shall be regulated by the Assembly or by the Council and may be decided by a majority of the Members of the League represented at the meeting.

3. The first meeting of the Assembly and the first meeting of the Council shall be summoned by the President of the United States of America.

Article 6

1. The permanent Secretariat shall be established at the Seat of the League. The Secretariat shall comprise a Secretary-General and such secretaries and staff as may be required. . . .

Article 7

1. The Seat of the League is established at Geneva.

2. The Council may at any time decide that the Seat of the League shall be established elsewhere.

3. All positions under or in connection with the League, including the Secretariat, shall be open equally to men and women. . . .

Article 8

1. The Members of the League recognise that the maintenance of peace requires the reduction of national armaments to the lowest point consistent with national safety and the enforcement by common action of international obligations.

2. The Council, taking account of the geographical situation and circumstances of each State, shall formulate plans for such reduction for the consideration and action of the several Governments.

3. Such plans shall be subject to reconsideration and revision at least every ten years.

4. After these plans have been adopted by the several Governments, the limits of armaments therein fixed shall not be exceeded without the concurrence of the Council.

5. The Members of the League agree that the manufacture by private enterprise of munitions and implements of war is open to grave objections. The Council shall advise how the evil effects attendant upon such manufacture can be prevented, due regard being had to the necessities of those Members of the League which are not able to manufacture the munitions and implements of war necessary for their safety.

6. The Members of the League undertake to interchange full and frank information as to the scale of their armaments, their military, naval and air programmes and the condition of such of their industries as are adaptable to warlike purposes.

Article 9

A permanent Commission shall be constituted to advise the Council on the execution of the provisions of Articles 1 and 8 and on military, naval and air questions generally.

Article 10

The Members of the League undertake to respect and preserve as against external aggression the territorial integrity and existing political independence of all Members of the League. In case of any such aggression or in case of any threat or danger of such aggression, the Council shall advise upon the means by which this obligation shall be fulfilled.

Article 11

1. Any war or threat of war, whether immediately affecting any of the Members of the League or not, is hereby declared a matter of concern to the whole League, and the League shall take any action that may be deemed wise and effectual to safeguard the peace of nations. In case any such emergency should arise, the Secretary-General shall, on the request of any Member of the League, forthwith summon a meeting of the Council.

2. It is also declared to be the friendly right of each Member of the League to bring to the attention of the Assembly or of the Council any circumstance whatever affecting international relations which threatens to disturb international peace or the good understanding between nations upon which peace depends.

Article 12

1. The Members of the League agree that if there should arise between them any dispute likely to lead to a rupture they will submit the matter either to arbitration or to inquiry by the Council, and they agree in no case to resort to war until three months after the award by the arbitrators or the report by the Council.

2. In any case under this article the award of the arbitrators shall be made within a reasonable time, and the report of the Council shall be made within six months after the submission of the dispute.

Article 13

1. The Members of the League agree that whenever any dispute shall arise between them which they recognise to be suitable for submission to arbitration, and which cannot be satisfactorily settled by diplomacy, they will submit the whole subject-matter to arbitration.

2. Disputes as to the interpretation of a treaty, as to any question of international law, as to the existence of any fact which, if established, would constitute a breach of any international obligation, or as to the extent and nature of the reparation to be made for any such breach, are declared to be among those which are generally suitable for submission to arbitration.

3 [adopted after 1919]. For the consideration of any such dispute, the court to which the case is referred shall be the Permanent Court of International Justice, established in accordance with Article 14, or any tribunal agreed on by the parties to the dispute or stipulated in any Convention existing between them.

4. The Members of the League agree that they will carry out in full good faith any award that may be rendered, and that they will not resort to war against a Member of the League which complies therewith. In the event of any failure to carry out such an award, the Council shall propose what steps should be taken to give effect thereto.

Article 14

The Council shall formulate and submit to the Members of the League for adoption plans for the establishment of a Permanent Court of International Justice. The Court shall be competent to hear and determine any dispute of an international character which the parties thereto submit to it. The Court may also give an advisory opinion upon any dispute or question referred to it by the Council or by the Assembly.

Article 15

1. If there should arise between Members of the League any dispute likely to lead to a rupture, which is not submitted to arbitration in accordance with Article 13, the Members of the League agree that they will submit the matter to the Council. Any party to the dispute may effect such submission by giving notice of the existence of the dispute to the Secretary-General, who will make all necessary arrangements for a full investigation and consideration thereof.

2. For this purpose, the parties to the dispute will communicate to the Secretary-General as promptly as possible, statements of their case with all the relevant facts and papers, and the Council may forthwith direct the publication thereof.

3. The Council shall endeavour to effect a settlement of the dispute, and if such efforts are successful, a statement shall be made public giving such facts and explanations regarding the dispute and the terms of settlement thereof as the Council may deem appropriate.

4. If the dispute is not thus settled, the Council either unanimously or by a majority vote shall make and publish a report containing a statement of the facts of the dispute and the recommendations which are deemed just and proper in regard thereto.

5. Any member of the League represented on the Council may make a public statement of the facts of the dispute and of its conclusions regarding the same.

6. If a report by the Council is unanimously agreed to by the members thereof other than the Representatives of one or more of the parties to the dispute, the Members of the League agree that they will not go to war with any party to the dispute which complies with the recommendations of the report.

7. If the Council fails to reach a report which is unanimously agreed to by the members thereof, other than the Representatives of one or more of the parties to the dispute, the Members of the League reserve to themselves the right to take such action as they shall consider necessary for the maintenance of right and justice.

8. If the dispute between the parties is claimed by one of them, and is found by the Council, to arise out of a matter which by international law is solely within the domestic jurisdiction of that party, the Council shall so report, and shall make no recommendation as to its settlement.

9. The Council may in any case under this article refer the dispute to the Assembly. The dispute shall be so referred at the request of either party to the dispute provided that such request be made within fourteen days after the submission of the dispute to the Council.

10. In any case referred to the Assembly, all the provisions of this article and of Article 12 relating to the action and powers of the Council shall apply to the action and powers of the Assembly, provided that a report made by the Assembly, if concurred in by the Representatives of those Members of the League represented on the Council and of a majority of the other Members of the League, exclusive in each case of the Representatives of the parties to the dispute, shall have the same force as a report by the Council concurred in by all the members thereof other than the Representatives of one or more of the parties to the dispute.

Article 16

1. Should any Member of the League resort to war in disregard of its covenants under Articles 12, 13 or 15, it shall, *ipso facto*, be deemed to

have committed an act of war against all other Members of the League, which hereby undertake immediately to subject it to the severance of all trade or financial relations, the prohibition of all intercourse between their nations and the nationals of the Covenant-breaking State, and the prevention of all financial, commercial or personal intercourse between the nationals of the Covenant-breaking State and the nationals of any other State, whether a Member of the League or not.

2. It shall be the duty of the Council in such case to recommend to the several Governments concerned what effective military, naval or air force the Members of the League shall severally contribute to the armed forces to be used to protect the covenants of the League.

3. The Members of the League agree, further, that they will mutually support one another in the financial and economic measures which are taken under this article, in order to minimise the loss and inconvenience resulting from the above measures, and that they will mutually support one another in resisting any special measures aimed at one of their number by the Covenant-breaking State, and that they will take the necessary steps to afford passage through their territory to the forces of any of the Members of the League which are co-operating to protect the covenants of the League.

4. Any Member of the League which has violated any covenant of the League may be declared to be no longer a Member of the League by a vote of the Council concurred in by the Representatives of all the other Members of the League represented thereon.

Article 17

1. In the event of a dispute between a Member of the League and a State which is not a member of the League or between States not members of the League, the State or States not members of the League shall be invited to accept the obligations of membership in the League for the purposes of such dispute, upon such conditions as the Council may deem just. If such invitation is accepted, the provisions of Articles 12 to 16 inclusive shall be applied with such modifications as may be deemed necessary by the Council.

2. Upon such invitation being given, the Council shall immediately institute an enquiry into the circumstances of the dispute and recommend such action as may seem best and most effectual in the circumstances.

3. If a State so invited shall refuse to accept the obligations of membership in the League for the purposes of such dispute, and shall resort to war against a Member of the League, the provisions of Article 16 shall be applicable as against the State taking such action.

4. If both parties to the dispute when so invited refuse to accept the

obligations of membership in the League for the purposes of such dispute, the Council may take such measures and make such recommendations as will prevent hostilities and will result in the settlement of the dispute.

Article 18

Every treaty or international engagement entered into hereafter by any Member of the League shall be forthwith registered with the Secretariat and shall, as soon as possible, be published by it. No such treaty or international engagement shall be binding until so registered.

Article 19

The Assembly may from time to time advise the reconsideration by Members of the League of treaties which have become inapplicable and the consideration of international conditions whose continuance might endanger the peace of the world.

Article 20

1. The Members of the League severally agree that this Covenant is accepted as abrogating all obligations or understandings *inter se* which are inconsistent with the terms thereof, and solemnly undertake that they will not hereafter enter into any engagements inconsistent with the terms thereof.

2. In case any Member of the League shall, before becoming a Member of the League, have undertaken any obligations inconsistent with the terms of this Covenant, it shall be the duty of such Member to take immediate steps to procure its release from such obligations.

Article 21

Nothing in this Covenant shall be deemed to affect the validity of international engagements, such as treaties of arbitrations or regional understandings like the Monroe doctrine, for securing the maintenance of peace.

Article 22

1. To those colonies and territories which as a consequence of the late war have ceased to be under the sovereignty of the States which formerly governed them and which are inhabited by peoples not yet able to stand by themselves under the strenuous conditions of the modern world, there should be applied the principle that the well-being and development of such peoples form a sacred trust of civilisation and that

securities for the performance of this trust should be embodied in this Covenant.

2. The best method of giving practical effect to this principle is that the tutelage of such peoples should be entrusted to advanced nations who, by reason of their resources, their experience or their geographical position, can best undertake this responsibility, and who are willing to accept it, and that this tutelage should be exercised by them as Mandatories on behalf of the League.

3. The character of the mandate must differ according to the stage of development of the people, the geographical situation of the territory, its economic conditions and other similar circumstances.

4. Certain communities formerly belonging to the Turkish Empire have reached a stage of development where their existence as independent nations can be provisionally recognised subject to the rendering of administrative advice and assistance by a Mandatory until such time as they are able to stand alone. The wishes of these communities must be a principal consideration in the selection of the Mandatory.

5. Other peoples, especially those of Central Africa, are at such a stage that the Mandatory must be responsible for the administration of the territory under conditions which will guarantee freedom of conscience and religion, subject only to the maintenance of public order and morals, the prohibition of abuses such as the slave trade, the arms traffic and the liquor traffic, and the prevention of the establishment of fortifications or military and naval bases and of military training of the natives for other than police purposes and the defence of territory, and will also secure equal opportunities for the trade and commerce of other Members of the League.

6. There are territories, such as South West Africa and certain of the South Pacific Islands, which, owing to the sparseness of their population, or their small size, or their remoteness from the centre of civilisation, or their geographical contiguity to the territory of the Mandatory, and other circumstances, can be best administered under the laws of the Mandatory as integral portions of its territory, subject to the safeguards above mentioned in the interests of the indigenous population.

7. In every case of mandate, the Mandatory shall render to the Council an annual report in reference to the territory committed to its charge.

8. The degree of authority, control or administration to be exercised by the Mandatory shall, if not previously agreed upon by the Members of the League, be explicitly defined in each case by the Council.

9. A permanent Commission shall be constituted to receive and examine the annual reports of the Mandatories and to advise the Council on all matters relating to the observance of the mandates.

Article 23

Subject to and in accordance with the provisions of international Conventions existing or hereafter to be agreed upon, the Members of the League:

  (a) will endeavour to secure and maintain fair and humane conditions of labour for men, women and children, both in their own countries and in all countries to which their commercial and industrial relations extend, and for that purpose will establish and maintain the necessary international organisations;
  (b) undertake to secure just treatment of the native inhabitants of territories under their control;
  (c) will entrust the League with the general supervision over the execution of agreements with regard to the traffic in women and children, and the traffic in opium and other dangerous drugs;
  (d) will entrust the League with the general supervision of the trade in arms and ammunition with the countries in which the control of this traffic is necessary in the common interest;
  (e) will make provision to secure and maintain freedom of communications and of transit and equitable treatment for the commerce of all Members of the League. In this connection, the special necessities of the regions devastated during the war of 1914–18 shall be borne in mind;
  (f) will endeavour to take steps in matters of international concern for the prevention and control of disease.

Article 24

1. There shall be placed under the direction of the League all international bureaux already established by general treaties if the parties to such treaties consent. All such international bureaux and all commissions for the regulation of matters of international interest hereafter constituted shall be placed under the direction of the League.

2. In all matters of international interest which are regulated by general Conventions but which are not placed under the control of international bureaux or commissions, the Secretariat of the League shall, subject to the consent of the Council and if desired by the parties, collect and distribute all relevant information and shall render any other assistance which may be necessary or desirable.

3. The Council may include as part of the expenses of the Secretariat the expenses of any bureau or commission which is placed under the direction of the League.

Article 25

The Members of the League agree to encourage and promote the establishment and co-operation of duly authorised voluntary national Red Cross organisations having as purposes the improvement of health, the prevention of disease and the mitigation of suffering throughout the world.

Article 26

1. Amendments to this Covenant will take effect when ratified by the Members of the League whose Representatives compose the Council and by a majority of the Members of the League whose Representatives compose the Assembly.

2. No such amendments shall bind any Member of the League which signifies its dissent therefrom, but in that case it shall cease to be a Member of the League.

APPENDIX II

RESOLUTIONS CONCERNING THE ECONOMIC WEAPON ADOPTED BY THE LEAGUE ASSEMBLY 4 OCTOBER 1921

1. The resolutions and the proposals for amendments to Article 16 which have been adopted by the Assembly shall, so long as the amendments have not been put in force in the form required by the Covenant, constitute rules for guidance which the Assembly recommends, as a provisional measure, to the Council and to the Members of the League in connection with the application of Article 16.

2. Subject to the special provisions of Article 17, the economic measures referred to in Article 16 shall be applicable only in the specific case referred to in this article.

3. The unilateral action of the defaulting State cannot create a state of war: it merely entitles the other Members of the League to resort to acts of war or to declare themselves in a state of war with the Covenant-breaking State; but it is in accordance with the spirit of the Covenant that the League of Nations should attempt, at least at the outset, to avoid war, and to restore peace by economic pressure.

4. It is the duty of each Member of the League to decide for itself whether a breach of the Covenant has been committed. The fulfilment of their duties under Article 16 is required from Members of the League by the express terms of the Covenant, and they cannot neglect them without breach of their treaty obligations.

5. All cases of breach of Covenant under Article 16 shall be referred to the Council as a matter of urgency at the request of any Member of the League. Further, if a breach of Covenant be committed, or if there arise a danger of such breach being committed, the Secretary-General shall at once give notice thereof to all the Members of the Council. Upon receipt of such a request by a Member of the League or of such a notice by the Secretary-General, the Council will meet as soon as possible. The Council shall summon representatives of the parties to the conflict and of all States which are neighbours of the defaulting State, or which normally maintain close economic relations with it, or whose co-

190

operation would be especially valuable for the application of Article 16.

6. If the Council is of opinion that a State has been guilty of a breach of Covenant, the minutes of the meeting at which that opinion is arrived at shall be immediately sent to all Members of the League, accompanied by a statement of reasons and by an invitation to take action accordingly. The fullest publicity shall be given to this decision.

7. For the purpose of assisting it to enforce Article 16, the Council may, if it thinks fit, be assisted by a technical Committee. This Committee, which will remain in permanent session as soon as the action decided on is taken, may include, if desirable, representatives of the State specially affected.

8. The Council shall recommend the date on which the enforcement of economic pressure, under Article 16, is to be begun, and shall give notice of that date to all the Members of the League.

9. All States must be treated alike as regards the application of the measures of economic pressure, with the following reservations:

(a) it may be necessary to recommend the execution of special measures by certain States;

(b) if it is thought desirable to postpone, wholly or partially, in the case of certain States, the effective application of the economic sanctions laid down in Article 16, such postponement shall not be permitted except in so far as it is desirable for the success of the common plan of action, or reduces to a minimum the losses and embarrassments which may be entailed in the case of certain Members of the League by the application of the sanctions.

10. It is not possible to decide beforehand, and in detail, the various measures of an economic, commercial and financial nature to be taken in each case where economic pressure is to be applied.

When the case arises, the Council shall recommend to the Members of the League a plan for joint action.

11. The interruption of diplomatic relations may, in the first place, be limited to the withdrawal of the heads of Missions.

12. Consular relations may possibly be maintained.

13. For the purposes of the severance of relations between persons belonging to the Covenant-breaking State and persons belonging to other States Members of the League, the test shall be residence and not nationality.

14. In cases of prolonged application of economic pressure, measures of increasing stringency may be taken. The cutting-off of the food supplies of the civil population of the defaulting State shall be regarded as an extremely drastic measure which shall only be applied if the other measures available are clearly inadequate.

15. Correspondence and all other methods of communication shall be subjected to special regulations.

16. Humanitarian relations shall be continued.

17. Efforts should be made to arrive at arrangements which would ensure the co-operation of States non-Members of the League in the measures to be taken.

18. In special circumstances and in support of economic measures to be taken, it may become advisable:

   (a) to establish an effective blockade of the seaboard of the Covenant-breaking State;

   (b) to entrust to some Members of the League the execution of the blockade operations.

19. The Council shall urge upon all the States Members of the League that their Governments should take the necessary preparatory measures, above all of a legislative character, to enable them to enforce at short notice the necessary measures of economic pressure.

BIBLIOGRAPHY

I have tried where possible to include only books which are easily available. There are a number of interesting books on the League which are alas out of print and unobtainable except at a few large libraries.

1. *General Introductions to the League of Nations*

Books

WALTERS, F. *A History of the League of Nations*, Oxford University Press. London, 1952.

A detailed narrative account of the League's history, which is an invaluable source of reference to the League's many activities.

ZIMMERN, A. *The League of Nations and the Rule of Law, 1918–35*. Macmillan. London, 1936.

One of the best analyses of the origin and working of the League.

WEBSTER, C. K. & HERBERT, S. *The League of Nations in Theory and Practice*. Allen and Unwin, London, 1933.

A useful assessment of the League in the 1920s.

CLAUDE, INIS, Jnr. *Swords into Ploughshares*, Random House, New York, 1956.

An interesting analysis of the League, and of the United Nations, by a political scientist.

MILLER, D. H. *The Drafting of the Covenant*, 2 vols., Putnam, New York, 1928.

A detailed account of the drafting of the League Covenant at Paris in 1919, by the legal adviser to the American Delegation in Paris.

AUFRICHT, H. *Guide to League of Nations Publications: A Bibliographical Survey of the Work of the League, 1920–1947*, Columbia University Press, New York, 1951.

Articles

NIEMAYER, G. 'The Balance Sheet of the League Experiment' in *International Organisation*, **16**, no. 4, 1952.

REYNOLDS, P. 'The League of Nations', in *The New Cambridge Modern History*, vol. XII, revised edition, *The Shifting Balance of World Forces*. Cambridge University Press, Cambridge, 1968.

A recent, succinct historical survey of the League of Nations.

2. The League as an International Organisation

Books

BURTON, M. *The Assembly of the League of Nations,* University of Chicago Press, Chicago, 1941.
A detailed examination of the development of the League Assembly.

HUDSON, M. *The Permanent Court of International Justice, 1920–42,* Macmillan, New York, 1943.
A history of the P.C.I.J. established under article 14 of the League Covenant, and of the development of international law under the League.

HALL, D. *Mandates, Dependencies and Trusteeship,* Carnegie Endowment for International Peace, Washington, 1948.

WRIGHT, Q. *Mandates under the League of Nations,* University of Chicago Press, Chicago, 1930.
A detailed study of the operation of the mandates system in the 1920s.

MACARTNEY, C. *National States and National Minorities,* Oxford University Press, London, 1934.
An examination of the League machinery for the protection of minorities and of its operation.

ALCOCK, A. *The History of the International Labour Organisation,* Macmillan, London, 1970.

PHELAN, E. J. *Yes and Albert Thomas,* Cresset Press, London, 1936.
A personal appreciation of the head of the I.L.O. by one of his British assistants.

Articles

CARLTON, D. 'Britain and the League Council Crisis of 1926', in *Historical Journal,* 1968.
An examination of the crisis involving the admission of Germany to the League Council.

HARDINGE, LORD. 'The League of Nations' in *The Quarterly Review,* no. 241, January 1924.
The impressions of a leading British diplomat of the organisation and working of the League Assembly of 1923.

3. The League and Peaceful Settlement

Books

BARROS, J. *The Corfu Incident of 1923 : Mussolini and the League of Nations.* Princeton University Press, New Jersey, 1965.
A detailed analysis of the Corfu crisis of 1923.

BARROS, J. *The Aland Islands Question: Its Settlement by the League of Nations,* Yale University Press, New Haven, (Conn.), 1968.

An exhaustive account of the Aland Islands dispute and its settlement.

BARROS, J. *The League of Nations and the Great Powers: The Greek–Bulgarian Incident of 1925*, Oxford University Press, London, 1970.
A detailed examination of a dispute settled by the League in 1925.

BASSETT, R. *Democracy and Foreign Policy*, Cass, London, 1968.
An account of the Manchurian crisis of 1931 as viewed by the British Parliament, press and public.

THORNE, C. *The Limits of Foreign Policy: The League, the West and the Far Eastern Crisis of 1931–33*, Hamish Hamilton, London, 1972.

4. The League of Nations and Disarmament

Books

CHAPUT, R. *Disarmament in British Foreign Policy*, Allen and Unwin, London, 1935.
An analysis of British disarmament between 1919 and 1934 and its relationship with League disarmament schemes.

ROSKILL, S. *British Naval Policy Between the Wars*, vol. 1: *The Period of Anglo–American Antagonism, 1919–29*, Collins, London and Glasgow, 1968.

Articles

CARLTON, D. 'Disarmament with Guarantees: Cecil, 1922–7' in *Disarmament and Arms Control*, III, 1965.

5. Attitudes to the League of Member States

Books

MCCALLUM, R. B. *Public Opinion and the Last Peace*, Oxford University Press, London, 1944.
An interesting assessment of British public opinion in the 1920s towards the Treaty of Versailles and the League of Nations.

MILLER, K. *Socialism and Foreign Policy: Theory and Practice in Britain to 1931*, Nijhoff, Hague, 1967.
An analysis of socialist attitudes in Britain to a wide range of international issues, including the League of Nations.

CARLTON, D. *Macdonald versus Henderson: The Foreign Policy of the Second Labour Government*, Macmillan, London, 1969.

CARTER, G. *The British Commonwealth and International Security*, Ryerson, Toronto, 1947.
An account of the policies of the British Dominions towards the League of Nations.

VERMA. *India and the League of Nations*, Bharati Bhawar, Patna, 1970.
A rather dull account of Indian representation and policies at Geneva.

6. *Biographies and Autobiographies with some League interest*

SEYMOUR, C. *The Intimate Papers of Colonel House*, 4 vols. Benn, London, 1926–28.
Contains interesting material on the origins of the League during the first world war.

CECIL, VISCOUNT. *A Great Experiment*, Cape, London, 1941.

CECIL, VISCOUNT. *All the Way*, Hodder and Stoughton, London, 1949.
Two autobiographies of Lord Cecil, of which the first contains much information about the history of the League.

HAMILTON, A. *Henderson*, Heinemann, London, 1938.
This biography of the Labour foreign secretary contains much material about his activities at Geneva.

MIDDLEMAS, K. & BARNES, J. *Baldwin: A Political Biography*. Weidenfeld. London, 1968.

MURRAY, G. *The League of Nations Movement: Some Recollections of the Early Days*, London, 1955.
The David Davies Memorial Lecture, 1955.

PETRIE, SIR C. *The Life and Letters of the Right Hon. Sir Austen Chamberlain*, 2 vols., Cassell, London, 1939–40.

ROSKILL, S. *Hankey, Man of Secrets*, Vol. 2. Collins. London and Glasgow, 1972.
The diary extracts published in this volume reveal much about British Government policy towards the League.

SALTER, A. *Memoirs of a Public Servant*. Faber, London, 1961.

SALTER, A. *Slave of the Lamp: A Public Servant's Notebook*, Weidenfeld. London, 1967.
These two books contain the reminiscences of a prominent member of the League Secretariat.

INDEX